The Lion, the Eagle, and Upper Canada:
A Developing Colonial Ideology

The Lion, the Eagle, and Upper Canada

A Developing Colonial Ideology

JANE ERRINGTON

McGill-Queen's University Press
Kingston and Montreal

Legal deposit 3rd quarter 1987
Bibliothèque nationale du Québec

Printed in Canada

This book has been published with the help of a
grant from the Social Science Federation of Canada,
using funds provided by the Social Sciences and
Humanities Research Council of Canada.

Canadian Cataloguing in Publication Data

Errington, Jane, 1951–
    The lion, the eagle, and Upper Canada
    Bibliography: p.
    Includes index.
    ISBN 0-7735-0603-9
    1. Canada – Politics and government – 1783–1791.*
    2. Canada – Politics and government – 1791–1837.*
    3. Canada – History – 1763–1867. I. Title.
    FC3071.E77 1987   971.03   C87-093747-2
    F1058.E77 1987

to WE and ESE

Contents

Illustrations

Acknowledgments

This volume would not have been possible without the willing assistance and encouragement of a great number of individuals and institutions and I would like to thank at least some of them here. The Canada Council provided support for the research and writing, in the form of doctoral and postdoctoral fellowships. A grant from the Advisory Research Committee of Queen's University and from the Arts Division of the Royal Military College of Canada funded most of the final preparation of the manuscript. The librarians and archivists at the Public Archives of Canada, the Public Archives of Ontario, Queen's Archives, and the Douglas Library at Queen's uncomplainingly gave me their time and help, and the maps and cartoons are reproduced with the kind permission of these repositories and the Anne S.K. Brown Military Collection, John Hay Collection, Brown University Library, The New York Historical Society, and the Lilly Library, Indiana University. In addition, I would like to thank the *Journal of Canadian Studies* and George Rawlyk and the *American Review of Canadian Studies* for permission to include material which appears in chapters 3 and 4.

Helen McEwen's humour and patience never waned through the typing and seemingly endless revisions and corrections, and Mary Alice Thompson was good enough to read and make suggestions on parts of an early draft. Thanks are also due to my colleagues at Queen's University and the Royal Military College of Canada for their encouragement throughout. My biggest debt here is to George Rawlyk, my supervisor and friend, whose guidance, patience, prodding, and continuous encouragement made sure that this project was finished and contributed materially to the final product. And last but by no means least, it is impossible to say how much I appreciated the farm folk, for providing respite and periodically putting things back into perspective, and my parents who were and are always there.

The Lion, the Eagle, and Upper Canada

Introduction

"Twenty-six years ago," Richard Cartwright, an influential and prosperous merchant in Kingston wrote in 1810, "this province was ... a howling wilderness, little known and less cultivated." When the American loyalists arrived after 1784 to take up the land promised by their king, there had been nothing "except the movable hut of the wandering savage" and "the solitary establishment of the trader in furs." Yet in the intervening years, Cartwright proudly observed, "I have seen the wilderness ... converted into fruitful fields, and covered with comfortable habitations. I have seen about me thousands, who without any other funds than their personal labour, begin to denude the soil of its primaeval forests, in possession of extensive and well cultivated farms and abounding in all substantial comforts of life." And perhaps more importantly, Cartwright continued, "I have seen the foundations laid of institutions and establishments for the promoting of knowledge and diffusing of religious instruction." Indeed, to Richard Cartwright and to the thousands of other men and women who had shared the trials of the early years, the transformation of Upper Canada from a wilderness frontier to a settled and increasingly prosperous province was truly "a scene which the benevolent mind must dwell upon with peculiar complacency."[1]

The history of the development of early Upper Canada is generally retold as the triumph of hardy British-American settlers over both the "howling wilderness" and the destructive influence of American democracy and republicanism. Alone and penniless, the story goes, a motley collection of farmers and artisans, labourers and merchants, and a few doctors, lawyers, and clergymen, abandoned their homes and possessions, forsook friends and family, and in defiance of the American Revolution, trekked north to the uncharted wilderness to start their lives anew. Here, against innumerable odds, the loyalists

founded a new British society in North America.[2] For though short
of material goods, these ardent British subjects, it has been asserted,
did bring with them a legacy of British conservatism and vehement
anti-Americanism which coloured all their activities in the new colony. One noted historian contends that "the sheer hatred of those
who lost property, suffered indignities, lost members of their families, lost their homeland, lost the war ... congealed into permanence"
after 1784. Early residents of Upper Canada were determined to
establish and to maintain "a counterrevolutionary society on the
borders of a revolutionary one."[3] And this legacy, it is presumed by
some, gave to Upper Canada and later to English-speaking Canada
a proclivity to political and social conservatism which the province's,
and after 1867, the nation's proximity to the United States only
reinforced. In short, the development of early Upper Canada and
the beliefs of its loyalist residents laid the foundations of an English-
speaking society which, from the beginning, indiscriminately rejected all things American while embracing eighteenth-century British conservative values and traditions.

Such historical interpretations are, not surprisingly, widely accepted by a people whose national identity has traditionally rested
on the belief that they are fundamentally different from their southern republican neighbours. Though Canadians and Americans share
a language, and to a large degree a continental economy and culture,
Canadians nonetheless take pride in the fact that their society is not
American. From the beginning, it is proudly asserted, Canadians
have guarded the "true liberty" of the people. The loyalists, by re-
jecting the precepts of unrestrained democracy and republicanism,
set the groundwork for a community which accepted the primary
importance of social order and respect for authority. Individual
rights and liberties, it is frequently and often self-righteously maintained, can only really be guaranteed in a society which first under-
takes to ensure peace, order, and good government – not in one
which puts the individual's right to life, liberty, and the pursuit of
happiness first. And the fundamental differences evident in the national institutions of today rest firmly in the traditions of the past.

Certainly there are few scholars who would deny that many of the
early loyalists were, in the broadest sense of the word, conservative.
It is often forgotten, however, that a number of those who arrived
in 1784 and after were not in any real sense British. And though
the American Revolution was a pivotal event in their lives, it was not
the only factor which influenced their attitudes and beliefs about
their new home. Moreover, the first arrivals to Upper Canada were
not alone in the 1780s. In addition to the few traders and the "wan-

dering savages," the American refugees also had the advantage of having British troops garrisoned in the area, which provided them with both a sense of security and a focus for settlement. Furthermore, by the mid-1790s the loyalists were being joined by an increasing number of American pioneer settlers in search of cheap fertile land. And throughout the early years, almost all Upper Canadians actively maintained contact with friends and families who had stayed behind in the republic. Indeed, Upper Canada between 1784 and 1828 was a colony of both Great Britain and the United States. Its creation and development over the first forty-five years depended on the continuing social, cultural, economic, and political support of these two nations, to the extent that inhabitants of this "far flung frontier" could often see "little ... that was uniquely" theirs.[4] The political and social institutions established in Upper Canada after 1784 and the attitudes and beliefs of its political, social, and economic leaders were rooted in their understanding of the mother country and of the republic to the south. The earliest Upper Canadians may have set the parameters of the conservatism of later Canadian society. Yet it was not a conservatism which rejected out of hand its American neighbours or unquestioningly embraced its British heritage. The story of early Upper Canada and the development of a colonial ideology is the story of a community which consciously accepted its dual heritage. Influential residents attempted to use the best of both worlds – the old and the new – in laying the foundations of their new society. Moreover, Great Britain and the United States provided these colonists with constant points of reference with which to gauge their own development.[5] Yet, even in the beginning, perceptions of the United States and Great Britain and of their importance to the development of the colony varied from one region to another and from one group of settlers to another. And colonial ideology inevitably changed over time, evolving in response to changing domestic circumstances and to the colonists' knowledge of altering world affairs.

For the most part, the majority of Upper Canadians between 1784 and 1828 – the farmers, the mechanics, the artisans, and the labourers – seemed to take their continuing connections to Great Britain and the United States for granted. Generally uneducated, most did not have the time or the inclination, other than perhaps in times of crisis, to reflect on anything which did not directly impinge on their daily struggle for survival. It was really only the few educated and articulate leaders of Upper Canada who were both conscious of and concerned about the colony's social, political, and economic development and about its relationship to the world outside its boundaries. Yet, even among the colonial elites, there was no common understanding of either the United States or Great Britain or, in fact, of what type of society they hoped to build in Upper Canada. And the often conflicting views of the two "imperial" components of Upper Canada engendered much of the bitter political debate which periodically erupted after 1791.

In its simplest terms, the debate which preoccupied leading Upper Canadians throughout the formative period revolved around the central issue of whether Upper Canada was to be a British or an American society, or a careful amalgam of both. For the province to become and remain a bastion of British liberty, some asserted, it must consciously reject all political or social ideas or institutions which were in any way tainted by American republican ideals. In short, for many, to be an Upper Canadian was to be "not American." Throughout the period, there were others, however, who argued that only by acknowledging the Americanness of the colony and, indeed, by carefully adopting certain economic, social, and political ideas from south of the border could Upper Canadians be expected to remain loyal members of the British Empire. These differences of opinion were clearly the result of two fundamentally divergent views of the United States and particularly of its social and political situation. The issue was further complicated, however, by equally divergent attitudes towards the political and social situation prevailing in Great Britain. At different times, some leading Upper Canadians asserted that the colony must carefully imitate the traditions and institutions of her illustrious mother country. Possessing the very *image* of the British constitution, it was contended, Upper Canada could and should develop as closely as was possible into a little Britain. To others, however, such assumptions were not only impractical, they were dangerous. Certainly all colonial leaders between 1784 and 1828 were committed to the creation of a strong British community in Upper Canada and readily acknowledged the immeasurable benefits that were to be derived from the British constitution. But considering the demographic and physical circumstances of the colony, many stressed that it was both reasonable and sufficient to apply only the *principles* of that time-tested constitution and to emulate the *spirit* of Great Britain.

These viewpoints were very rarely argued in such stark, black-and-white terms. Most often specific circumstances demanded that the individual's or group's position be qualified or couched in rather general and seemingly nebulous rhetoric. Moreover, positions shifted, sometimes radically, over time and in response to a particular issue. For example, as shall be seen, to be vehemently anti-American did not necessarily imply that one stood up for the "little Britain" interpretation. Indeed, what is particularly fascinating is how the divergent views of Great Britain and the United States intersected, and how arguments and ideology evolved and were applied to a myriad of specific issues. As is the case today, many Upper Canadians in the formative years found a collective colonial identity in comparing themselves to the two nations which had given them life.

It was the original group of merchant-loyalist leaders, in the colony since 1784, who initially argued that Upper Canada was as much an American as a British colony. Though men like Richard Cartwright, Robert Hamilton, and John Stuart had fought and suffered (and, incidentally, in the long run profited) as a result of their commitment to the empire, they recognized that the new province and its people were, in the broadest sense of the word, American. Both loyalists and the later American settlers were by choice and by inclination men of the New World. Though Cartwright and his associates clearly had strong political and emotional ties to the empire, they saw no contradiction between this and their commitment to the New World and to their old homeland. Thus, they asserted, the principles of the British constitution and British traditions had to be carefully and judiciously applied to meet the specific needs of the New World community. At the same time, the loyalist leadership actively promoted the use of American ideas and practices in their new home.

The largely British-born officials who arrived after 1791 found it almost impossible to accept such views. The United States, many vehemently believed, was the quintessence of disloyalty, rebellion, and betrayal, and, from the beginning, they seemed determined to cut off all ties with the republic. Moreover, they asserted, the colony had to be purged of its Americanness, and John Graves Simcoe, in particular, wanted to create a little Britain in its stead.

During the first twenty-five years of development, the ideological divisions between the two groups did gradually narrow. At heart, the local leadership groups of the two oldest settlements, Kingston and Niagara, and the colonial leadership at the new capital in York had many beliefs in common. And as the threat of American invasion increased in the first decade of the nineteenth century, they presented a relatively united front in defence of the empire and of their conservative values. Yet what is clear is that, throughout the period, many prominent Upper Canadians also considered themselves part of a conservative community which spanned the border. Over the years, strong ideological, social, and economic ties had developed between the members of the colonial elites and federalists in the United States. And as Upper Canadians mounted a defence of their homes in 1812, they did so as much in terms of their American as of their British heritage.

Such apparent unanimity of purpose among various colonial leaders did not survive the war. In 1815 the old divisions reemerged with far greater complexity and vehemence. Moreover, the experiences of that ordeal, the gradual social, economic, and political integration of the colony and just the passage of time all brought new issues to the fore that demanded new solutions. And it was quite natural that as the second generation began to take command of the government, their views differed at times quite radically from those of the original loyalist-British leadership. Between 1815 and 1828 the now relatively broadly based tory leadership which supported the colonial administration in York persisted in their attempt to arrest the influence of the United States on provincial society. Unlike their government predecessors, however, men like Rev. (later bishop) John Strachan and his young student, Attorney General John Robinson, argued that Upper Canada was not and could not become a re-creation of Great Britain. On the basis of their understanding of events at home, these men continually argued that political leaders had to carefully apply the *principles* of the British constitution. To emulate British practice too closely, they believed, was to open the door to radicalism and republicanism. It was the growing forces of reform which now argued both for continuing ties with the United States and for all the rights and privileges of Englishmen as were to be found in the very *image* of the British constitution. They asserted that without this Upper Canadians would become increasingly discontented and would inevitably fall into the outstretched hands of the United States.

The shifting and increasingly complex political beliefs articulated in Upper Canada in the 1820s were in large part a response to the particular circumstances of the time. Taxation, immigration, powers in government, and citizenship – all these issues demanded attention and all evoked considerable controversy. As politics began to impinge increasingly on the lives of the majority of the colonists, prominent individuals took various positions which they undoubtedly believed would gain them the most support. Yet, in the debates in the House of Assembly and in the ongoing controversies which preoccupied the newspaper editors, it is evident that the divisions in the colony stemmed not just from political opportunism. The 1820s witnessed the emergence of a debate which was concerned with the very nature of Upper Canada itself and who had the right to call themselves Upper Canadians. The terms of the debate rested firmly on two differing world views.

It is clear, therefore, that in order to have some appreciation of the evolution of Upper Canadian beliefs, and particularly of the development of political ideology, it is first necessary to come to grips with the various and changing perceptions that different groups of colonial leaders had of the United States and of Great Britain during the formative period of Upper Canadian development. Prominent residents were themselves aware of the continuing impact that these two nations had on their everyday lives and on the social and political issues of the time. Yet it must be remembered that the beliefs of early Upper Canadians and their perceptions of others were also very much a product of their own peculiar circumstances. We must not shift our focus so as to ignore the importance of local and colonial situations within which the ideology was worked out and applied.

The study of perceptions and of developing ideologies is difficult at the best of times. Depending on the sources available and considered, and invariably on the mindset of the viewer, even contemporary analysts are constantly at odds as to what some political or economic leaders really meant or what one group or party of citizens really believes today. All too often, the presumption that some conscious system of beliefs must exist becomes, on examination, a self-fulfilling prophecy. This problem of interpretation, of attempting to get into the mind of an individual in the hope of understanding "what they really meant," is doubly hard for the historian of early Upper Canada. Between 1784 and 1828 relatively few residents had the time, the inclination, or the ability to commit their thoughts and activities to paper and little of what was then written has survived. More importantly, the specific context and circumstances in which experiences were recorded gave particular meaning and connotations to words and phrases which are foreign to the twentieth-century historian. Yet one cannot, as so many have done, short-circuit the process by defining at the outset an Upper Canadian ideology, finding the evidence to support it, and then presuming that this provided the foundation of later developments and attitudes in the colony. Rather, like the anthropologist and ethnologist, the historian must accept that early Upper Canada is a foreign world and translate its historical records accordingly.

To do this with any degree of success, one must first attempt to understand the land and the people and the society which gave rise to the development of a conscious system of beliefs. No society (and this is equally true of its beliefs) is a homogeneous, static entity. Early Upper Canada between 1784 and 1828 was a "dynamic product of the activities of its members"; and it was a product, moreover, which was "profoundly shaped by the images the participants [had] of their own and other performances."[6] To understand the changing mind or minds of the early colonists, one must therefore first collect evidence of their behaviour. This includes the everyday, nonverbal activities of various individuals, the public record, including tracts and addresses, and the private communications of articulate members of the society. In the case of early Upper Canada our knowledge of the everyday lives and activities of the majority of pioneers is still sadly incomplete. Only an extensive study of popular culture in all its aspects, including religion, gender, occupation, mobility, and lifestyle of the inarticulate majority of residents, will provide us with some appreciation of their attitudes and beliefs.[7] Almost no attempt has been made here to grapple with this very large and complex problem. There is, however, a relative wealth of public and private communications which show in an articulate form the ideology of those writing. When examined in the context of the time, the audience, and the particular circumstances, such records provide an invaluable insight into the gradual development of an Upper Canadian ideology. For it is clear that the political, economic, and social leaders of Upper Canada did have and did consciously articulate a system of political and social beliefs which encompassed a rational and logical interpretation of their past and prescribed actions for their future. This is not to presume that such beliefs were accepted by all Upper Canadians. Indeed, the evidence suggests that from time to time the majority of Upper Canadians were actively antagonistic to the colonial leadership.

This study is an attempt to understand what some Upper Canadians, those few individuals who were recognized as leaders of their communities, actually believed about themselves and about others, particularly the United States and Great Britain, and how their views of themselves intersected and depended upon their views of others and changed over time. This is a study of Upper Canada from "the top" – a study of the articulate elite, who cannot, it is clear, be considered as a homogeneous whole but rather as a number of heterogeneous groups. It is likely that the views chronicled here did at times reflect those of many Upper Canadians, perhaps a large majority. At other times, and perhaps most of the time, however, the views of the elite mirrored their own self-centred concerns, nothing more and nothing less.

PART ONE

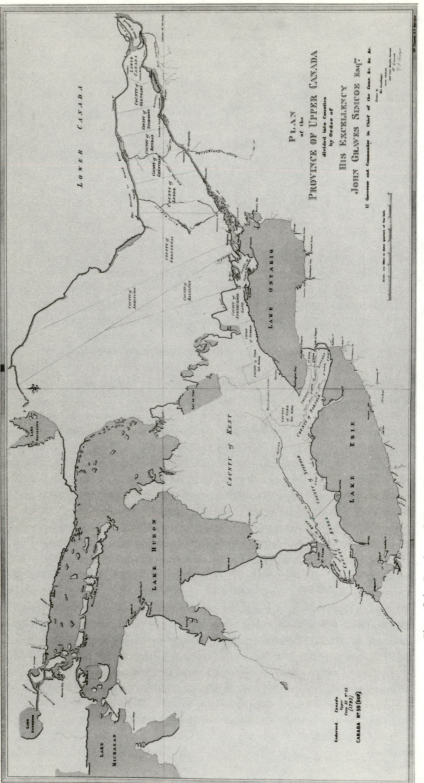

1 Plan of the Province of Upper Canada, 1793 (Special Collections, Douglas Library, Queen's University)

CHAPTER ONE

The Land and the People

In January 1791, shortly after his appointment as lieutenant governor of Upper Canada had been confirmed, John Graves Simcoe confidently predicted in a letter to a friend that the new colony was "destined by nature, sooner or later to govern the interior world."[1] There, in the virgin wilderness of North America, he believed he could build a new British society. It would be a bastion of imperial power and might – a society worthy of its king and of its heroic loyalist origins which would not only replace, but would eclipse that which had been lost in the thirteen colonies.

Yet as Simcoe and his entourage finally made their way up the St Lawrence eighteen months later to begin this formidable task, images of a bustling, prosperous community must have been far from their thoughts. All that could be seen from the decks of the bateau was a seemingly endless and impenetrable barrier of rocks and trees. Only occasionally did a few small clearings with a solitary mill or a rude log cabin or rough fields of corn and vegetables mark the presence of the almost 10,000 settlers who had arrived in the past ten years.[2] Even the British garrisons at Kingston and Niagara and the two small communities which had sprung up around them gave little indication of future greatness or prosperity. In 1792 Upper Canada was a wilderness frontier. Its hardy pioneer settlers lived with their backs to the wilds and the harsh landscape was an ever-present companion which dominated their lives and thoughts and concerns. Inevitably, it also had a continuing impact on the evolution of colonial society, an influence which was far beyond Simcoe's or any other individual's control, and which proved to be instrumental in determining the contours of that society.

By the time Simcoe stepped off the boat at Kingston dock in July, he must have also begun to realize that the wilds of Upper Canada were not the only or perhaps even the most formidable barrier to the fulfilment of his dreams. Though their presence was hardly noticeable in 1792, the few thousand settlers already in the province had long since begun to lay the foundations of a new society. Between 1784 and 1792 a number of small isolated communities had been established along the north shore of the St Lawrence River and the lower Great Lakes. By 1792 each one had developed its own distinct character, reflecting the variety of customs, traditions and expectations of its residents; and this uniqueness was encouraged and perpetuated by the hundreds of miles of bush and water which divided one from another. In fact, it was impossible to speak of one Upper Canada in 1792. There were a number of Upper Canadas. Yet not one of these communities lived up to Simcoe's expectations of what the colony should be like and he soon found that reshaping them would prove far more difficult than he had anticipated.

There is no question that most Upper Canadians in 1792 were men and women of "humble origin."[3] Some were loyalists who had moved north to take refuge from the turmoil of the American Revolution. A few were Britons and Europeans who had come to seek their fortune; a growing and soon overwhelming number of new Upper Canadians were restless Americans, who were searching for a new land and opportunities.[4] In the early years, few residents of the colony had capital or assets or any formal knowledge of law or government. Fewer still seemed to have given much conscious consideration to the kind of society they were building on the frontier. It might be expected that in the light of this, most Upper Canadians would have enthusiastically endorsed Simcoe's plans; one would presume that at least the loyalists, who in 1792 were still in the majority, would have welcomed his arrival. Such was not to be the case, however.

Though Upper Canada was officially and administratively a British colony, its residents in 1792 were a heterogeneous mixture of Germans, Scots, Dutch, English, and French (not to mention the substantial Amer-Indian portion of the population). English was the official language of the colony; yet often it was German, Gaelic, Dutch, and French which could be heard on the streets of its tiny villages and on the farms in the back country. Even as late as 1810, one resident observed somewhat ruefully that the population of Upper Canada was still "composed of persons born in different states and nations, under various governments and laws, and speaking several languages." Before Simcoe's vision could be realized, Upper Canadians had to be assimilated "into one congenial people";[5] and yet those frontier conditions which once had seemed so conducive to the implementation of his plans in fact tended only to perpetuate the diversity of cultures and languages.

Most Upper Canadians during the formative years of settlement were pioneer farmers who had come to the colony to better their lot and the prospects of their children.[6] Clearing the land, planting and harvesting, and attending to the myriad of tasks necessary to sustain life demanded all their time and effort. Particularly in the early years, when roads were almost nonexistent and the few trails often impassable, visits even to one's closest neighbours were infrequent occasions to be appreciated to the full. Certainly few Upper Canadians had any time to give serious consideration to anything beyond their immediate needs. Throughout much of the first twenty-five years of colonial development, an individual's community was confined to those in his or her family and to the few settlers he or she met occasionally at the mill, at work parties, or at social occasions. In this largely oral society, dependent on face-to-face communications, the individual defined him or herself not by social caste or rank but by location, by culture, by language, by religion, and by his or her place in the family. And this was reinforced by tradition and the rituals of life on the frontier.[7] Indeed, to a casual observer, there was little to distinguish rural settlements in the backwoods of Upper Canada from those on the frontiers of New York or the New England states. There was certainly no visible sign that the backwoods of Upper Canada was British.

It was really only in the few tiny villages of the colony that there was any real indication that Upper Canada was a British colony. As Simcoe stepped outside St George's Anglican Church in Kingston after being sworn in as the first lieutenant governor of Upper Canada in July 1792, there was before him the beginnings of an urban community. The dusty streets were undoubtedly busy with people. In the taverns, residents were probably discussing the events of the day over a dram. The shops too would have been full of men and women buying goods from overseas and from the United States. Like their counterparts in the backwoods, the lives of the residents of Kingston and Niagara and later York were governed by tradition and ritual. But these were quite different from the traditions and rituals which prevailed in rural Upper Canada. In Kingston and Niagara residents were part of a more closely knit society. They enjoyed within easy walking distance the amenities of a church, a tavern, a few shops, and many neighbours. They also enjoyed the benefits which could be obtained by living in close proximity to a permanent British force.

In the early years, the towns of Upper Canada were "the garrison centres of the Empire,"[8] and with the walls of forts silhouetted against the skyline, no resident could forget this fact. To the townspeople, the British forts represented order and deference. And the tradition and protocol which determined the relationships of the men who lived behind the palisades were soon partially mirrored on the streets of the town. In fact, by the time Simcoe arrived, each village already exhibited the rudiments of an economically and socially differentiated and stratified society.

To Isaac Weld, visiting in 1797, and to other travellers to the colony, this was first apparent in the architecture and physical layout of these colonial settlements. In Niagara and Kingston, Weld noted, "the houses with few exceptions are made of wood" and "those next to the lake are poor." But he found that in Niagara, "at the upper end of the town, there are several very excellent dwellings, inhabited by the principal officers of government." In Kingston, there were even a few houses made "of stone and brick."[9] In addition each town in Upper Canada soon had an Anglican church where, weekly, the Church of England minister endeavoured to inculcate the habits of a suitable godly subordination. Court-houses and jails were built to deal with those who broke the laws and defied the customs of society. And in York, after 1800, the government erected a special building to house the lawmakers of the colony. These buildings, large and relatively imposing and often set apart from the rest of the town, represented the authority of their residents – the principal merchants, professionals, and government officers of Upper Canada. It was these men, together with the British officers at the garrisons, who made and administered the laws. It was these men, the politically effective minority, who controlled much of the day-to-day lives of most of the townspeople of Upper Canada. It was here that Simcoe found in 1792 the few Upper Canadians who were also concerned about the future of the colony.

The prominence and influence of the first leaders of Upper Canada could be traced back to their early relationships with the British military authorities during the revolution. Most were loyalists and many, like Thomas Markland, Robert Macaulay, and Richard Cartwright, Jr, had actually joined the British forces on the battlefield. In addition, Cartwright, together with his business partner, Scotsman Robert Hamilton, had competently and unobtrusively kept the garrisons supplied with provisions. Others, like Rev. John Stuart and Rev. Robert Addison,[10] after fleeing the revolution, had ministered spiritually to the British forces. As the influence of the British military diminished after 1784, these already respected, enterprising, and educated young men had quite naturally begun to assume political as well as economic power within their local communities. Gradually, their control of trade, of the courts, of the local militias, and of the church had solidified so that by 1792 they were the unrivalled leaders of their towns, a position which was strengthened by various administrative and political appointments – to land boards, the Legislative Council, and as magistrates – made in the next few years. In addition, the merchants of Kingston and Niagara were consciously part of a strong business community which spanned the colony.[11]

The arrival of Lieutenant Governor Simcoe and his retinue in 1792 added a new and, for some, a foreign element to the already existing leadership in Upper Canada. The authority of these British-born and educated officials was derived from the explicit mandate of the British government. Experienced in administrative and military activities and relatively wealthy, these newly appointed colonial officers expected to dominate not only the government but all society in Upper Canada. They had behind them the force of law and tradition and ahead of them lucrative networks of patronage. Socially and politically, Simcoe and his successors assumed that they stood at the apex of the new colonial community.

The new lieutenant governor discovered, however, that the members of the local leadership groups were often reluctant to accept his authority or his grandiose plans without question. Many had supported one of their own, Sir John Johnson, for lieutenant governor and were undoubtedly disappointed by Simcoe's appointment. Moreover, Cartwright and Hamilton and a number of others soon came to resent the airs and influences of these self-styled "Englishmen of education"[12] who consciously attempted to exclude them from the best society of York. And as shall be seen, the indigenous leaders of Upper Canada quickly took exception to many of Simcoe's policies.

Initially, however, contact between the two groups, the indigenous and administrative elites, was quite limited. Divergence in occupation, background, and expectations for the colony itself made personal and social relations between the two groups difficult at best. In addition, particularly after the capital was moved to York in 1796, the government officials found themselves physically and psychologically isolated from the rest of the colony. Indeed, throughout much of the early period, the authority and influence of all groups, including the colonial administration, was severely restricted by the same wilderness conditions which isolated all Upper Canadian settlements.[13]

It is within this context of a diverse mixture of peoples and cultures, of communities isolated from each other by the frontier, and by varying experiences and expectations, that the attitudes and ideologies of the Upper Canadian elites gradually evolved. It is far too much to expect to find in Upper Canada the basis of a British community where all or even most actively espoused allegiance to the king and British traditions. The majority of residents in Kingston, Niagara, and York, like those in the backwoods, had few personal or social ties with the British establishment. Most were North Americans primarily concerned with the everyday problems of making a living. Many favoured not the Church of England but the Methodist meeting-house. Socially they looked not to the forts or the big houses but to the local taverns for their amusements. And the culture of the majority was not based on the written traditions of British life but on the oral traditions of their old homes in the United States or Great Britain. The physical isolation imposed by the frontier only served to accentuate these divisions. In the early years, most Upper Canadians undoubtedly only wanted to be left alone, to rebuild their lives by recreating patterns and traditions and customs of their former existence. With their friends and relations living south of the border or across the Atlantic, few had any reason to visit settlements in other parts of the province. Even most townsfolk had little inclination to look beyond the village limits. And various attempts from the outside to interrupt and change the flow of community life were often vehemently resisted.[14] This is not to say that the leaders of the colony did not share broadly defined economic, social, and political interests and particularly a devout attachment to the mother country. Yet even they could not escape the physical and psychological isolation endemic to the frontier and often their attitudes and concerns sharply differed.

Isolation characterized Upper Canadian life until after the War of 1812. Within twenty years of Simcoe's arrival, however, the population of Upper Canada had increased significantly; new settlers had opened up new areas and older farmlands had developed into well-tended and prosperous holdings. The towns too had grown, and their influence had begun to be felt in the surrounding areas. By 1810 Kingston and Niagara and York were bustling little communities, each with a weekly market, and, in Kingston and Niagara in particular, constant activity at their docks. In addition, narrow dirt tracks now radiated from the village centres, joining the enterprises of the towns to the settlements in the immediate area. Increasingly farmers brought their goods to the local markets, often accompanied by their wives and children who shopped and met their friends and neighbours.[15]

The culture of a backwoods society nevertheless persisted. In 1812, while some farmers prospered, with their land cleared and fully productive, others were only beginning the pioneer cycle of planting and harvesting. As had been the case twenty years before, there was still no typical Upper Canadian and certainly no typical Upper Canadian ideology. Leading residents continued to articulate various points of view, mirroring the preoccupations, attitudes, and values of groups of people with varying experiences.

The impact of their immediate environment was, however, only one of the factors which contributed to the development of widely differing viewpoints among Upper Canadians. For though they did not, in these early years, share any real sense of a common colonial identity, many continued to feel a kinship with those they had left behind. And despite the fact that they had chosen to establish themselves on the northern frontier of the United States, Upper Canadians obviously had not totally divorced themselves from the larger world. Through their newspapers and correspondence, in government reports and, for a few, by infrequent trips to the outside, prominent colonists maintained contact with friends and associates in Lower Canada, in Great Britain, and in the United States. Between 1791 and 1812 these international contacts exacerbated the already existing divisions between one Upper Canadian community and another. More importantly, these extracolonial connections were largely responsible for the differing understandings of the nature and needs of their own society which developed among the various colonial elites.

CHAPTER TWO

And This Shall be a British Province

On 17 September 1792 Lieutenant Governor John Graves Simcoe opened the first session of the new legislature of Upper Canada. "I have summoned you together," he announced to the joint sitting of the House of Assembly and Legislative Council, "under the authority of an Act of Parliament of Great Britain passed in the last year," to execute "great and momentous Trusts and Duties." "The wisdom and beneficence of our Most Gracious Sovereign and the British Parliament," he declared, had bestowed on the colony "the blessings of our invaluable Constitution ... and all the forms which secure and maintain it." Now, he proclaimed, Upper Canadians had to exercise that same manner of "Patriotism" which they had so conspicuously shown during the American Revolution. "With fostering care" and "due deliberation and foresight" they must begin to lay "the foundation of Union, of Industry and Wealth, of Commerce and Power" which would "last through all succeeding ages."[1]

The members of the House were "sensibly flattered by the strong testimony of His Majesty's paternal tenderness" and grateful for this opportunity to share in shaping the future of their homes. In a spirit of unanimity and enthusiasm which, on the surface at least, prevailed throughout the session, the Upper Canadian legislators, "as fellow subjects of the British Empire," formally pledged their support to their king, to the constitution and to the "British senator soldier," John Graves Simcoe, who had been sent to lead them. The "numerous and Agricultural people" of Upper Canada would reap the full benefits of "the British law and the munificience ... of his Majesty," the legislators declared. And they committed themselves to improving the already "favourable situation" of the province.[2]

Yet, as they sat on their camp stools listening to the lieutenant governor, the elected representatives of the House of Assembly and the appointed members of the Legislative Council must have reflected, at least momentarily, on the incongruity of their situation. Only seven years before, a good many of them had been penniless refugees without homes, without friends, and without a country. Now they were respected members of their communities – prominent and popular enough to be chosen by their peers to represent them and to make those crucial decisions which would determine the legal and social foundations of a new society. The seeming absurdity of their personal situation was only accentuated by their surroundings. The formality and pomp and circumstances of this and subsequent sessions of the legislature were surely more fitting in the stately halls of London than in a camp tent hastily erected in the wilderness of Upper Canada. The members, though British subjects, were also North Americans, who in a few weeks would put aside the formalities, forget the rituals, and return to their homes to take up once again the toil of pioneer life. There were few present, however, who would have denied the central importance of the moment. The meeting of the colonial legislature symbolized that essential unity which existed between the corridors of power in Westminster and the backwoods of Upper Canada. It was a graphic representation that the loyalist response to the American Revolution had not been forgotten or wasted. Upper Canadians were, in the fullest sense of the word, Britons. Inevitably, this fact would have a profound impact on the future evolution of an Upper Canadian ideology. Simcoe and the members of the House of Assembly and the Legislative Council in 1792 and in subsequent sessions of the government were certainly sincere in their ardent addresses of allegiance to the crown and to the unity of the empire. From the beginning, however, it was clear that the colonists' commitment to the mother country and their support of the administration's policies were tempered by the circumstances of their new homes on the northern frontier and by the strong attachment that many of them continued to feel for the land and people of the new republic. The indigenous leaders of Upper Canada were consciously Anglo-American and their plans for the colony were shaped by their dual heritage. Such sentiments were neither shared nor understood by Lieutenant Governor Simcoe or by his immediate successors. The administrators sent from London were of another world. Their perceptions of the colony and of its needs were far different from the collective understanding of the colonial leaders of Niagara and Kingston. Thus it was also inevitable that the meeting of the Old

World and the New, of the formal and stylized proceedings of Parliament and the immediate and ever-present demands of pioneer life epitomized in this first session at Niagara would lead to tensions.

Writing to his business associate and friend in London, Isaac Todd, in October 1792 after the first session of the legislature had been prorogued, Richard Cartwright, Jr, rhetorically asked, "To what is to be ascribed the present state of improvement and population in this country? Certainly not to its natural advantages, but to the liberality which Government has shown towards the loyalists who first settled it." The "Government" he was referring to was that of King George III and his Parliament in Britain. Its "liberality," as Cartwright proceeded to explain, included a host of material benefits received by the colonists – "the money spent by the numerous garrisons and public departments established amongst us, ... the demand for our produce," and most importantly, "the English laws and form of Government." In short, Cartwright stated, "His Majesty in his Benevolence" had provided "a comfortable asylum for the unfortunate loyalists reduced to poverty and driven into exile by their attachment to Britain."[3]

There were few in Upper Canada in 1792 who could ever really forget the crucial role that Great Britain had played and continued to play in their lives. It had been their continued allegiance to the king which had forced a number of them to unceremoniously abandon their homes in the republic and make the long trek north. Few seemed to regret their decision, however, for in recognition of their sacrifice and to compensate them at least partially for their losses the mother country had provided the loyal Americans with a new home. Here loyalists and even the later American immigrants had been given free land and the tools and supplies necessary to tide them over the initial painful stages of resettlement. Here British troops had provided protection, enabling Upper Canadians to build their homes and businesses secure from the terrors of the wilderness and unhampered by the lawlessness usually endemic in pioneer life.[4] Moreover, in its determination to ensure the colony's survival, the British government continued to provide incentives and capital to stimulate the local economy. Throughout the first twenty-five years of settlement, quit rents and taxes were negligible.[5] Annually, capital was injected into the economy through payment to half-pay officers; after 1800 the loyalists began to receive cash settlements to compensate them for their losses incurred during the revolution.[6] And throughout the period, the British garrison provided local farmers, shopkeepers, artisans, and tavern owners with ready markets for their goods and services. It would seem that in 1792 Upper Canadians had much to be thankful for.

Yet, as the colony matured and residents prospered, it is likely that the majority of Upper Canadians began to take such benefits for granted. Many loyalists undoubtedly came to accept British aid as theirs by right. And those restless American settlers who gravitated to the colony after 1792 to take advantage of the situation soon came to presume that such policies were only proper and just. Indeed, by the time Simcoe arrived, the British connection, so necessary to their everyday existence, had probably become an unconscious part of most colonists' lives. The backwoods farmer had little time to reflect on the political nature of his community and for most Upper Canadians, months would often go by without any direct contact with government officials, personnel from the fort, or anyone or anything to do with Great Britain. Even in Kingston and Niagara, where residents came into daily contact with the red-coated soldier, the presence of the garrison was probably soon taken for granted.

It was really only the prominent citizens of the three principal towns who had any real understanding or conscious appreciation of the advantages that membership in the empire conferred on the colony (as well as on their own personal situation). As one resident observed, "the benevolent intentions of the British government" and the king continued "to be exemplified in every measure that would tend to promote" Upper Canadians' prosperity. To members of the colonial elites, however, the material benefits they received were of secondary importance. The greatest advantage that membership in the empire provided for all Upper Canadians was the principles and practices of British parliamentary traditions. This constitution had "stood the test of time"[7] and leading Upper Canadians were confident that its traditions would furnish the foundations on which their new society could safely rest. As important to many, at least personally, however, was their attachment to their beloved sovereign, King George III, who personified all that was good and just in the world.

At the beginning of June each year, Upper Canadians celebrated the birthday of their king. In honour of the occasion the local militias were mustered; the officers and men of the forts offered their official tribute at review; and for all in the colony the day was an occasion for rejoicing, at home, in church, and, undoubtedly for a great many, in the local taverns. As the *Kingston Gazette* reported in 1812, the Fourth of June was given to acknowledging with "effusions of loyalty ... the numerous benefits which have been conferred upon us by His Majesty's Government."[8]

To the leaders of Upper Canada, King George III represented the very essence of all that they had fought to preserve during the long years of the American Revolution. The patriots, in order to assert their independence, had in 1776 symbolically killed the king and denied any kinship with the empire. The loyalists, though well aware of the numerous problems that plagued the relationship between the thirteen colonies and the mother country had been unable and unwilling to take this last crucial step. They could not accept that "the King, the Lords and the Commons" had "laid a regular plan to enslave America."[9] Thus, rather than condone patricide, they had chosen to move to a new land. It was only to be expected, therefore, that George III was still of crucial symbolic importance for many in Upper Canada after 1784. To these loyal British Americans, he was still their father; he was the head of the family of English-speaking peoples and the leader of a mighty empire of which they wished to remain a part. Moreover, George III gave the colonists, and particularly their leaders, a unique identity, one distinct from that of their wayward cousins in the south.

Their own experiences after the revolution confirmed to those who were assembled at Niagara in the fall of 1792 that their king was the "Protector of Nations." "In this remote but flourishing part of Your Majesty's Dominion," the House of Assembly declared in 1793, "we have found shelter by Your Majesty's paternal care and tenderness."[10] King George III and his Parliament had not only provided succour and support for those loyal subjects who had been driven from their homes; he also personally represented all those qualities which had been lost in their old homes in the United States and which many hoped to instil in the colony. As head of a family of Britons, he symbolized order, virtue, and piety. This all-powerful father was wise and just; he animated "his subjects to noble and benevolent deeds" and Upper Canadians were exhorted in his name to suppress "vice, immorality, and profaneness."[11] In fact, many believed that it was only under their sovereign's guidance that the province might eventually "merit the Divine Providence and favour, without which no Nation or individual – though ever so mighty – can expect to prosper." With the active support of the king, Upper Canadians once again had "the happiness to be free"[12] and could now proceed to establish a society far superior to that which was emerging south of the border.

The importance of the king in maintaining the liberty and virtue of his people seemed to be reinforced by newspaper and government reports of the steady deterioration of European affairs after 1790. The Upper Canadian elite "marked the progress of that unruly spirit of innovation and turbulence"[13] which prevailed in France with considerable regret. Deprived of their own "mild and beneficent Sovereign," the people of France had fallen prey to insidious leaders who threatened the peace of all Europe.[14] When news of the outbreak of war between France and Britain was received in April 1793 colonial concern intensified. Though "at a distance from the scene of the conflict" and "removed from the immediate consequences of the dangers," prominent residents, as members of the empire, were, nonetheless, extremely interested in the king's attempts to keep Great Britain secure. They were well aware that in the long run their own safety and security "depended on hers [Britain's]."[15]

Throughout the twenty years of European war, Upper Canadian newspapers were filled with detailed accounts of the numerous British battles against "the great violence and the almost universal anarchy of France."[16] Throughout, though somewhat anxious, Upper Canadians remained confident that Great Britain would prevail. Profuse addresses proclaiming Upper Canadians' loyalty and the love they had for the king annually emanated from the colonial capital. As Britons, leading Upper Canadians took pride in "the famous and successful stand" that the king's armies were making against French tyranny.[17] In 1798 they rejoiced at the defeat of the French fleet and the following year were gladdened by "the Glorious, Glorious News" of Nelson's victories.[18] Clearly the king and his Parliament were "the terror of their enemies." Under the inspiration of King George III, the British force was "towering in its strength" and presented "a monument of glory"[19] for all the world to emulate. And between 1793 and 1815, it was continually implied, Britain's battles in Europe were Upper Canadians' battles and the empire's triumphs were shared by all the colonists.

This was graphically illustrated in a Thanksgiving sermon given in 1799 to commemorate Nelson's victory at the battle of the Nile. To Bishop Jacob Mountain, head of the Church of England in the Canadas and to other colonial leaders, it was "our" army and "our" navy which, with the assistance of divine Providence, had defeated the forces of the French. The bishop stressed that "we form an integral part of the Empire and with it we must stand or fall."[20] To the colonists the European war was but another example of His Majesty's defence of liberty and justice and all those principles for which they themselves had sacrificed so much. All were proud, if somewhat relieved, in 1802 when peace was finally attained.[21] However, the prediction of some that Britain and France would never be at war again was dashed a year later as the empire once more prepared "to take up the cause which was that of all humanity."[22]

And as hostilities resumed Upper Canadians once more stood if only vicariously beside their comrades in arms across the Atlantic.

Throughout the Napoleonic Wars, Upper Canadian legislators, "influenced by a strong and uniform principle of attachment to your Majesty's person and government,"[23] were determined to take what limited action they could in support of the cause. As Lieutenant Governor Simcoe declared in 1794, "it is our duty to provide against all exigencies, and to place ourselves in a capacity to resist all innovations whatever." All must be vigilant and, he continued, perhaps with more confidence than was warranted, "I have the firmest reliance that the inhabitants of this Province will unite with every subject of the British Empire" and defend their homes, their king and their constitution against all "unjustifiable hostilities."[24] Five years later, the members of the Assembly, to show "their devoted attachment to the cause of justice," voted to send a small contribution to the king from surplus provincial revenues. In addition, colonial leaders periodically took measures to ensure internal security and peace in the province. For example, in 1804, fearing the influx of Frenchmen from the United States and the "introduction of French principles" into their new homeland, the House passed an act "to guard against the insidious designs of hostile aliens."[25]

For the most part, however, the European war was more of symbolic importance than of immediate and pressing practical concern to most Upper Canadian leaders. The actual battle for order, justice, and stability against the forces of anarchy and mob rule was primarily a European affair. And Upper Canadians were happy for it to remain so. Indeed, when the Anglo-French conflict threatened to involve Upper Canadians directly in 1806 and 1807, a surprising number of colonists, including members of the elite, were clearly reluctant to take an active part. Yet even when their duty as British colonists did finally force them to take up arms in 1812 against friends and neighbours in the United States, most influential Upper Canadians still considered themselves fortunate to live under the rule of King George III. He was without question "the best of Kings."[26] And though by the time of his golden jubilee, age and illness had reduced George III to a mere figurehead, pathetically irrational, the special message sent by the members of colonial government reaffirmed their whole hearted loyalty and emotional attachment to their king. "With gratitude and thankfulness," the Upper Canadian legislators declared in March 1810, "we acknowledge ... a most special blessing which had accompanied and adorned your Majesty's reign. Attached to Your Majesty's person and government, happy in the enjoyment of that invaluable constitution which we possess and grateful for the bounty which we in this Province have received from Your Majesty's hands .... We ... do most fervently implore the great ruler of Princes, that He may be graciously pleased to preserve Your Majesty's valuable life, and to permit Your Majesty long to be the Father, the Protector, and the King of your people."[27]

It must be noted, however, that not all or perhaps even a majority of Upper Canadians shared this strong emotional attachment to George III. The colony seemed to become increasingly Americanized as the first decade of the nineteenth century unfolded. Its inhabitants and many of their social customs resembled those of New York and New England at the time, rather than what one might expect in a purely British province. As shall be seen, after 1800 the provincial elite expressed a growing concern about the loyalty of Upper Canadians, a concern which implicitly questioned the population's commitment to their king. Whether in fact such widespread concern was well founded is as yet unknown. Too little is understood about the popular culture and beliefs of the majority of Upper Canadians to make any concrete conclusions possible in this regard. It may be that many residents if not antagonistic were at least apathetic to the pro-British stance of their leaders. Certainly only the few prominent Upper Canadians would have expressed the importance of the king in such stylized rhetoric.

Nonetheless, the king did symbolize to thousands of Upper Canadians – especially to many loyalists and newly arrived British immigrants – the glory and might of the British empire. Moreover, his and, implicitly, their stand against the forces of tyranny and anarchy was not just on behalf of the British cause in Europe. It was also a righteous defence of all those principles for which they and their mother country had once suffered in the American Revolution. It was, in fact, a defence of "that noble form of government"[28] which Upper Canada had been fortunate enough to inherit from Great Britain.

In 1810 one leading Upper Canadian observed that "Under the Epitome of the English constitution, we enjoy the greatest practical political freedom."[29] With its mixed and balanced form of representative and appointed assemblies, led by an independent monarchy, the British constitution, it was believed, effectively guaranteed the liberty of all subjects while at the same time ensuring "the subordination necessary to civilized society." In Britain and in Upper Canada, neither the tyranny of the crown nor the tyranny of the people could gain a position of ascendancy. As one colonist remarked, "no man's personal property ever was endangered by the power of the Governor," for "the Governor *cannot* become oppressive or formidable to the liberties of the individual."[30] To the leaders of the colony, however, "the blessings which flowed from the possession of a constitution approaching as nearly as our local situation will permit to the British constitution"[31] included far more than the mere structure and procedures of parliamentary government. Its principles could provide the ideological blueprint for the colony's future social and political development. For only the British constitution, "which neither innovation can impair, nor anarchy deform," would ensure that Upper Canadians and Britons all over the world would establish a just society and remain "a great, free and happy people."[32]

As so many Canadian historians have argued, all members of the Upper Canadian elite in the early period were in the broadest sense of the word conservative. They believed that all civilized societies were founded on a social and religious compact. The true happiness of man was ultimately attained by the individual's deference to authority – both God's and man's.[33] Thus, as the balance in government between the crown, the executive, and the legislative branch had to be carefully guarded, so too, it was felt, must each member of the community recognize and accept his or her place in the social order.

Their experiences during and after the American Revolution and their knowledge of the deteriorating situation in France strengthened prominent residents' determination to "inculcate a love of order, harmony and union" in the colony. In their old homes they had watched with dismay as the natural order of society had disintegrated under the impact of what loyalists and others conceived to be the uncontrolled passions of the people. In France "the spirit of innovation and turbulence" was also causing "universal anarchy."[34] Colonial leaders considered themselves "good citizens and lovers of Rule and Order," and from the very beginning they attempted to forestall "all innovations whatever, flowing from modern and unjustifiable principles." In particular, in their roles as legislators, they tried to prevent the madness of those "who exercise authority over the French nation"[35] from flourishing in Upper Canada. "Norval" was certainly not alone in his beliefs when he wrote to the *Upper Canada Gazette* in August 1800 that only "by submitting to civil order, by placing enlightened men in their councils, by the *wisdom* of their legislature and by *strengthening* the executive arm" could Upper Canadians share in the personal liberty which was the legacy of all true Britons.[36] It was the duty of all in positions of influence to encourage and to instil "the regular habits of piety and morality" among people. "Public and private felicity" were essential. The principles of subordination and of "good order and decorum"[37] had to be promoted and accepted by the great body of people before Upper Canada could ever hope to match the greatness of Great Britain. Only then, prominent Upper Canadians believed, could the constitution "which the Mother Country has given us" be preserved "uncontaminated."[38]

It soon became clear, however, that colonial leaders disagreed, often sharply, on how such accepted truths were to be put into practice. Particularly after Lieutenant Governor Simcoe arrived, political life in Upper Canada was rocked with heated debate on what it meant to be British and to have the benefits of the time-honoured constitution. It was a controversy which had its roots in two different world-views and particularly in the divergent and often conflicting perceptions of king and country held by the two primary elite groups in Upper Canada.

John Graves Simcoe and those men who were sent from Westminster after 1791 were in the fullest meaning of the word British. Their ideas and beliefs had been shaped by their experiences as Englishmen, born and educated there and serving an English king. To these men George III was a very real person and British battles in Europe were of personal and immediate concern. Most had made no personal or lasting commitment to Upper Canada and it is likely that, with the exception of John Graves Sincoe, few would have come to the colony if they had been offered positions elsewhere. In comparison with other imperial postings, Upper Canada was a little-known backwater, lacking both prestige and comfort. It was a wilderness to be ruled. Home to them was in England and they expected to return there to family and friends once their professional duties in the New World were completed. Often considerably older than their colonial counterparts and at the end of their careers, these imported officials generally had little knowledge of and even less interest in this young frontier posting. As they saw it, their appointment to Upper Canada was to govern the country for the ultimate benefit of the empire and of the king.[39]

Prominent residents of Kingston and Niagara who had come to the colony in its earliest years had, on the other hand, never crossed the Atlantic, and most could not share in any sense of personal involvement either with the king or in the war with France. To the indigenous leadership of Upper Canada, the king and the constitution represented ideals to be lived by, symbols of all that they had fought and sacrificed so much for and which they now hoped to preserve in their new home. Their personal knowledge of King George III and of the British constitution was at best second-hand, resting on their experiences as American loyalists and colonists. It was to North America and not to Europe that the original elite was wholly committed. Most colonists had consciously chosen Upper Canada as a new home for themselves and for their children. As Richard Cartwright expressed it in a letter to Isaac Todd in 1794, "All my prospects, as well for myself as my family, are confined to this Province; I am bound to it by the strongest ties, and with its welfare my interest is most essentially connected."[40] By the time Simcoe arrived, these enterprising and ambitious men had already invested seven years of their lives in establishing a place for themselves for the future.

Certainly the British-American settlers were grateful to George III for granting them this "asylum"; it was a "mark of peculiar favour" that had been awarded to them as a result of their "attachment to their sovereign."[41] It was a reward, many also believed, that had been well earned. And they undoubtedly assumed that the creation of the separate colony of Upper Canada in 1791 was an implicit acknowledgment of their right to take an active part in determining its future. No one questioned that the new British colonial officials had both administrative and military expertise and the mandate of the British parliament to govern. But they were outsiders. They did not possess that invaluable first-hand knowledge of the colony which the original residents had so painfully gained. And they showed themselves to have little real appreciation of the land and the people who had already settled the new province.

"A Government should be formed for a Country," wrote Richard Cartwright, "not a country strained and distorted for the Accommodation of a preconceived and speculative scheme of Government." To Cartwright and Hamilton and other prominent residents in Upper Canada, it seemed only logical that the physical conditions prevalent in the colony should dictate the actual workings of its government and society. "The maxim to follow nature, not to force it," Cartwright wrote to Isaac Todd in 1792, "is as proper for our guide in politics as in all other concerns."[42] But within a year of the first legislative session, it was evident that Simcoe had chosen not to recognize the peculiar conditions of this new land or to follow the suggestions of experienced advisers.

From the beginning, the lieutenant governor was determined that Upper Canada was to be a *British* society in fact as well as in name. As far as was humanly possible, he intended to create a little Britain in the North American wilderness. Almost a year before he arrived in Kingston, Simcoe had written to Sir Henry Dundas, the British colonial officer in London, that he planned to make Upper Canada's

"Establishments, Civil and Military" the epitome of those at home. Moreover, he maintained, "the utmost Attention should be paid that British Customs, Manners, and Principles ... be promoted and inculcated."[43] Simcoe even suggested the establishment of an Upper Canadian aristocracy made up primarily of British-born officials. Though he had to abandon this last endeavour, Simcoe and other members of his entourage were nonetheless determined to transplant other trappings of British society to the frontier. And this desire to start anew by recreating the Old World society undoubtedly formed at least part of Simcoe's reasoning for moving the colonial capital from Niagara to York.

In his letters home, the lieutenant governor constantly stressed that both Niagara and Kingston were vulnerable to any military incursions from the United States. Perhaps more important, however, was the need to physically separate the colonial administration from the influence of the already existing merchant oligarchy in the two older towns. In a report to Henry Dundas in the fall of 1793, Simcoe stated that it was essential that "the seat of Government should be situated in the internal part of the colony ... in order to induce habits of civilization and obedience to just Government, and to cherish the Spirit of Loyalty to His Majesty, and attachment to the British Nation."[44] Here, away from the insidious influence of the new republic to the south and removed from the already entrenched American-born leaders of Upper Canada, Simcoe might be able to realize his dreams.

Richard Cartwright and other prominent Kingstonians were understandably disappointed that their community had not been chosen as the permanent seat of government. In a letter to Todd written directly after the plans for the new capital were announced, Cartwright commented rather cryptically that Simcoe "was a little wild in his projects." The lieutenant governor "expects more in a few years than can happen in a decade." Indeed, Cartwright judged after reviewing Simcoe's proposals that the lieutenant governor "seems to be satisfied with nothing less than ... a second London." The Kingston merchant explained that "even at York, a town lot is to be granted in the front street only on condition that you shall build a house of not less than forty-seven feet front, two stories high and after a certain order of architecture ... It is only in the back streets and alleys that the tinkers and tailors will be allowed to consult their taste and circumstances in the structure of their habitations." To Cartwright, these attempts to recreate Great Britain on the shores of Lake Ontario were both misguided and dangerous. The decision was really only "a piece of political Quixotism ... perfectly Utopian."[45]

In addition to the expense involved, Cartwright noted that the move would only take the government further from the people it was intended to serve. To the men who had watched their compatriots in the thirteen colonies rebel against what many loyalists had considered the misguided administration of colonial officials, such plans were viewed with considerable trepidation.

This was only one of Simcoe's policies that upset the Anglo-American leaders. In 1793 Cartwright condemned the new Marriage Act. Its attempt to enforce the virtual establishment of the Church of England when nineteen out of twenty Upper Canadians were not adherents of that church was, he believed, "as impolitic" as it was unjust.[46] A year later, he and his friend Robert Hamilton jointly recorded their objections to the proposed Judicature Act. Their address to the Legislative Council pointed out that with its scattered population and poor state of communications, the colony could not physically accommodate the imposition of the British court system. "Such measures," they explained, "were inconsistent with the colony's geographical position and must shock the habits and prejudices of the majority of its residents."[47] In his annual assessment for Todd after that session, Cartwright's criticisms were even harsher. Simcoe was "not attending sufficiently ... to the spirit of the Constitution," he wrote. Rather he "thinks every existing regulation in England would be proper here." Cartwright complained that "he seems bent on copying all the subordinate establishments without considering the great disparity of the two countries in every respect." By 1794 it was feared by a growing number of influential Upper Canadians that rather than securing the colony for Great Britain, the politics and policies of the new lieutenant governor would "unquestioningly be sowing the seeds of Civil discord and perhaps laying the Foundation for future Revolution."[48]

In the light of such criticisms, it is not surprising that Simcoe's initial distrust of the first settlers of the colony intensified over his five-year tenure as lieutenant governor. He was frequently exasperated by Cartwright's and Hamilton's public opposition, and he went so far as to complain to Dundas that these men were obviously "avowed Republicans." He believed it was *their* views which were "diametrically opposite to the British constitution."[49] Despite this criticism, the two merchants continued to push their proposals forward while at the same time defending their own actions to friends and officials in Quebec and London. For as Cartwright explained to Todd, "I cannot look tamely on and see measures pursued that by sowing the seeds of discontent among us may ultimately avert us from the favour of Great Britain, which is so necessary for our prosperity." Surely, the leaders of Kingston and Niagara believed, their appointments to the Legislative Council and to other administrative bodies in the colony were "from a desire on the part of the officials in London to avail themselves of their knowledge of the country and acquaintance with the inhabitants, derived from long residence and familiar intercourse with them." It was their duty, therefore, to "assist in forming such laws as might be most applicable to the situation in the colony"[50] even if that led them into repeated confrontations with the lieutenant governor.

Such antagonism between the British and some of the British-American leaders of the colony was perhaps inevitable in the early years of Upper Canada's development. Simcoe undoubtedly feared that the British-Americans were too attuned to the New World. Though he acknowledged that they had chosen to remain loyal to the crown, most of the loyalists *had* been born and educated in an America which had rebelled and he believed that the treasonous sentiments of the patriots could not have failed to adversely colour the thinking of even the most ardent loyalist. For their part, the Anglo-American leaders of Kingston and Niagara saw no reason to disregard the lessons that they had learned directly and indirectly during the revolution. Moreover, men like Cartwright knew the nature of the people who had come to Upper Canada; they knew the land "where intercourse between the different districts is casual at best and where for five months of the year, the most populous parts of the Province could more easily communicate with Europe than with the seat of our Government."[51] In applying the principles and ideals of the British constitution, people like Cartwright believed that legislators must always remain conscious of the unique circumstances of the particular community. They had no desire to recreate a little Britain for they were also North Americans. The first settlers anticipated and worked towards the creation of a new and unique British-American society, one that incorporated the best of British ideals and American practice.

Relations between the various leadership groups in the colony did begin to improve after Lieutenant Governor Simcoe left the colony in 1795. Gradually, as the social and political divisions among Britons and Americans began to break down, friendships ripened between officials in York and residents of Kingston and Niagara. Under the administration of General Hunter and Lieutenant Governor Gore, the often unsolicited advice which continued to flow from Niagara and Kingston began to meet a more receptive audience in York. By 1812 the personal and ideological gulf between the executive and leading Anglo-Americans had narrowed considerably.[52] Even then, however, some differences in outlook persisted. The concerns of the regional leaders of Kingston and Niagara continued to be focused on the immediate needs of the new land and of their respective communities. Their commitment to their king and to Great Britain remained strong but their interest in imperial affairs outside the colony was still secondary. It was only when the colony was itself threatened from without or when the authority of its leaders was challenged from within, as seemed to be the case in 1807, that the importance of their British heritage was consciously articulated. Most of the time, it was taken for granted and only brought forth in the annual sessions of the colonial legislature or on those special occasions which were celebrated throughout the year.

Yet for those living in the towns of Upper Canada, the British forts were a constant reminder of the colony's dependence on the mother country. In local Anglican churches, in the legislature, on the militia field, and even in the taverns, ordinary colonists voiced their loyalty to king and country. Many provincial leaders wondered whether these occasions, with their formal and stylized professions of allegiance, had any real influence on the attitudes of the largely American-born settlers. Nevertheless, the very performance of the rituals and the repetition of what were often seemingly meaningless words must have had some impact, if only a peripheral one, on the minds of many colonists. At one level of understanding at least, all Upper Canadians were forced to acknowledge, in actions as well as in words, that Upper Canada was, indeed, a British colony.

The point must be stressed, however, that to most residents Upper Canada was not just a British colony: it was their home. Certainly the colony's membership in the empire and its allegiance to the king were vitally important, particularly to prominent Upper Canadians. Their British heritage set them apart from and, some believed, above the treasonous actions of old associates in the United States. Indeed, their commitment to the king and constitution was what made them Upper Canadians rather than Americans. But in addition to being British subjects, Upper Canadians were also Americans living in a North American community. For the original settlers in the province, the legacy of the British constitution was constantly being tempered by their "Americanness." Moreover, their understanding of how the British constitution, which they revered, should be applied to their particular situation was inevitably influenced by their evolving perceptions of the new republic to the south.

CHAPTER THREE

Upper Canada – an American Community?

In 1805 Richard Cartwright of Kingston made what seems to have been one of several trips back to his old home in the United States. Though perhaps still haunted by the painful memories of his hurried flight from the thirteen colonies almost thirty years before, he none-theless found this journey to Albany a "pleasant one." "The Country I have traveled through," Cartwright reported to his son, "affords a variety of the most beautiful Prospects and the Improvements that have been made in every Part of it since I visited it before are far beyond anything I could have imagined."[1] That Richard Cartwright, a fervid loyalist-refugee of the revolution and a pillar of society in Upper Canada, could look with approval on the American republic is perhaps surprising to the many scholars who have characterized the early colony as a bastion of British conservatism and the home of virulent anti-Americanism.[2] Yet prominent and not so prominent Upper Canadians of this early period often voiced their satisfaction with and approbation of the rapid economic and social advancements being made in the United States. This admiration did not blind the colonial elite, however, to the central factors which had prompted many to abandon their homes in the 1780s. Republicanism and a democratic government did foster political factions and dissent and often bitter personal controversy. All too often in the United States public virtue and private morality were lost sight of amid the din created by an ill-informed populace and unscrupulous politicians. Such disorder, colonial leaders firmly believed, was "injurious to the peace and happiness of society." Thus, though there was much in the United States "worthy of immitation," it was also clear to many influential Upper Canadians that "the states are far from furnishing proper models in everything."[3]

Perhaps the best way to characterize colonial attitudes towards their southern neighbours is to describe them as ambivalent. Although Upper Canada was politically and, for many, emotionally a British colony, no resident before or indeed after the War of 1812 could have realistically denied that it was also a North American community. Her land and her people were largely American; a number of her social institutions and practices were patterned after those in the United States; and, most importantly, the colony's proximity to and continuing dependence on the United States made it impossible to indiscriminately reject all things American. Certainly the revolution had fostered a wariness and a distrust of the United States which was never really overcome in later years. Yet there also existed in the minds of many Upper Canadians (as indeed there exists today without any apparent contradiction) an admiration for and openness to American ideas and developments. After 1784 community leaders carefully and discriminatingly selected American models for use in their new home. At the same time the United States provided a constant reminder of what Upper Canadians had to try to avoid. In fact, throughout the whole period in question the United States, the province's closest and most accessible neighbour and the former home of so many of its residents, became the colonists' immediate and constant point of reference. It was a yardstick which Upper Canadians frequently used to measure their own success. Inevitably the colonial view of the American republic also came to influence greatly the elite's vision and understanding of their own society and of their position within it.

The American Revolution, as has often been said, created not one nation, but two. Yet the rough and imprecise political demarcation of the northern limits of the new republic had little real impact on the minds of many of its people. Initially, Upper Canada was intended as a home for loyal British subjects. Within a few years, however, the distinctly "loyalist" character of the northern colony was all but lost amid the "sudden and so great ... influx" of American immigrants who were taking part in "the traditional American search for better lands and a perfect home."[4] By 1812 residents and travellers both observed that, particularly in the western districts of the colony, "the loyalist element was scarcely noticeable amongst the diversity of people who had come to take up land or engage in trade." Even in the heartland of loyalism, the Kingston area, it was reported that "a great portion ... are persons who evidently have no claim to the appellation loyalists."[5] In its early years Upper Canada was demographically at least an American community.

    The growing Americanness of Upper Canada was reinforced by

the physical proximity of the two nations. New York and the New England states were Upper Canada's closest and most accessible neighbours. News, mail, and travellers from Europe and, indeed, from the most easterly sections of British North America arrived most quickly and easily through Boston or New York.[6] And Richard Cartwright was not the only Upper Canadian who made frequent journeys south. Though the loyalist residents of Upper Canada had consciously spurned the political outcome of the revolution, they had not cast aside friends and family who remained behind. Soon after the revolution, one traveller noted that "passions [had] mutually subsided" on both sides of the border, and even between some of the most loyal British-Americans and those Americans who had actively "espoused the cause of the Republic" the natural feelings of "consanguinity, amity and personal friendships were revived."[7] This was only to be expected; Americans and Upper Canadians "were still interesting objects to each other." Particularly at Niagara and Kingston and along the St Lawrence "the most social harmony" soon prevailed "between gentlemen on the American side and those on the British side" and many Upper Canadians and Americans frequently exchanged visits for business and pleasure, regardless of the state of international affairs.[8]

The continuing personal contact across the border was supplemented by increasingly lucrative economic associations between merchants. Within ten years of the end of the revolution, whiskey, rum, salt, seeds, and tobacco (to name only a few commodities) regularly flowed from New York and the New England states to Upper Canadian markets or along the St Lawrence to Montreal and Quebec.[9] In return, colonial merchants exported potash and some flour south, and before 1800 a few had even won profitable contracts supplying those American garrisons on the south shore which had been unable to rely on their own farmers for produce.[10] Initially, trade north and south was carried on unhindered by customs duties or tariffs and provincial merchants actively lobbied before the turn of the century to keep the border free of all restrictions. Yet even the levying of colonial import duties after 1800 and the imposition of an American embargo seven years later did little to hamper what was already "one of the most important sources of prosperity to the colony."[11]

Throughout the first twenty-five years of settlement, there seems little doubt that prominent loyalists and other Upper Canadians still considered themselves an integral part of a North American community which spanned the border. Even the governing elite of York could not escape being influenced by the proximity of the United States – for the republic was, until well after the War of 1812, Upper

Canada's window on the world. And it is perhaps the nature of this basic communications link which had the greatest continuing impact on evolving Upper Canadian attitudes and understandings.

Largely isolated from other parts of British North America and, until the war, from each other, prominent Upper Canadians from 1790 onwards relied on the United States for much of their knowledge of affairs outside their local communities. Only the colonial administrators regularly received reports from London and these were months out of date and often lacked detail. Thus most interested Upper Canadians, forced to find a more reliable and comprehensive source of news and information, quite readily turned to American gazettes.[12] This propensity to look south of the border for the most up-to-date and topical information was made clearly apparent when the few local newspapers began to appear after 1793.

Like fellow editors in the republic, Upper Canadian printers did not always specify the sources of their information; but it was certainly not unusual to read the general byline "from the United States" or "taken from American newspapers" preceding reports from England, Europe, the Maritime colonies, and sometimes even from Quebec. With increasing frequency, Upper Canadian editors began to acknowledge that their accounts of European affairs were generally reprinted from a New York newspaper, often the *New York Daily Advertiser*; American congressional reports were frequently drawn from the *National Intelligencer*. Even the editors of the official government newspaper (published in York after 1798), the *Upper Canada Gazette*, were forced to agree with printers in Kingston and Niagara that, like travellers and mail, European and British news reached the colony fastest through New York, Philadelphia, and Boston. A source analysis of the *Kingston Gazette* from its first publication in September 1810 to just after the war in June 1815 confirms this. Approximately 75 per cent of all news printed by editor Stephen Miles originated in the United States; and even the official closing of the border after war was declared did not stop Miles from relying on American sources for most of his European reports.[13]

More important, however, was the type of American sources which Miles seems to have specifically preferred. Almost all reports in the *Kingston Gazette* which originated in the United States were taken from federalist newspapers, those journals which, after 1800, supported the major opposition party in the United States. At first glance, this might suggest that since New York and the New England states were the heartland of conservative America, it was their newspapers which were most readily available in Upper Canada. However, the nonfederalist reports appearing in the *Kingston Gazette* and in other colonial newspapers indicate that this may not have been the case. In fact, Miles seems only to have been following a trend which had been firmly established by previous colonial editors. The Tiffany brothers, editors of first the *Canada Constellation* and then the *Niagara Herald* at the turn of the century in Niagara, and John Bennett, the editor of the *Upper Canada Gazette* in York, appeared to look quite consciously for accounts which most closely expressed the viewpoint of their readers. For the most part, this preference was implied merely by naming the specific journal; for example, a report would be taken from the *Albany Gazette* or from the *Baltimore Federal Republican*. However, when John Cameron took over the *Upper Canada Gazette* in 1807, he explicitly informed his readers that he was pleased to have opened "a regular correspondence with the *Federal* Printers in the United States" for his "early intelligence of continental and foreign affairs."[14] It would seem, therefore, that Miles's and other colonial editors' preference for reports from the American conservative newspapers was a measured and conscious one. And considering the highly dependent financial position of colonial newspapers at this time, it can be argued that this preference reflected the prevailing view of their limited constituency of wealthy, articulate, influential Upper Canadians.[15]

Thus before the War of 1812 and indeed throughout and after the war, influential colonists not only considered themselves part of a North American community but specifically part of a conservative American community. There was developing in Upper Canada, as was emerging in New Brunswick at the same time, a "federalist-loyalist alliance" which provided much of the ideological underpinnings of the colonists' evolving view of their neighbours. Not only did Upper Canadians rely on the federalist press for most of their information about what was happening in the United States, but both their positive and "negative stereotype[s] of republican America"[16] were also largely borrowed from federalists south of the border.

In 1796 Gideon Tiffany, then editor of the *Upper Canada Gazette* still published in Niagara, confidently predicted that "we look to the time as not far distant when our wilderness shall have been converted into well cultivated fields."[17] From the outset, Upper Canadians believed that the future of the new colony depended on the development of its agricultural potential. As one anonymous Kingstonian commented in 1810, "in a political view" agriculture "is important and perhaps the only firm and stable foundation of greatness." "As a profession," he continued, "it strengthens the mind without enervating the body. In morality, it tends to increase virtue without introducing vice. In religion, it naturally inspires piety, devotion and dependence, without the tincture of infidelity." Moreover, he concluded, it was "a rational and agreeable amusement to the man of leisure, and a boundless force of contemplation and activity to the industrious."[18] The salutory effects of an agricultural life were clearly evident as Upper Canadians looked across the Atlantic. The colonists believed that it was Great Britain's hardworking farming population who were the economic mainstay of its "power and opulence"[19] and the foundation of its superiority in the world. If carefully nurtured and developed, Upper Canada too could share in this prosperity. But it was apparent that though Great Britain might be the ideal to be followed, her agricultural techniques had little to offer the Upper Canadian pioneers. Rather it was to the United States, "where the soil and climate are similar,"[20] that colonists had to turn for models of *how* this rural prosperity was to be accomplished.

From the very beginning, colonial leaders recognized that only "the Americans understood the mode of agriculture proper for the new colony."[21] And though some leading Upper Canadians had reservations about admitting so many American settlers, most in the early years did approve of the economic benefits of Lieutenant Governor Simcoe's "patriot policy"[22] of 1792 which encouraged farmers from south of the border to move to the virgin Upper Canadian wilderness. "Being from necessity in the habit of providing with their own hands many things which in other countries the artisan is always at hand to supply, they [the Americans] possess resources in themselves which other people are usually strangers to," Richard Cartwright commented in a letter to the then lieutenant governor, Richard ard Hunter, in 1799. Though Cartwright was one of those who was concerned about the deleterious effect of so many Americans on the political development of the colony, he realized that only these settlers "would boldly begin their operations in the wilderness ... the dreary novelty of the situation would appall a European."[23]

The native ingenuity of these new settlers was not enough, however, to ensure that the new lands would become fully productive. Through their travels and their reading of American newspapers and journals, leading Upper Canadians were made aware of the new agricultural techniques being developed south of the border – developments which could easily be introduced into the northern province. And the vehicle most suited to transmit these ideas, it was realized, was the burgeoning Upper Canadian press. Even if newspapers were not directly available to the majority in the colony, the information they contained was soon passed on by those who came to market, to the tavern, and to the other informal occasions which drew residents together.[24]

Throughout their years of publication, the *Canada Constellation*, the *Niagara Herald*, the *Kingston Gazette*, and even the *Upper Canada Gazette* devoted a great deal of space to articles on planting and harvesting, and a host of other matters of specific interest to farmers.[25] Most of these were taken from a wide selection of American publications and from the papers of various American agricultural societies. For example, a letter from one Joseph Cooper of New Jersey to a friend in Philadelphia, reprinted in the *Kingston Gazette*, gave specific directions on the best method of tilling soil.[26] Upper Canadian farmers received explicit instruction on the keeping of bees from the *Boston Register*; relying on an unnamed American newspaper, the editor of the *Upper Canada Gazette* provided a detailed discussion of how potatoes were cultivated in Ireland and the United States leaving no doubt that the latter method was far more appropriate in the northern colony.[27] And in support of already stated colonial policy, the Upper Canadian press gave considerable attention to the growing of hemp with advice taken from the New York Agricultural Society and various American journals.[28] In addition, residents of the Niagara district, of York, and later of Kingston, obviously aware of the advantages communities south of the border were gaining from local agricultural societies, began to establish their own societies after 1800.[29] Both implicitly and explicitly, the Upper Canadian farming population was urged to use these new proven techniques in order to clear more land and to increase their agricultural production. Constantly reminding readers of the progress being made south of the border, the press emphasized that it was "in the combined interests of patriotism and self interest"[30] for the colonists to exert themselves. One article on orchards published in the *Kingston Gazette* in 1811 was most explicit in this regard. "Our inhabitants, it is hoped, are too ambitious to be outdone in any laudable exertions by their neighbours in the United States."[31]

Improving agricultural techniques was not the only concern that Upper Canadians and many Americans had in common. Both were trying to open up the frontier to settlement and to further national development. South of the border, however, the process had been going on for over 100 years and it was realized that the Americans had accumulated valuable experience of how best to confront a host of problems. Thus, over the years, the new British colonists looked to the United States for examples of how roads should be built and maintained and how land and water transportation generally could be improved. One contributor to the *Canada Constellation* recommended, for example, that York institute a Stump Law, a statute found on the books of many American towns, to ensure clear passage on the capital's lanes and encourage proper maintenance of town lots. Another resident in Kingston suggested that Upper Canadians "should learn a useful lesson from their neighbours" and have a national census taken in the colony to aid in determining the proper number of representatives in the House of Assembly and in assessing taxes.[32] Through the pages of Upper Canadian newspapers, colonial readers also followed with interest American developments in manufacturing and improvements of local and national services. Of particular concern and use to the British-Americans was how their southern cousins coped with fires, a problem which plagued both societies.[33] Upper Canadians were also interested in early American attempts to combat various diseases and excessive drinking, procedures which began to be employed in the colony after the War of 1812.[34] As fascinating for many prominent colonists was the rapid industrial growth of the United States.[35] One article in the *Upper Canada Gazette* told of a new factory for the spinning and weaving of hemp which had just been built outside Philadelphia. In 1811 the *Kingston Gazette* noted the establishment of a new state prison in New York.[36] The same paper even considered the American proposals to build the Erie Canal joining Lake Erie to the Hudson River "praiseworthy,"[37] though it was realized that the canal would seriously undermine traditional colonial trade routes. Perhaps the most telling comments, however, were those which appeared in the *Kingston Gazette* in late 1810 concerning the creation of a local bank. American examples were expressly used both to support and to oppose the proposal, for, as one resident stated, the situation in the United States "is nearly similar to our own." Certainly the banks in Utica, New York, and other American centres were far more appropriate examples than any British ones. Moreover, as one contributor somewhat cryptically concluded, "there are many among us capable of correcting me if I have mistated a single fact."[38]

These constant references to American practices and models were in part a recognition of the great progress being made in the United States. Though Upper Canadians realized that their own development was not keeping pace, there seemed to be little resentment of American advances. Indeed, with few exceptions, the northern observers recognized and applauded the American spirit of enterprise and native ingenuity. Soon, Upper Canadians believed, they too would enjoy the benefits of such improvements and prosperity. As the editor of the *Upper Canada Gazette* confidently predicted as early as 1796, "the great Franklin" might well wish to return 100 years hence "to see how wonderful have been the improvements in the American world."[39]

Leading Upper Canadians were always conscious, however, that material prosperity, though important in itself, could not ensure the political and social survival of the colony. Proximity to the United States and the admittance of so many "good" American settlers was in fact a double-edged sword. Though the United States provided the much-needed technical innovations and the personnel to maintain and develop the colony to its fullest potential, the very presence of these settlers and the proximity of the republic also threatened Upper Canada's continued existence as a distinct and, many believed, superior society.

In 1784 many leading Upper Canadians had chosen not to become citizens of a republican democracy because they could not, emotionally or intellectually, accept its rejection of the monarchy and the British constitution. In the late 1780s, however, the colonists' actual understanding of the new American system and its implications was relatively uninformed. Preoccupied with their own backbreaking attempts to establish new homes, Upper Canadians had little time to consider broad political and social issues. The little news that did appear in the first colonial newspaper, the *Upper Canada Gazette*, reflected its readers' preoccupation with the situation in their own colony and in Great Britain. Yet Upper Canadians could not and did not remain isolated on the northern frontier for long. As contact with friends and family was renewed and American newspapers became more readily available, their interest in and concern about American affairs deepened. In part, this was a result of the growing impact that European affairs and especially the French Revolution were seen to have on American politics. More immediately, however, Upper Canadian interest was sparked by the destructive effects that "democracy" was having on American society itself.

Particularly after 1796, parties and factions seemed to be destroying any stability and balance which postrevolutionary America had achieved. Relying increasingly on the federalists of New York and the New England states for their news and understanding of the impending disaster, Upper Canadians watched fearfully the apparent decline and downfall of the republic. The colonists' concern was neither disinterested nor, as time went on, uninformed. The failure of the American "experiment," it was believed, threatened all in the vicinity. Moreover, Upper Canadians' understanding of development south of the border influenced to a large degree their vision of their own society; it provided a coherent explanation not only for the troubles to the south but also for the political dissension growing in Upper Canada after 1800.

While the federalist elite was in command in the United States, many Upper Canadians believed that it was guiding "the American experiment of representative democracy"[40] with restraint and some success. By 1796, however, it was clear that the fragile tranquillity and stability which had been so tenuously attained under George Washington and other federalist leaders was in jeopardy. "Factions and rebellions" were invading the republic and between 1796 and 1800 many Upper Canadians watched the rise of the new "republican party" to prominence with growing anxiety. In their efforts to challenge the policies and the political supremacy of the federalists, the so-called "Virginian Oligarchy" was "dividing the people from the government."[41] And though as late as August 1800 some in the colony still expected the federalists to win the upcoming presidential election, reports of the growing divisions in the federalist ranks and the complications evident in the electoral system caused others to be more doubtful. The American people were becoming "the tools of factions," it was judged, and the pawns of political opportunists.[42] Increasingly interested northern observers began to predict that if such political infighting continued the United States would be humbled and whatever remained of liberty would be lost. By February of 1801 there were few in Upper Canada who were really surprised at Jefferson's victory.[43]

There is no question that for a number of prominent Upper Canadians the republican victory of 1800 was of only passing interest and certainly of little consequence. Many of the British-born officials and immigrants, like the recently arrived John Strachan, supposed that though "the politics of the United States had undergone considerable change ... the general measures of that Government will undergo no greater change than a change of ministry in Britain." Strachan's somewhat simplistic view of the American system of government was initially coupled with a latent admiration of the new republic and its people. Certainly, he commented in March 1801 that "the President and Sub-Presidents are both noted republicans; the federalist party is split in two."[44] It was only gradually, as his residence in the colony lengthened, that Strachan gained some real appreciation of the growing rift between the federalists and the republicans. It was then that he began to acquire a marked antipathy to the United States.

"The character of the Americans is generally speaking bad," he remarked in a letter to his old Scots friend James Brown in 1807, "and craft and duplicity is too much resorted to even in their public measure."[45] Believing that he had "profitted" by his "neighbourhood to Democracy," he explained to his friend in 1809 that "the mass of people are more corrupted than a person of your excellent heart can well imagine." The men of "this new nation are *vain* and *rapacious* and without *honour*," and the official encouragement of "licentious liberty" keeps them "at a constant boil." Even in Upper Canada, so heavily populated with American-born settlers, Strachan had concluded in 1803, "there is a most lamentable want of what we [he and Brown] call independent or respectable people ... In point of fact," he proclaimed, "they are brutes."[46]

By the end of the decade, Strachan even went so far as to propose what was at that time a rather novel explanation of the differences between Upper Canadians and Americans. In perhaps the first explicit articulation of the myth of "the true north strong and free," which would become so important to Canadian imperialist thought some seventy-five years later,[47] Strachan argued that Canada, because of its geographical location and climate, was inherently superior to the United States. In a veiled reference to the republic, he asserted that inevitably "governments of southern countries were despotic and slavery was rife." Upper Canada and, implicitly, Great Britain, on the other hand, "being among the northern nations" were the true homes of liberty and justice. The souls of their residents, he pronounced, "are raised to exertion by their native storms; among them all the different branches of knowledge are carried to the highest perfection." To Strachan, it seemed clear that "the natives of colder and more severe climates far surpass the inhabitants of the milder sky."[48] This explanation notwithstanding, Strachan had by the end of the decade come to believe firmly in the evil consequences of a republican form of government. The type of government under which one lived "has a direct influence on the manner of the people,"[49] he wrote in the *Kingston Gazette* in 1811. A number of Strachan's contemporaries had come to this realization a decade before. Certainly it was this assumption which had caused so much alarm when news of the republican victory had reached the colony.

Naturally accepting the federalist viewpoint of the situation, many influential colonists in Kingston and Niagara came to believe in 1800 that "the Americans are now destined to be torn into faction – and to live in perpetual disorder."[50] Unlike Washington, whose life had "been dedicated to virtue," Thomas Jefferson among other things "countenanced the abolition of the Christian Sabbath." In the United States, "public tranquility, public harmony and public justice"[51] were lost, destroyed by republican anarchy and the rule of the mob. From their knowledge of the ancient republics of Athens and Rome, whose downfall could be attributed to the natural "consequences of an elective government,"[52] many of the indigenous leaders of Upper Canada, echoing their federalist friends, fully expected that history was bound to repeat itself. "A dreadful spirit of division" had split the country "into two distinct peoples," it was reported, and "revolution, and perhaps a bloody one seems not far distant." To many on both sides of the border, it seemed clear that the United States "had reached the end of a rising curve of the cycle."[53]

It was this second, perhaps more informed view of a people divided, of good and bad Americans battling for political supremacy, which tended to prevail in Upper Canada over the next fifteen years. The evidence suggests that most of the indigenous elite did not share the harsh and almost complete condemnation of the American people that Rev. John Strachan frequently expressed. The disastrous decline of the United States, they believed, was the result of the depravity of the republicans. And as the plight of the federalists worsened, Upper Canadians continued to be sympathetic to their dilemma. "I sincerely pity the virtuous and well disposed part of the community in that country," wrote one Upper Canadian in the *Kingston Gazette* in 1812. "For seven years" they have suffered and "they are still suffering under the unjust and unprincipled measures of their Government." They "are making the noblest effort by every laudible means in their power to counteract the baneful effects of their tyrannical and ruinous policies."[54]

By 1812 even the young Scottish minister had come to appreciate the Upper Canadian-federalist point of view. Over the past twelve years he too had made important personal contacts with people south of the border and, together with other British residents, his views had been significantly shaped by those around him. Though increasingly antagonistic to the United States, he now accepted without question that it was the federalist party which possessed "all the worth and talent in the United States." Sympathy did not mean approval, however, for Strachan continually wondered what good these citizens could perform in a perverted and tyrannical system.[55]

Many other leading Upper Canadians had begun to share Strachan's fears that even the best efforts of the federalists would not be able to postpone disaster. Most now judged that "the violence of their political parties, their abusive attacks upon each other's characters and the scurrility of too many of their publications" were all too characteristic of republican democracy. "Their democratic system," wrote one contributor to the *Kingston Gazette*, "fostered an uncontrollable spirit of party ... the rage of their parties has become intolerable."[56] Moreover, the numerous reports from south of the border of violence, crime, and political intrigue all pointed to a society where, with the firm control of the federalists now gone, stability was permanently lost.[57]

The worsening situation in the United States was a constant reminder to leading Upper Canadians of what, at all costs, had to be avoided in the northern colony. Upper Canada had been given a form of government far superior to that of the republic; but the evils of levelling, of factions and of political and social strife were still painfully evident in the colony. And while, at the official level, the Upper Canadian legislature consciously strove to subdue "French principles," local newspapers warned of the more immediate dangers from the south.

An ever-present and growing cause of concern among some of the colonial elite and particularly those in Kingston and later in York was the large number of American settlers who lived in Upper Canada. As early as 1795, travellers noted that "the spirit of independence which prevails in the United States" was beginning to "gain ground" in Upper Canada. Indeed, many new arrivals seemed to retain "ideas of equality and insubordination"; a number expressed "a determined partiality to the United States" and many were generally judged to be "bad citizens."[58] It was apparent that these pioneers had not come to Upper Canada because of their preference for the British form of government. "It is not to be expected," Cartwright wrote to Lieutenant Governor Hunter in 1799, that "a man will change his political principles, or prejudices by crossing a river." And Cartwright counselled that in the future "the greatest precaution ... should be used to exclude improper persons"[59] from entering the colony.

Not all leading Upper Canadians shared these concerns, however. In one of the few instances when Robert Hamilton and Cartwright were clearly at odds, Hamilton, William Dickson, and other Niagara merchants categorically asserted that political allegiance had little to do with developing the North American economy. As his biographer, Bruce Wilson, notes, Hamilton, because of his own interests in land speculation and the forwarding and portaging enterprises, fully supported Simcoe's policy on American emigration and actively lobbied colonial authorities to keep the border open.[60] Only a few in the Niagara area questioned such ideas. One resident did note that there were "a few uneasy souls, admirers of republicanism and revolution" in the area in 1801 and, he feared that their presence was "much to the prejudice"[61] of the colonial government. Most in the western region, however, fully supported their leaders' understanding of the situation.

Though before the War of 1812 not all colonial leaders were agreed on the desirability of unrestricted American immigration, most were increasingly aware that, like the federalists in the United States, they were surrounded by a population which threatened their leadership and the basic principles of order and deference on which the society was founded. In the United States such democratic impulses, it was argued, had led to a general levelling and to a disintegration of social order. Upper Canadian leaders were determined to forestall such developments in their homeland.

An article in the *Niagara Herald*, printed just after the news of Jefferson's election had reached the colony, sounded the first warning. Explicitly pointing to recent events south of the border, the editors declared that "there cannot be a greater judgement befall a country than such a dreadful spirit of division." Political parties made people "greater strangers ... more adverse to one another than if they were actually two different nations." Thus perhaps one of the most significant lessons that Upper Canadians learned as they watched American politics was that "A furious party spirit when it rages in its full violence exerts itself in civil war and bloodshed; ... In a word it fills a nation with spleen and rancour, and extinguishes all the seeds of good nature, compassions and humanity."[62]

It is not surprising, therefore, that in the elections for the House of Assembly in the first decade of the nineteenth century, most Upper Canadian candidates placed a high premium on their independence from any party or faction. "Actuated by motives remote from the Pursuits of Ambition or the Schemes of self-interest," candidates requested support so that they could enact "wise and beneficial laws for the good of society." Electors were exhorted to vote prudently, to elect a "gentleman" "who has honesty and an independent spirit" to represent them. He need not be popular but, it was asserted, he had to have ability and judgment and be expected to fulfil his "sacred duty" to uphold the "general good and general harmony" of society.[63] The appeal of William Weekes, a recently arrived Irishman running for a seat in the House of Assembly in 1804, was indicative of many of the period. At the conclusion of his *Address to the Free and Independent Electors of the East Riding of York*, he stated, "I stand unconnected with any party, unsupported by any influence and unambitious of any patronage."[64]

Yet, a year later, it was the same William Weekes who, together with Joseph Willcocks and Justice Thorpe, became the centre of a controversy which appeared to threaten the very fabric of Upper

Canadian society.[65] In a by-election in 1805, Weekes (once clerk to the controversial Aaron Burr, who had reportedly caused the split in the federalist party which many felt had resulted in its electoral defeat in 1800) once again offered himself as a candidate; but this time he intended to represent "the interests of the People." At approximately the same time the newly arrived Justice Thorpe consciously began a campaign to direct and redress the grievances of many Upper Canadians concerning land policies and the colonial administration. Within a year these two men and their small group of associates became identified as champions of "the people" against the tyranny of the government.[66] And for the first time in Upper Canada's short history, the established leaders of the colony discovered themselves under fire and their authority seriously challenged. For many prominent colonists the situation was all too reminiscent of political developments south of the border and this served to reinforce their identification with their "ideological brethren" to the south, the American federalists.

The Weekes-Thorpe controversy had started innocuously enough. Robert Thorpe arrived in the colony in September 1805 fully expecting to be appointed chief justice of Upper Canada and firmly convinced that he had both the necessary talent and a duty to rectify the evils of the present colonial administration and "conciliate the people" to the government. Initially, Justice Thorpe restricted his activities to conducting an active and lengthy correspondence with the Colonial Office and advising sympathetic representatives of the people, including William Weekes, on how best to bring certain concerns of interest "to the people" before the House of Assembly.[67] Though colonial leaders considered such activities totally "outside the accepted bounds"[68] of colonial politics and clearly suspicious, it was not until Lieutenant Governor Gore arrived and refused to countenance Thorpe's ideas that the controversy flared into vitriolic debate. Keenly disappointed at being bypassed for the chief justiceship, aggrieved that the lieutenant governor had failed to take his advice, and increasingly isolated from York society, Thorpe took his campaign directly to the people, using both the bench and, after Weekes's death at the end of 1806, a seat in the House of Assembly as vehicles to attract support. Between October 1806 and November 1807, Thorpe and his "Party," including William Wyatt, recently dismissed as surveyor general, and Joseph Willcocks, editor of the *Upper Canada Guardian*, formed an opposition group which actively agitated against the colonial administration.[69]

At first the *Upper Canada Gazette* in York, following the lead of the colonial legislature, tried to ignore the situation publicly at least.

Prominent Upper Canadians were not loath, however, to express their growing concern privately to each other. The activities of this cabal of "outrageous demagogues"[70] were almost treasonous, one anonymous Upper Canadian recorded in a private sketch of the conduct of Justice Thorpe. By their public addresses and increasingly through their newspaper, the *Upper Canada Guardian*, Thorpe and his associates were encouraging active discontent among the people and partisan and irresponsible opposition to the government. To the established leaders of Upper Canada there seemed no question that, left alone, the general populace would have remained loyal and relatively acquiescent. It was the renegade justice who was at the centre of unrest and "the principal mover of all factions and turbulence in the province." The Irishman had perverted the court from acting as a hall of justice to being a "vehicle of private spleen and malice."[71] Most discounted Thorpe's public pronouncements of loyalty and concern for the welfare of the colony. Rather it was contended that only "personal vanity and infatuation" directed his "irrational activities."[72] By his actions Thorpe had created an opposition party which was consciously setting out to destroy order and good government. Few colonial leaders considered that Thorpe had any heartfelt concern for "the interests of the people."

By the summer of 1809 the Upper Canadian elite found that their privately expressed concerns and various attempts to control the situation were largely ineffectual. News of the growing unrest in the colony was beginning to reach London; moreover, "the diabolical machinations of a desperate cabal of Irishmen," with their "treasonable allusions to the American revolution" threatened "to reduce the province to the same folorn condition"[73] which prevailed in the United States. At no time did the leaders of the colony attribute Thorpe's activities to the *direct* influence of American republican ideas. Some did suspect that Joseph Willcocks had personal and political connections with radical American republican editors. Most of the colonial elite, however, identified Thorpe with the radical United Irish movement.[74] He was characterized as "a friend and associate of the celebrated [Thomas Addis] Emmett,"[75] once a radical leader of the United Irish movement and after 1803 a noted American republican; moreover, many of Thorpe's Upper Canadian associates were Irishmen who also shared their leader's proclivities for rebellious Irish thought. By the fall of 1807 there seemed little doubt that Thorpe was heading a "Democratic Party" based on "republican principles"[76] and the effect of this man upon the minds of the American settlers, who "from habit and education" were "ready enough to second the views of factions,"[77] was potentially disastrous.

Yet even Justice Thorpe's suspension and eventual departure from the colony at the end of 1807 failed to alleviate the situation. The controversy continued, fuelled by comments in the *Upper Canada Guardian* and the appearance of a pamphlet written by John Mills Jackson defending the justice's stand. In March 1810 the House of Assembly was unable to ignore the situation any longer, and it publicly denounced Jackson's *View of the Province of Upper Canada*. "It contains a false, scandalous and seditious libel," they judged, "manifesting the tendency to alienate the affection of the people from His Majesty's Government in the Province."[78] That same year, two private pamphlets also appeared in defence of the colonial government. Both Richard Cartwright, in *Letters of an American Loyalist to His Friend in Great Britain*, and an anonymous settler, in *A Letter to the Right Honourable Lord Castlereagh*, condemned the actions of the "few desperadoes" and their attempts to "impress the public mind with an unfavourable opinion of its Government."[79] Both authors stressed that even in these perilous times Upper Canadians, by virtue of their constitution, enjoyed "the greatest practical political freedom."[80]

These attempts to negate Thorpe's support in the colony, and more significantly to convince the imperial parliament that the colony was loyal and committed to the crown, did not, however, still the fears of civil unrest. In 1810 it had become painfully clear to some in Upper Canada that the colony was too American. In the eyes of many colonial leaders, the threat posed by democracy and its attendant factionalism to the internal security and well-being of the British province was only compounded by the menacing policies of the republican administration south of the border. By 1810 a growing number of influential Upper Canadians had come to believe that they were fighting for the very existence of the colony.

The pernicious effect of faction on the political life of Upper Canada was not the only American development which concerned prominent colonists. By 1800 they discovered that republican ideas were also invading the religious and educational institutions of the new province – the two forums which should have been the bulwarks of society's authority. Unless these institutions were safeguarded by ensuring that the right type of school, run by the right men and the right church (in this case the Church of England) was established, it was feared that they would in fact become agents of republican discontent and active disaffection.

Between 1784 and 1815 all attempts to establish the Church of England in the colony proved unsuccessful. Neither the government nor the Society for the Propagation of the Gospel was willing to financially support or actively promote the expansion of the church. By 1812 there were still only six Anglican clergymen in Upper Canada, far too few to adequately serve the growing population. What was particularly upsetting to many colonial leaders, however, was that for most Upper Canadians the deplorable state of the Church of England was of little consequence. Reflecting their own past experiences in America, most residents preferred the ministrations of itinerant preachers from the United States and particularly the young and enterprising Methodist and Baptist ministers who annually trekked north to the backwoods.[81]

These "preachers and fanatics," Richard Cartwright remarked in 1806, had "overrun the country." With their emphasis on individual salvation and mass participation, these "deplorable fanatics"[82] turned men's hearts away from constituted authority. Rather than supporting the "rationale doctrines of the Church of England," it was feared that the Methodists in particular were filling the people's minds with "low cunning" and with "republican ideas of independence and individual freedom."[83] And there seemed to be nothing that could be done to offset their pernicious influence.

Perhaps more insidious for some Upper Canadians was the influence that "democratic" ideas were having on the most vulnerable aspect of colonial society, the education of its youth. In the early years of the province's development, schools had been virtually nonexistent. As Richard Cartwright explained, most Upper Canadians' time was taken up with the "axe and the plough." The little education that was available was received at home; only a privileged few were sent to schools in Lower Canada or in the United States.[84] Gradually, however, "a spirit of improvement" began to spread throughout the colony. Local clergymen opened small classrooms to teach arithmetic and the classics. Prominent residents like Richard Cartwright began to engage tutors for their children. In 1807 the legislature established four district grammar schools[85] and by 1810 many residents were advocating the creation of common schools, as were to be found in both the United States and Great Britain, "to aid in the administration of justice," the assimilation of the colony's diverse population, and the establishment of a deferential society.[86] From the beginning, however, education in Upper Canada was plagued by a lack of suitable teachers and textbooks. In the prewar years, most masters and books came from the United States and the values they professed were often inimical to "inculcating [those] habits of subordination"[87] deemed to be one of the essential functions of any school system. Various attempts to rectify the situation proved unsuccessful. It was not, however, until a new academy of learning was opened in Ernest

Town, just outside Kingston, in 1811 that the full implications of this problem were realized.

The establishment of the Ernest Town school was first announced in the *Kingston Gazette* in April 1811. Its headmaster was to be Barnabas Bidwell, a recently arrived American. Initially, many must have been delighted at the opening of a new school. For some, however, approval was quickly transformed into horror when it was realized that Bidwell had once been an active member of the republican party in Massachusetts and was rumoured to be a fugitive from justice. "If training and talents were all that were requisite to qualify a man to be a teacher to an academy, it is then presumed that no exception could be taken to Mr. Bidwell," one anonymous resident noted in the *Kingston Gazette*. But "Vindex" found it "revolting to all sense of propriety and everything connected with our normal feelings" that "a malefactor, who has fled from the justice of his own country" should even be considered for the appointment. The rumour of Bidwell's illegal activities was only one and perhaps not the most important reason for "Vindex's" objection. He pointed out that in the United States Bidwell was "a distinguished partisan of democracy in the most unqualified sense of the word." Surely, "Vindex" commented, "it would be hardly possible for those who should be placed under his tuition to escape the infection of his political tenets, which are hostile to the fundamental principles of our government."[88] It seemed that the evil influence of democracy had invaded even this heartland of loyalism.

A number of residents were unconcerned, however. One member of the school committee publicly defended Bidwell's appointment in the next issue of the *Gazette*. He assured possible patrons of the Ernest Town Academy that Bidwell's political beliefs had no bearing on his abilities and would not interfere with his teaching. And despite further protests from "Vindex," Bidwell retained his post.[89] Nonetheless, the Bidwell affair must have confirmed some of the worst fears of influential residents in the area. Not only did many of the so-called late loyalists retain their sympathy for the republican cause but evidently even some of the local leaders of the Kingston region were willing to condone and actually to encourage such ideas.

By the end of 1811 these ongoing concerns about the invasion of American democratic ideas into colonial society became submerged under a far more pressing and immediate fear of direct military invasion from the United States. Throughout 1811 and 1812 the *Upper Canada Gazette* and the *Kingston Gazette*, the only two colonial newspapers still regularly published, were dominated by news of the escalating tensions between Great Britain and the United States. It seemed inevitable that Upper Canada would soon be drawn into the fray. For residents in Kingston and Niagara the prospect was particularly daunting. For twenty years they had maintained close personal and economic relations with American friends. They had relied on the United States for guidance on how to develop the colony. They depended on the United States for most of their news and it was from federalist-American reports and perceptions that they continued to draw most of their own understanding of the political situation in which they were now enmeshed. During the first decade of the new century, that sense of community, which rested on the common heritage and occupations of the leaders at Kingston and Niagara and the federalists in the United States, and on the continuing contact between them, had strengthened and matured. Prominent Upper Canadians believed that they not only shared the attitudes and beliefs of their American conservative friends but also the danger of being overwhelmed by republican troublemakers. For articulate Upper Canadians, far too much of their daily lives was affected by their relations with the United States for them to welcome the coming war or to condemn indiscriminately all American actions.

Even the British-born leaders of York and other British immigrants were dismayed by the prospect of war. Though many had initially been antagonistic to the United States, over the years their anti-Americanism had become somewhat muted. Like the leaders of Kingston and Niagara, they too were dependent on American sources for their news. After 1807, if not before, they also consciously showed a preference for federalist sources and came to accept many of the American conservative explanations of both world and American events. For the most part, influential Upper Canadians in the prewar years looked to the United States with a relatively informed and discriminating eye. It was only to be expected, therefore, that Upper Canada's response to the impending conflict would be marked by ambivalence.

CHAPTER FOUR

The Steady Decline to War

Professor A.R.M. Lower has observed that "Canada has lived her life under the shadow of two great nations, from which nations she has drawn the source of her life."[1] Early Upper Canadian leaders were certainly well aware of their dual heritage and of their continuing dependence on both Great Britain and the United States for the political, economic, and social well-being of the colony. Most of the time these influences coexisted in the colony without any apparent contradiction or tension. Upper Canadians were British subjects who lived in America; from the beginning, British and American ideas and beliefs were inextricably interwoven in the fabric of Upper Canadian society and life, to the point where it is often difficult to untangle the threads to examine each separately. Yet, from time to time, Upper Canadians could not help becoming conscious of the apparent contradiction of their position and of their evolving ideology. The colony had been created, not by amiable cooperation, but out of a bitter confrontation between Great Britain and the United States. Though the Treaty of Paris had brought peace, it had not ensured harmony between the two nations. The revolution had left bitter memories among the protagonists, a spirit of antagonism that was exacerbated by the problems of translating the terms of the peace treaty into the realities of new boundaries and renewed diplomatic relations. Often the colonists' continuing allegiance to the crown was not, on the surface at least, in any way compatible with their ongoing relationship with their southern neighbours. Nonetheless, Upper Canada's unique relationship with the two powers and her continuing reliance on both for material and ideological sustenance persisted.

The strength of the fabric that was gradually becoming Upper Canada was most evident in the way colonists responded to the various crises in British-American relations between 1784 and 1815. From the beginning, Upper Canadians were determined to maintain their vital ties with both nations. After 1784 they worked hard to reestablish amiable relations along the border. Gradually local differences of jurisdiction and of trade were resolved and friendly contacts renewed. What Upper Canadians found much more difficult and eventually impossible to defuse, however, was the mounting international tensions between Great Britain and the United States, fostered by the contagion unleashed by the French Revolution and subsequent Napoleonic Wars.

Throughout the early years, leading colonists unquestioningly supported the mother country in her battles against Napoleon, even though these were ostensibly confined to the European arena. After 1800 Upper Canadians were aware that the federalists in the United States also supported the British fight against tyranny. Yet North American conservatives could not avert American republicans' growing support for the French cause. Moreover, it was soon discovered that there was little that could be done to prevent an all-out military confrontation in North America. Yet, even as war threatened and eventually ravaged the colony, it only confirmed the colonists' prevailing understanding of the United States and Great Britain and of Upper Canada's relationship with both. Upper Canadians were British-Americans. Their allegiance to the crown and the unity of the empire complemented the personal and ideological ties that bound them to the federalists in the United States. While they joined the British in the struggle against "anarchy" and "French principles," they also consciously joined federalist associates in their battle against the seemingly tyrannical and unjust government of the republicans. In fact, the nature of the escalating crisis in the first decade of the nineteenth century and the parameters of the international situation served only to encourage leading Upper Canadians to remain true to their dual heritage.

Writing in the first issue of the *Kingston Gazette* in September 1810, an anonymous settler commented that relations between the United States and Upper Canada were difficult at the best of times. Problems of jurisdiction created by "an unmarked border" had plagued residents on both sides of the border since the establishment of the two communities. By 1810 the war in Europe only exacerbated this ongoing concern. Inhabitants "are in danger of becoming habituated to mutual prejudices, jealousies, reflections, reproaches and all that process of national alienation which had, in the progress of ages, rendered the British and French so inveterate in their hostility as to call each other natural enemies," the commentator wrote with concern. "Such a state of emnity between the inhabitants of the British province and the American citizens, is to be deprecated," he continued, for "it would lessen their enjoyment of life and check their prosperity."[2]

Upper Canadians had been preoccupied with this problem since soon after they had settled the lands north of the St Lawrence and the Great Lakes. Prudence demanded that colonists maintain good relations with their southern neighbours. Most lived only a few miles from the expanding and dynamic republic which could engulf them at any time. More important, however, many settlers had close personal and economic associations with people south of the border, relations which might be harmed or even severed if the two governments were at odds. Yet the very proximity of the United States which facilitated such close ties also inevitably led to periodic tensions between various border communities. Smugglers, criminals, and military deserters constantly took advantage of the propinquity of the United States and Upper Canada; and with an as yet largely undefined boundary, apparent infringements of national jurisdictions were inevitable.

During the early years, military dispatches from Kingston and Niagara frequently reported that British soldiers had deserted to the United States. Though some accounts gave no apparent reason for these desertions, others specifically charged that the Americans were actively encouraging British soldiers to leave their posts with promises of promotion and of higher pay in the American army.[3] Moreover, irritated officers often noted that their attempts to bring men back to justice had met with active opposition from both officials and civilians in the United States. For their part, American authorities accused irresponsible British officers of abusing American citizens and destroying their property. Particularly at Niagara at the turn of the century, tensions ran high.

The *Niagara Herald* reported in September 1801 the case of a British officer who, having crossed the border to take an offender into custody, had unintentionally killed a vital witness who had been attempting to escape. Only a month later, a British constable assaulted an American officer while trying to serve a writ.[4] While official protests and demands for justice were exchanged across the border, the American garrison was put on the alert. Yet to the editor of the *Niagara Herald* both incidents were but a tempest in a teapot. He explained to his readers that the real cause of the problem was the commander of the American garrison. He had imbibed too much of the "spirit of '76," Sylvester Tiffany declared, and was refusing even to enforce "the laws of his own country." Most Americans and Upper Canadians realized that the British were only doing their duty. And even those Americans who did not, the Niagara publisher concluded, were only "at their 'old game' "[5] of obstructing justice, falsely demanding reparations, and generally worsening an already difficult situation.

Such military problems along the border were compounded by civilian disputes over jurisdiction. Criminals were often active in one country only to escape apprehension and prosecution by crossing the border into the other. Counterfeiters seemed to be particularly active despite repeated attempts by the authorities of both nations to put an end to the practice.[6] Another ongoing concern emerged as trade increased across the Great Lakes and the St Lawrence. Though the problem was often one of mistaken jurisdiction, tempers nonetheless flared as officials of both nations frequently stopped vessels for apparent violations of trading regulations.

Far more disruptive, however, was the smuggling in which residents on both sides of the border were actively engaged. Enterprising Americans and Canadians were constantly taking advantage of the relatively open and usually unpatrolled border to bring whiskey, tea, and other goods to markets in Upper Canada. In the summer months, "crafts of all sorts and sizes crowded the River St. Lawrence."[7] In the winter, ice conditions permitting, sleighs laden with goods made the journey north and south. Various American attempts to close the border in 1807 and 1808 only encouraged this illicit trade, providing adventurous entrepreneurs with greater opportunities to increase their profits. As one United States customs officer at Sackets Harbour, NY, reported in 1809, "all the force I can raise is not sufficient to stop them." The smugglers, he noted, "appear determined to evade the law at the risk of their lives." Fearfully, the officer concluded, "my life and the lives of my deputies are threatened daily; what will be the fate of us God only knows."[8] Even the declaration of war in 1812 did not stop this profitable and illegal trade.

Many Upper Canadians undoubtedly benefited directly from these activities. A number realized, however, that smuggling threatened to disrupt peaceful relations between the two governments and they therefore called for its immediate cessation. Upper Canadians should show "a spirit of mutual liberality, candor and forbearance," it was asserted, for only "by preserving harmony and promoting good neighbourhood" could "the friends of both nations ... respectively increase their national prosperity."[9] By the fall of 1810, residents of Kingston and officials on the south shore of Lake Ontario had organized a cooperative effort to apprehend smugglers. "Such instances of the reciprocation of acts of justice and liberality," one contributor to the *Kingston Gazette* remarked with approval, "were much more condusive to mutual prosperity than a state of legislative counteraction and hostility." Another reader reminded Kingstonians that "in the preservation of peace, every member of the community has a degree of influence and a correspondent duty to perform."[10] "National difficulties" persisted, however, as a result of "the mutual incursions and acts of jurisdiction and other interferences of the subject of one government with the known and acknowledged limits of the other."[11] Moreover, most residents had no idea of the actual limits of their respective governments. Thus despite numerous recommendations that the boundary between the United States and the province be clearly defined, confusion prevailed until well after the War of 1812 when a joint commission finally settled the thorny issue.[12]

The periodic problems which erupted along the border were, for the most part, local concerns, touching only those living in Kingston, along the St Lawrence, and in the Niagara regions. Yet colonial officials, though physically isolated in York, could also not forget the growing giant to the south or the fact that isolated border incidents could easily escalate into a major international crisis. As a result, Lieutenant Governor Simcoe, who of all British officials during the period was perhaps most antagonistic to the United States, and his successors made numerous attempts to forestall and alleviate any grounds for local tensions. Early in the 1790s, for example, legislation was enacted to stop smugglers and counterfeiters. In addition, the government frequently called for residents to maintain and promote good relations with their American cousins.[13]

For most Upper Canadians, such official encouragement was unnecessary. It was in their best interests, personally and economically, to keep the border areas open and free of strife. They therefore did all in their power to ensure international cordiality. For example, just before the turn of the century, one settler in Niagara suggested that inhabitants of the area gather together for various sporting activities to supplement the already existing "intercourse of economic, friendship and sociability between the people of the province and those in the neighbouring part of the United States." A year earlier, the *Upper Canada Gazette* had reported with some pleasure that the American garrison had shown the colours and played the "British Grenadiers" on the occasion of the king's birthday. At that time the editor had remarked on "the uncommon unanimity which has attended the intercourse of the military in their extensive lines" on both sides of the border. Considering the proximity of the gar-

risons, such "unanimity ... was totally unexpected by all" and the
editor had fervently hoped that such "acts of civility" would "beget
a substantial friendship between individuals and which at length
pervades or unites even nations as a band of brothers."[14] These
various individual attempts to encourage civility and goodwill seemed
to be successful, on the local level at least; yet it became progressively
evident to leading colonists that harmony on the North American
frontier did not ensure peace between their respective governments.
As early as 1793 Upper Canadians and Americans found that despite
all their best efforts they were once again on the brink of war.

Open warfare between Great Britain and the United States had
ended in 1784; but the Treaty of Paris had not stopped the two
nations from jockeying for position on the western frontiers of North
America. Particularly between 1791 and 1794, relations between the
British and American governments grew increasingly strained. The
British government and its representatives in Upper Canada refused
to relinquish their forts in the west, claiming that the Americans had
not provided the loyalist refugees with compensation. Officials in
the United States countercharged that the British were encouraging
Indian uprisings which threatened American frontier settlements in
the west. Events in early 1794 only added more justification for the
heated controversy.

In the spring of that year, Lord Dorchester, the governor general
of British North America, delivered a speech to the western Indians
in which he reaffirmed Great Britain's brotherhood with her native
allies. At almost the same time, Lieutenant Governor Simcoe completed the construction of a new fort at Miami (near present-day
Toledo), in what Americans had always considered to be their territory.[15] The government of the United States regarded both actions
as an open challenge to their nationhood. A report from an Albany
paper, reprinted in the *Upper Canada Gazette* in July 1794, explained
the attitude that many Americans took to the situation. "Our restless
British neighbours," it declared, "have, by their insulting and
unwarranted intrusions induced us to commence defensive operations." It was therefore necessary for the United States to proceed
to "a total conquest" of the west and "a reduction of the interior
posts of the Upper Provinces." Only this, it was angrily proclaimed,
"will effectively prevent any further inroads of either British or
savage intruders in our peaceful frontiers."[16] American officials began
to stop all boats and goods from entering Upper Canada from the
south. Simultaneously, General "Mad Anthony" Wayne and a con-
tingent of American troops began to advance on British forts on the
western frontier.

Prominent Upper Canadians apprehensively watched as imperial officials responded. "The militia of Detroit and Niagara were drafted" and British reinforcements were rushed to Detroit. Richard Cartwright reported in a letter to Isaac Todd that he was "in full expectation that war would be kindled among us immediately." And he continued, "however an American war might terminate in a national point of view, it must at all events, be ruinous to this Province."[17] It was with considerable relief, therefore, that influential colonists learned in October 1794 of the success of special American emissary John Jay's mission to Great Britain. "Mr. Jay is to return with the olive branch,"[18] Cartwright joyfully wrote to Todd. Gradually tensions between the American and colonial and British governments eased and, for a time at least, peace and harmony once again prevailed in North America.

The resolution of the North American controversies in 1794 had little impact, however, on British-American relations generally, for another point of contention had already emerged which would prove to be far more divisive. In 1793 the new republican government of France had declared war on Great Britain. Almost immediately, the government of the United States had proclaimed its neutrality. Official neutrality, however, did not reflect the growing sympathies in the United States for one or other side of the conflict. Indeed, by 1794 differing American perceptions of the French Revolution were beginning to amplify "the already existing internal disagreements in the country."[19] The so-called "Democrats" led by Thomas Jefferson soon became identified by both American *and* Upper Canadian observers as the "French faction" – strong supporters of the new European republic. The federalists, on the other hand, relying on a combination of British conservative reports and their own presuppositions regarding the problems of unrestrained democracy, condemned the French Revolution and its consequences. This stand by the federalists undoubtedly contributed greatly to the growing empathy between influential Upper Canadians and conservative Americans; certainly it heightened the colonists' antipathy to republicanism.

Between 1794 and 1800 Upper Canadians watched with interest and some concern as American neutrality was buffeted by the combined pressure of the European conflict and internal political divisions. Much of the time "a good understanding" seemed to exist between the republic and Great Britain. The so-called "Anglo-Federalists" (or "monarchial party," as it was pejoratively called by the republicans)[20] clearly considered that the French Revolution was "an insurrection against all nations, a war against all laws of society, and vastly more dangerous to the peace and happiness of the world than the partial revolt of a few counties in the United States of America." They openly supported "the glorious and successful stand that Great Britain has singly made against the ferocious and desolating tyranny of France." Like prominent Upper Canadians, the federalists "contemplated with increased attachment and reverence and pride, the great nation" which "all alone ... has kept her stand and singly braved the storm that has laid low so many of the distinguished powers of the world."[21] Indeed, it seemed in 1796 that "a closer amity than the one existing now" would be impossible to attain. Some Upper Canadians and federalists even suggested, in the light of the repeated reports of French violations of American sovereignty, that the United States would be "pushed into a general combination"[22] and declare war on France. But Franco-American relations remained "in a state of uncertainty." By 1797 the republican opposition in government was beginning to apply considerable pressure on the federalist administration to reach an accommodation with France. And despite "the continuance of the degradation of their commerce,"[23] some Americans were actually taking up the French standard.

The increasingly vocal stand of the Anglo-federalists in support of Great Britain strengthened the ideological ties which bound influential Upper Canadians to the North American community. Not only did the federalists and the Upper Canadian elite share basic attitudes towards society and the state, they also now had a common enemy. For them the "French influence," despite its defeat at the polls in 1796, clearly continued to infect American political and social life and threaten the stability and very survival of the republic. To Englishman William Cobbett (then living in the United States) and to many Americans in the late 1790s, the root of the problem was that "there were too many Frenchmen" in the country.

An article reprinted from Cobbett's *Porcupine Gazette* in the *Upper Canada Gazette* explained in 1798 that the Frenchmen in the United States were obviously "jacobins and known enemies of ... peace and security." The Anglo-American editor advocated that these men, most of whom had attached themselves to the republican party, should be expelled before their "seditious" influence could predominate and they themselves become a vanguard for French invasion forces in the future.[24] Both federalists and Upper Canadians agreed that the French "had to be guarded against." "Their acts of seduction," many feared, would divide the American people from their Upper Canadian associates and shake the "whole fabric of society."[25] The presence of French aliens in the United States, however, was not the most pressing concern. To the leaders of Upper Canada, the root of political and social upheaval south of the border lay in the strengthening forces of the republican party. By 1798 the republicans had shown themselves to be "the friends of France more than of their own country." They had become willing agents of the French government and it was reported that "some of the base traitors have even declared that in the event of war, they will join France."[26] Before the turn of the century, influential Upper Canadians quite naturally believed that if the republicans ever attained power, they would weaken the government of the United States and leave the nation open to a French invasion.

The republican victory in 1800 was therefore viewed by the federalists and many Upper Canadians as potentially disastrous to all of North America. Not only would the United States now "be cursed with all the evils of anarchy"[27] which resulted from the democrats' encouragement of factions; but, it was feared, all of the continent would be subject to the pernicious French influence. Statements by public officials on both sides of the border stressed that in the United States the door was now open to revolution, to mob rule, and to anarchy. And if the French succeeded in the United States, Upper Canadians fully expected that they too would be engulfed by the forces of republicanism. Soon after Jefferson's victory, predictions of an American "war with England"[28] began to appear in the colonial newspapers and some Upper Canadians feared that their hopes for future peace and prosperity were doomed.

In the short term, Upper Canadian and federalist concerns about disorder and armed conflict seemed to be unfounded. Peace in Europe in 1802 dampened tensions in America. As the members of the House of Assembly commented in their reply to the speech from the throne that year, Upper Canadians "feelingly rejoice in the common happiness of Europe on its deliverance from the calamities of war." For the next five years there seemed to be "the strongest proof ... of the sincere intention of the British government to cultivate the lasting friendship of the United States."[29] And these intentions were apparently reciprocated by the American government. Yet the seeds of a potential conflict remained. In the spring of 1803 war between Great Britain and France resumed. Four years later, in the summer of 1807, the *Upper Canada Gazette* reported, on the authority of the *Richmond Enquirer*, the recall of the British ambassador, Erskine, from Washington. And that July, with the sinking of the American frigate *Chesapeake* by the British *Leopard*, the tranquillity of the past six years was irrevocably broken. Old tensions between Great Britain and the United States were renewed and new antagonisms flourished. By the end of the summer, Upper Canadians were again living in fear of the imminent outbreak of war with the United States. This time, however, the danger from outside the colony was compounded by the internal unrest generated by the activities of Justice Thorpe.

Though the colonists did not fully realize it at the time, the *Chesapeake* affair was the first step on a road which would lead them to war. No one in the province would welcome the prospect; but, welcome or not, Upper Canada had to be prepared to face the ordeal. As prominent Upper Canadians hurriedly began to make the colony ready, they found themselves forced to reconcile their continuing allegiance to the king with their ongoing relationship to the American republic. In the process, many leading colonists consciously showed themselves to be Anglo-Americans, unwilling to give up their association with either nation.

The first public report of the *Chesapeake* affair in Upper Canada was a short and rather innocuous comment in the *Upper Canada Gazette*, 25 July 1807. "It is to be feared," the editor wrote, "that there was too great tenacity on the one side and precipitancy on the other; it is devoutly to be hoped that a friendly investigation and discussion of the points will prevent" the interests of Great Britain and the United States which were "so intimately blended, from rupture, injury or diminution." For the next six months, Upper Canadians joined "their friends in the United States" who, like themselves, were "the descendants of Englishmen" and "advocates of common sense and reason,"[30] in desperately hoping that a rupture could be avoided. Any conflict, North American conservatives believed, "would be impolitic, ruinous and extremely to be deprecated."[31] Yet the loud protests and repeated calls from the federalists for prudence and forbearance did not stop the American government from sounding the alarm and making preparations for war. By the end of 1807 hopes that the differences between the United States and Great Britain would "soon be adjusted"[32] began to fade and the Upper Canadian government had no alternative but to call the colony to arms.

The most pressing concern of colonial leaders in 1807 and 1808, as it was to be in 1812, was that the majority of Upper Canadians would be but hesitant combatants; indeed, it was feared that many might well refuse to fight at all. Most residents had no political or emotional attachment to the king or the British Empire. A majority of colonists had only recently arrived from the United States and would be loath to take up arms against their former compatriots. Moreover, their natural reluctance to fight was being encouraged in

1807 by the activities of Justice Thorpe. There was ample evidence that many settlers were "weak enough to be misled by Thorpes Acts and Cajoleries."[33] It was feared that too many believed that the colonial administration was inept and that the colony was mismanaged; to expect their wholehearted support for the British cause was unrealistic. Yet without complete cooperation prominent Upper Canadians knew that the province was doomed. All that they had fought for during the revolution and all that they had struggled to establish in their new homes would be lost. Thus, to protect not only their own positions of influence but, what was more crucial, to ensure the preservation of their society, colonial leaders set out to counteract internal disaffection and encourage all colonists to enthusiastically take up arms in the colony's defence.

In a speech to the local militia in December 1807, Richard Cartwright explained that as Great Britain had been forced into a war with France so too might Upper Canadians be forced to battle "a country where the ruling Party holds in abhorrence such even of their fellow subjects as are opposed to the extravagances of Democracy." "Honest men and loyal subjects are bound to be angered" by the American government's actions, he stated unequivocally. "Honour and gratitude and duty" demanded that the colonists "exert themselves in the cause of their country." By defending themselves, Cartwright told his audience, they defended the cause of Great Britain, a mother country which had given them "a Soil of no common fertility that furnished to the industrious every necessity of life." He went on, "We live in the most unbounded security of our homes and property without being at any charge for our Judicial Establishment. We enjoy every benefit of the best regulated Government ... without being called upon to defray any part of the Expense. ... These are the benefits conferred on us alone and cold and worthless must be the heart on which they fail to make an impression."[34]

For the next four years, the leaders of Upper Canada, in an attempt both to answer the accusations of Justice Thorpe and to engender a spirit of pride and gratitude among the settlers, carefully prepared statements on the many benefits that the colonists actually received from the British connection. Parliament had provided land at virtually no expense; the colonists paid no taxes; the justice system was fair and honest, and, as Richard Cartwright and others stressed, in Upper Canada the colonists enjoyed "the greatest practical political freedom."[35] It was realized, however, that these benefits alone would not persuade the majority of settlers to take up arms against their old homeland. As has been previously noted, most colonists had little contact with the colonial government and the British connection played little conscious part in their lives. Indeed, even for the leaders themselves, the benefits of the membership in the empire provided only part of the rationale for their willingness to participate in another North American war. For, like the majority in the colony, many prominent Upper Canadians were Americans, and their American heritage and their own understanding of the United States also played an essential part in their response to the impending conflict.

"What can we expect," Cartwright asked, "if America was successful in its invasion?" Addressing the militiamen assembled in Kingston in December 1807, he warned that "the former Animosities and Persecutions against the Adherents of Loyalty ... would be revived with more Vigour. ... We should be made to feel every injury and indignity that personal and political enmity should dictate to vulgar minds, armed with power and secure from Impunity."[36] The leaders of the colony pointed out to the population at large that it was "the blind and misguided party" – the republicans – who threatened to bring about war. "The French Influence" threatened to sever "the ties of interest and affection which ought so powerfully to unite"[37] the colonists and their neighbours in the United States. Implicitly, Upper Canadian settlers were urged to join the British *and* their federalist friends in the United States in a virtuous battle against Franco-republican tyranny and oppression.

Thus while colonial leaders consciously turned to Great Britain for military support and for inspiration to stave off the menace from the south, they also appealed to the strong Upper Canadian-federalist tradition in the colony to galvanize its inhabitants into action. The "most enlightened and patriotic citizens" of the United States realized that war would harm American commerce and "ultimately the existence of their independence." It was pointed out that the federalists believed that their own government should "accept all honourable terms and never fight in so ruinous a war for doubtful, much less unjust claims."[38] As the *Upper Canada Gazette* reported, one congressman had even written to the president that "we are doing no good. I fear we are about to plunge the nation into the most dreadful calamities, unnecessarily and wantonly. ... We are, in my opinion, violating the great rights of the people."[39]

From 1807 to the outbreak of war in 1812, the colonial press presented in considerable detail the American conservative opposition to the policies of the national administration. In part, this was undoubtedly intended to demonstrate to the majority of Upper Canadians that in preparing to battle the forces of tyranny and republicanism from the south, they would be joining their American friends. Settlers could take pride and defend their new homes, for in doing so they would be remaining true to their old homes and beliefs. But the presentation of federalist news and commentary also reflected the elites' own beliefs that their cause was just. Certainly they did not accept or attempt to foster among the colonists as a whole an indiscriminate anti-Americanism. Indeed, influential Upper Canadians saw no conflict between their commitment to the British Empire and an ongoing relationship with an American community of conservatives.

Upper Canadian preparations for war in 1807 and 1808 were premature and some American reports appearing in the *Upper Canada Gazette* in March 1808 even suggested that the "DANGER" of the French influence on American councils was "NEARLY OVER" and North Americans could shortly expect that the United States would declare war on France.[40] Such rumours were unfounded, however, and tension between the United States and Great Britain remained high. For though the government of the United States had not declared war on Great Britain, the republican administration, after a special and what Upper Canadian and federalist observers considered a "secretive" session of Congress, imposed an embargo on all American ports. Some feared, as an article from the *Boston Gazette* printed in the *Upper Canada Gazette* in December 1807 warned, that "it would put an end to all the negotiations for Peace and make a War inevitable."[41]

Throughout the winter and early spring of 1808, it was noted that American newspapers "teemed with news of the ill effects"[42] of the embargo. As the editor of the *Upper Canada Gazette* reported, American merchants were discontented and seamen were unemployed. A report from Schenectady claimed that four-fifths of all Americans were distressed by the actions of their government. "The merchants of Boston ... are generally determined not to comply" with the new regulations, it was reported, and many federalists expected that the people would not submit "to unconstitutional, ruinous and tyrannical laws, enforced at the point of a Bayonet."[43] The embargo "pitted Americans against Americans"[44] and there were a number of prominent federalists who publicly voiced their disappointment with their government's actions. In the spring of 1808 the *Gazette* reprinted a letter received from Congressman Timothy Pickering defending the rights of the British government to take their own subjects off American ships and deploring "the unnecessary and unjust actions of the President and national administration." A year later, the Massachusetts legislature received a letter from John Quincy Adams, advocating that the embargo be lifted. If not, Adams concluded, "democracy

A typical federalist view of the embargo in 1807 which was shared by leading Upper Canadians (New York Historical Society)

dies for ever in the east."[45] Another member of Congress went so far as to predict that civil war was imminent. Throughout 1808 and 1809 public opposition to the actions of the republican administration grew. In Rhode Island, in Massachusetts, and along the eastern seaboard and in northern New York, merchants, businessmen, and politicians publicly denounced their national government for its base attempt to appease Bonaparte.[46]

There was one resident of Kingston who welcomed the slight inconvenience that the American regulations placed on Upper Canadian commerce. In an unsigned article in the *Kingston Gazette* in January 1811, he commented that the embargo forced Upper Canadians to form "habits of using our great outlet for the purpose of exports and imports." He added that it "gives a spring to business here, and promotes a spirit of enterprise which if rightly directed and applied, will be useful and salutory to this country."[47] However, most Upper Canadians deplored the psychological and emotional effects of the embargo on Upper Canadian-American relations. The editor of the *Upper Canada Gazette* noted that it would not force the colonial government "to an unworthy compromise of national honour." But, he continued, it did cause unwarranted hardship on both sides of the border.[48] The opposition to the embargo demonstrated to the many Upper Canadians who were still hoping for a lasting peace that a majority of Americans did not support the ill-founded policies of their administration. Perhaps as important to Upper Canadians, however, was that the aftermath of the *Chesapeake* affair also confirmed the ill effects that a "bland and misguided party"[49] could have on any government.

In the United States, according to one American publication, the people who were naturally "worthy of the fraternity and friendship" of all Upper Canadians had been "sacrificed on the altar of French influence." Despite the "atlean efforts" of the virtuous federalists, the United States had succumbed to disorder wrought by political parties and the "Virginian faction."[50] Some Upper Canadians came to believe that this factionalism was endemic to the "evil system" of republicanism. Yet Upper Canadians could not in 1807 and 1808 feel too superior, for many believed that even under the British constitution "irresponsible" demagogues like Justice Thorpe and destructive political factions were causing havoc.

The repercussions of the events of 1807 and 1808 echoed through the minds of Upper Canadians for the next three years. Apprehensively, they watched as negotiations between the United States and Great Britain proceeded at a painstaking pace. In the newspapers, rumours of war between the two English-speaking powers were confused with reports that an American war with France would shortly be declared.[51] Nonetheless, it was becoming increasingly evident that the federalists were having less and less influence on their own government's policies. The political decline of the federalists did not, however, sever the bonds of the North American conservative community. Upper Canadians considered that American tories still had much to offer them. Prominent colonists continued to rely on the federalists for their information about international and American affairs and the federalists' viewpoint continued to provide the underpinning of much of Upper Canada's understanding of the developing crisis. Indeed, between 1808 and 1811 that sense of community which spanned the border was strengthened by a common response to deteriorating Anglo-American relations.[52] Yet during this period prominent Upper Canadians came to realize that the ideology and the actions of the American federalists provided only part of the answer to their own internal problems and those affecting the United States. As war approached, the colonial elite came to rely increasingly on the British connection to defend their independence and way of life.

In January and February 1812, after three years of uneasy peace, the leaders of Upper Canada once again believed that war was "at no great distance."[53] "We wish and hope for peace," Gen. Isaac Brock, president of Upper Canada, explained to the provincial legislature, but "it is nevertheless our duty to be prepared for war." He therefore called on the colonists' representatives to institute "a regular system of military instruction to the Militia" of the colony and generally to adopt "such measures as will best secure for the internal peace of the Country and defeat every hostile aggression." Brock assured the legislature that "the acknowledged importance of this colony to the parent State will secure the countinuance of her powerful protection." Nonetheless, "the task imposed upon you ... is arduous." "It is a task, however," Brock concluded, that "I hope and trust, laying aside every consideration but that of the public good, you will perform with a spirit of firmness, discretion and promptitude."[54]

During the next few months colonial leaders watched fearfully as relations between the mother country and the United States again deteriorated to the breaking-point. In their newspapers, Upper Canadians read about the heated debates in the American Congress concerning British-American relations. In March 1811 a new French minister arrived in Washington and many accepted the warning put forth by a contributor to the *Albany Gazette* and reprinted in the

Kingston Gazette that this was but another attempt "to widen the breach between the United States and draw that country nearer to France." "Step by step," both the federalists and Upper Canadians believed, "we are to be drawn closer to the vortex into which French ambitions is drawing everything in the European theatre."[55] That same month, North Americans were shocked and dismayed by reports of the confrontation between the American frigate *President*, and the British sloop *Little Belt*, a crisis all too reminiscent of the *Chesapeake* affair. "Ferocious consequences" were feared as President Madison declared that he had "a duty of putting the United States into armour to secure greater respect of America's mercantile flag."[56]

Despite the seriousness of the situation, the House of Assembly at the beginning of 1812 was reluctant to commit itself fully to a war footing. Members refused to pass measures to require militiamen to forswear allegiance to any foreign country before they were issued arms; they also denied the president's request to suspend the writ of *habeus corpus*.[57] To many colonial leaders this uncooperative attitude only increased their fear that if war was declared, "the great mass of people" would "join the American government."[58] Obviously, little had changed since the crisis of 1807. If anything, pro-American sentiments had strengthened. Most Upper Canadians were still reluctant to go to war, and it was often predicted that when war was declared many would flee back to their old homes. What was far more disconcerting was that some residents might decide to betray their new home by remaining in the province and actively supporting the American cause. Influential Upper Canadians once again, therefore, launched a propaganda campaign to convince the settlers that their homes were worth fighting for and that, despite apparently overwhelming odds, they could be victorious. Presenting arguments that had been developed over the previous five years, they contended that Upper Canadians should remain true to their dual heritage. The colonists must fight for "their sovereign ... their rights and privileges ... and fight for everything that is dear and sacred" to them; their wives, their children, their property, were all at stake.[59] And, as one confident settler wrote, "if the inhabitants are true to themselves" and implicitly to their federalist friends, "the wantonness and rapacity of the American democrats will meet with chastisement they will little calculate upon."[60]

The first call to arms was made by an anonymous "Canadian" writing to the *Kingston Gazette* in January 1812. This "most unnatural war," he wrote, was being forced by the designs of "the corrupt and venal speculators ... the avowed patrons of slavery and dealers in human blood" who were determined "to render a most acceptable service to Bonaparte." "I deprecate war, and above all this most unnatural war, and the disgraceful and corrupt motives which have led to it," he continued. "It will be a war waged in cooperation with a bloody Despot, who has wantonly trampled upon the liberties of Europe and deluged every country around him with the blood of its inhabitants." But all was not lost, "Canadian" reassured his readers. "If the inhabitants of this Province ... act with a degree of spirit and unanimity or if they are not greatly degenerated from what their ancestors were," victory was assured. For "supported by the well known courage and discipline of the British army," the residents of the colony, he predicted, "will form an impenetrable barrier and prove the safeguard and shield of their country."[61]

During the next six months, articulate Upper Canadians stressed that "the American who really loves his country cannot but deplore the wickedness and folly of his Government, who have thus dragged that nation into a war with the only country on earth which stands between them and universal despotism."[62] All "the best men in the nation, men of the greatest talents, courage and wealth"[63] in the United States opposed the war. Like their associates in Upper Canada, these Americans knew that it was the policies of the republican administration which had "destroyed their commerce, ruined the merchant, disheartened the farmer, palsied every incitement to industry and thrown the whole nation into a kind of palsy and despair."[64] Moreover, the republican government, "cunning pretenders to Liberty and equality," had "trampled on the rights of these citizens" and had "sold their country to our implacable Enemy." The federalists "were in danger" if "they uttered a syllable against the glorious war." In the light of such evidence, it was quite natural for leading Upper Canadians to believe that many Americans "with Washingtonian principles" would rather die "than stain their hands in the blood of an unjust war."[65]

Upper Canadians could not and did not "deny the Patriotism or courage of the American people." But, the leaders of the colony stressed, many Americans were just as reluctant as the colonists to go to war. "It is not to be supposed," they asserted, "that the yeomenry of that country will quit their comfortable homes and abandon their families and every tie in life to expose themselves to the bayonet or tomahawk in fighting the battles of Bonaparte, Madison and Co."[66] As a result, the American government would be able to recruit only "the most worthless part" of the population. Their army would "be composed of the refuse and scum of the earth, Renegades and Vagabonds ... savages of the worst description." And, of necessity, it would be commanded "by raw and inexperienced men who have probably never seen an engagement."[67] When Upper Canadians fought to defend their homes and their way of life, they would therefore not be battling American friends and relations but only those "corrupt and venal wretches"[68] who were leading the republic to rack and ruin.

More to the point, Upper Canadians, it was stressed "must take warning from the misfortunes" of their federalist friends. The colonists must "avoid the errors which have plunged" the Americans "from the height of glory to the lowest degradation, which have reduced them from prosperity and affluence to the lowest poverty and distress."[69] As Richard Cartwright, writing in the *Kingston Gazette* under the pen-name "Falkland," commented, "those amongst us who are capable of comparing their situation here with that of the inhabitants of any other country must see and acknowledge that their own is superior." As "brave and loyal people," Upper Canadians must therefore come forward and "rally round the Government."[70] Upper Canadians must defend their homes and a government and constitution which afforded them "the most perfect security of their persons and property." They would be supported by "the best disciplined troops in the world" who have a "confidence grounded upon the national glory." Their army would be led by "experienced officers who are perfectly acquainted with the country."[71] Moreover, their success was ordained by God and sanctified by the righteousness of their cause. Both self-interest and duty, it was asserted, compelled Upper Canadians to be "true to themselves," to the empire and to their old federalist compatriots. If not, they too, like their federalist friends, would be reduced "to a state of dependency and misery."[72]

While articulate Upper Canadians vigorously prepared the colonists to repulse an American invasion, they nonetheless continued to hope that "cold reflection and the dictates of justice" would "avert the calamities of war."[73] Following closely in the newspapers the negotiations between the two governments, Upper Canadians believed that the British government, at least, was seeking a peaceful resolution of their differences with the United States. The colonial papers also printed, often in full, reports of the mounting public and private opposition to the war in the United States. Simultaneously, however, Upper Canadians were receiving reports that the American army was being expanded and that the navy and local militiamen were preparing for war. As summer approached, it was clear that the wise counsel of the federalists had gone unheeded amidst the din of "party spirit." The "gilded wand of Napoleon"[74] was leading American policy against the wishes of the American people. And though the leaders of Upper Canada were sympathetic to the plight of their neighbours, as war drew closer they grew increasingly concerned about their own position. They were determined to defend their community and keep its residents secure from those evil forces which had already overwhelmed the United States.

Ironically, and perhaps appropriately, the first newspaper report that war had finally been declared came in an excerpt from an American newspaper reprinted in the *Kingston Gazette* on 23 June 1812.[75] A week later, Stephen Miles, on information received from Albany, confirmed the report. "It is pretty clearly ascertained," he wrote, "that war with the United States is no longer to be avoided." He therefore recommended to "every loyal subject and friend of his King and Country the dying admonition of the lamented and immortal Nelson, ENGLAND EXPECTS EVERY MAN WILL DO HIS DUTY."[76] On 4 July the editors of the *York Gazette* condemned the "rash step" that the American government had taken. It was not until the following week, however, that a proclamation by General Brock confirmed that Upper Canada and the United States were really at war: "I do hereby strictly enjoin and require all his Majesty's leige subjects to be obedient to the lawful authorities; to forbear all communications with the enemy or persons residing within the territory of the United States, and to manifest their loyalty by zealous co-operation with his Majesty's armed forces in defense of the Province and repulse the enemy."[77]

Neither official proclamations nor the eventual outbreak of hostilities, however, could force Upper Canadians to cut all ties with the United States. Individuals as well as goods and news continued to flow across the lakes and rivers. Upper Canadians continued to rely on the United States for their news, both of North America and of Europe.[78] Indeed, that sense of community and common cause which so many Upper Canadians shared with federalists south of the border was strengthened by their common, strongly critical response to the war.

The declaration of war seemed to have little impact on the lives of most Upper Canadians. Actual fighting in the first few months was restricted to the most western portions of the colony. In Kingston and York and surrounding areas, business continued as usual. Nonetheless, Upper Canadians in all parts of the colony felt the urgency of the situation. In the tiny capital of York, residents were inundated with district war reports, government regulations and proclamations, and all manner of rumours about the progress of the war. At the end of July 1812 Brock recalled the legislature and requested that it take measures to "protect and defend the Loyal Inhabitants" from the "machinations"[79] of the few traitors who were still in the colony. In Kingston, the militia was mustered; improvements finally began to be made to the town's fortifications and the dockyards were suddenly busy building ships to defend the lakes.[80] It was at this time that the first news of the fighting at Michilimacinac, at Detroit, and in the Niagara region began to appear in the *Kingston Gazette* and the *Upper Canada Gazette*. Even then, most could only watch apprehensively from a distance as British troops and the local militia engaged the American forces.

Indeed, many in the colony in the summer of 1812 continued to hope that an all-out confrontation engulfing the whole province might still be avoided. In mid-July a "Well-Wisher" urged those in Kingston not to be the aggressors. "Be watchful and vigilant at all points," he wrote, "and in the persevering spirit which had eminently distinguished the sons of Britain in Spain and Portugal, FIGHT BACK AND CONQUER" but "ONLY WHENEVER YOUR COUNTRY IS INVADED."[81] Upper Canadians realized that most south of the border also wished to forestall disaster. Stephen Miles reported in the *Kingston Gazette* on 21 July that the residents of the Canadas and Vermont and New York had agreed "to join in preventing individuals from committing outrage by plunder or otherwise." "Thus far," Miles continued, "we believe that inhabitants upon both sides had received little or no inconvenience from the approaching war."[82] Members of the House of Assembly, too, were still hesitant to grant Brock's request to suspend the civil rights of the colonists. Many Upper Canadians were evidently reluctant to provoke any further confrontation.

Throughout the summer and fall, the colonial press continued to give considerable attention to American opposition to the war. In Albany, the *Kingston Gazette* reported, "the utmost dismay prevailed ... on account of the contemplated hostilities ... which is everywhere deemed as unnecessary as unjust." In Boston, "the commercial part of the town" expressed its feelings "by all vessels hoisting their colours half mast." Upper Canadians noted that the people of Vermont refused to take up arms, and the government of Connecticut would not call out the militia, declaring that such actions would be illegal.[83] Upper Canadians read that even some members of the House of Representatives publicly condemned the administration, and the legislatures of New Hampshire, Connecticut, and Massachusetts were all opposed to the "mad Measures"[84] of Madison and Congress.

The federalists and the leaders of Upper Canada believed that "the President apprehends that he and the rest of Congress had outstripped the feelings and demands of the American public."

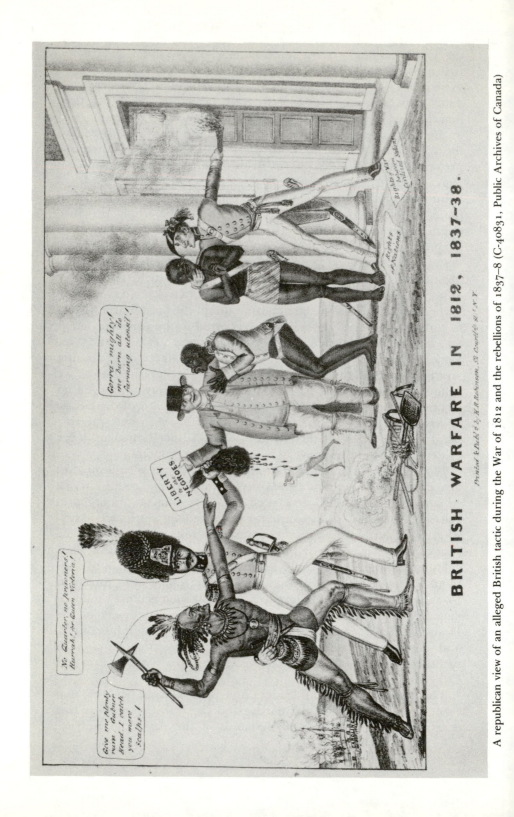

BRITISH WARFARE IN 1812, 1837–38.

Printed & Publd by H.R.Robinson, 52 Courtldt st N.Y.

A republican view of an alleged British tactic during the War of 1812 and the rebellions of 1837–8 (C-40831, Public Archives of Canada)

Moreover, "all his angry passions against Great Britain are enveloped with a fear of civil commotion or want of accord and support of the other constituted authorities in the United States."[85] It seemed clear that the predictions, first made after Jefferson's victory in 1800, that the United States would soon succumb to anarchy and chaos were finally being realized. In the American republic, "the tyranny of democracy ... had perverted the will of the majority."[86]

Thus, for the duration of the war, the Upper Canadian elite could not in all conscience condemn all Americans for their plight. Most, they believed, were individuals like themselves, caught in a situation not of their making. Indeed, most Americans, it was asserted, agreed that the war was being waged "without justifiable cause and prosecuted in a manner which indicates that conquest and ambition are its real motives."[87] To influential Upper Canadians, it was "that petty tyrant Madison" and his "weak as well as wicked administration" who were the enemy. These republican administrators, "the Virginian oligarchy," were "nearly akin to the deists and athiests of France ... men of hardened hearts, seared consciences, reprobate minds and desperate in wickedness."[88] It was these "minions ... of the Corsican Usurper" who were causing "the blood of American free men to flow to cement his power."[89]

Riots in the United States in the late summer of 1812 only seemed to confirm to many Upper Canadians the extent to which the French influence was causing "the decline and downfall of the American republic." A mob "instigated by the friends of the administration and completed by French democracy"[90] had destroyed the presses of the federalist newspaper, the *Baltimore Federal Republican*. The *Kingston Gazette* reported that "private property had been destroyed and the most brutal murders committed upon the most respectable individuals for daring to question the fallibility of men administering the government."[91] And this was not an isolated incident. Colonial newspapers recounted that elsewhere in Vermont "the right of free men is trampled down with impunity by an undisciplined soldiery." In Burlington, the commander of the American forces was prepared "to tar and feather those who were disrespectful of the government."[92] The measures of the Madison administration nurtured "mutual jealousies, separate and jarring interests," and "the seeds of ultimate disunion."[93] Upper Canadians watched as discontent in the United States mounted. The leaders of the colony asked each other and all the residents of Upper Canada, "is it reasonable for any individual in the province to expect greater protection from the United States than is granted to its own people? Will a government that does not cause to be respected either the lives or property of its own citizens 'come to protect' not to injure you?"[94]

During the war years, the *Kingston Gazette* (the only newspaper to continue relatively uninterrupted publication) drew a graphic picture of America as a country "on the road to ruin."[95] It was stressed that "the restrictive inhibitions" of their rulers "and the baneful consequences have sapped to its foundations the integrity" of all Americans. The republicans had "debauched the morals" of the community and "reared a mountain of corruption on the site of a temple of virtue."[96] The war was "sapping the wealth and prosperity of the land." American commerce was being destroyed, "cities ... laid to waste." War brought only "dishonour and suffering" to the United States. It divided the people and "threatened to destroy the union."[97]

Influential colonists also pointed out that "the decline of republicanism and national spirit" which marked "the tyrannical administration of Madison and Tompkins"[98] inevitably affected that country's efforts in the field. In the early months of the war, it was asserted that the American armies were disheartened by defeat. And to read both the federalist and Upper Canadian reports appearing in the colonial newspapers, it seemed that these early misfortunes were never overcome. In November 1813, for example, the Americans were soundly defeated at Williamsburg. Four months later, at Fort Niagara, "the strongest and most formidable position" that the Americans had held on the Canadian front was overrun. In June 1814 an anticipated easy victory at Montreal was transformed into a disgraceful fiasco.[99] Some Upper Canadians knew that the federalists attributed this "climax of folly and cowardice" to "the promiscuous scamperings of officers and men." Others laid the blame on "Cowardly Hull, the casconding Smith and the creeping Dearborn."[100] Certainly, as colonial leaders had predicted, the American generals were inept, the officers inexperienced, and their men reluctant combatants. However, all continued to believe that the root of the problem was in Washington. "The horrors and ruins of a dishonoured, unsuccessful war," proclaimed one American account, could be attributed to "the little man" and the "Virginian dynasty."[101] Many Americans charged that "if the Secretary of War had been honest and capable ... how very different would now be our ranks among the nations of the world." Instead, "our armies, starving, sickly, in despair and dying, are almost buried in the snows of the North." Both north and south of the border it was asked, "what apology have they to offer?"[102]

In contrast to this picture of American degradation and despair,

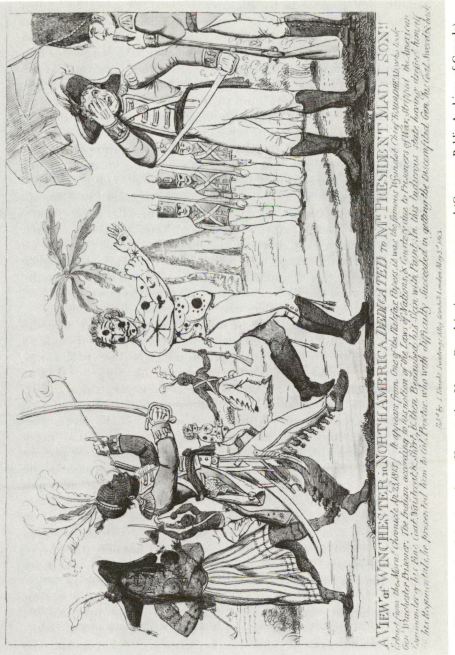

A VIEW of WINCHESTER in NORTH AMERICA DEDICATED to Mr PRESIDENT MAD—I SON!!

Extract from the Morn. Chronicle *Apr 23,1813.* It appears from One of the Halifax Papers, it was the famous Wyandot Chief ROUNDHEAD, who took Gen. Winchester Prisoner: The Indian according to his notion of the Laws of Nations, & courtesy due to Prisoners of War, stripped the American Commander of his fine Coat Waistcoat, Shirt, &c then Bedaubed his Skin with Paint. In this ludorous State having doctor'd himself, his Prisoner led him to Col. Proctor who with difficulty succeeded in getting the Discomfited Gen. his Coat, Swords &c back

Pub.d By J. Knight Sweetings Alley Cornhill London May 3 . 1813.

The ineptitude of the American officers makes Upper Canada's victory seem assured (C-23432, Public Archives of Canada)

there was the apparent unity of Upper Canada. According to the colonial newspapers, the British forces seemed to have rarely known defeat. The decisive Canadian victories at Michilimacinac, Detroit, and Queenston Heights were given extensive coverage in the local press. General Brock's leadership was "brilliant"; his heroic death at Queenston Heights was a tragedy for all Upper Canadians. As the "Father of his People," the general, Stephen Miles eulogized, was "watchful as he was brave" and his presence had "ensured a most glorious victory."[103] But no one forgot the "bold actions of our brave men."[104] The *Kingston Gazette* reported that "our militia have heard the voice and obeyed it, they have evinced by the promptitude and loyalty of their conduct that they are worthy of the king whom they served and of the constitution which they enjoy." The *York Gazette* observed, "it must afford infinite satisfaction to every Loyal Bosom that on every occasion, the militia of the Province has distinguished itself with an alacrity and spirit worthy of Veteran Troops. ... Such is the advantage of a good cause. Ours animates all classes, with alacrity, zeal and courage."[105] For the next three years, the *Kingston Gazette* was filled with reports of the courage and tenacity of the Canadian militia and the British army – all members of which showed "a spirit worthy of their ancestors."[106]

Upper Canadians were frequently reminded, however, that the militia and British troops were not alone in their determination to preserve the colony from the American invaders. The civilian population of the colony too was active in freeing "the country of traitors and the invading army."[107] In 1813 the Loyal and Patriotic Society of York was created both to encourage and to reward the loyalty, faithfulness, and industriousness of all settlers. At the ceremonies which announced its formation, one observer commented that "every man's ambition will be to employ himself most usefully in the present contest and caring not for the consequences, he will conserve by the most punctilious discharge of his duty, the safety of his country and his own individual honour."[108] Together, all Upper Canadians, "brave and noble people," were engaged in "the noble task of resisting unjust aggression." Publicly at least the colonists were determined "to preserve for themselves and their posterity not only their property but all those precious and unestimable privileges which are enjoyed in this Province as a member of the British Empire."[109]

For three years, the settlers were encouraged to take pride in their accomplishments; but they were never allowed to forget that the conflict in North America was only part of a larger global battle. Though months out of date, the very presence of European news in the York and Kingston newspapers implicitly reminded Upper

Canadians that while they fought American tyranny, Great Britain was battling and vanquishing the despotism of Napoleon. It was observed that "Britain was the only nation that upholds the real interest of State in defiance and opposition to the greatest tyranny that ever oppressed the world."[110] By her efforts, "Great Britain has done more honour to humanity than any nation that ever did or perhaps ever shall exist." Indeed, "the national temper" of Great Britain, which Upper Canadians implicitly shared, "seems to refuse all but the heroism of war."[111] And even though the mother country was battling for her very life in Europe she had not forgotten her loyal subjects in North America.

It was British leadership and trained British troops, prominent Upper Canadians acknowledged, that had enabled the local militia to turn back successfully the enemy. While the colonists fought in the interior, the British navy blockaded the coast. The *Kingston Gazette* provided detailed reports of the British invasion of Virginia and their victory at Washington.[112] While fresh troops arrived in Halifax in 1813, Upper Canadians read with some satisfaction that London society had formed a Society for the Relief of the Sufferings of the Inhabitants of Upper Canada.[113] To prominent Upper Canadians, the war had united all Britons in defence of their constitution. And their pride in their own accomplishments mounted as they came to consider the North American theatre of war as a vital part of the global battle for justice.

Upper Canadians, however, believed that even with the support of the brave British forces, they could not have been successful without the blessings of Divine Providence. The British victories, both at home and abroad, seemed convincing proof of the "triumph of virtue over vice, of a good cause over a bad one."[114] The fact that many Americans also saw the hand of God in the Upper Canadian victories only confirmed this belief. In the summer of 1813 the *Kingston Gazette* reprinted an excerpt from the *Boston Gazette*. "I am not superstitious," wrote one concerned federalist, "but when I consider the invasion of Russia and Canada by the allied powers of France and America, I constrain to believe in the justice and over-ruling providence of God who had declared that he will 'break the rod of the oppressors and scatter the nations' which delight in war."[115] "God is the source of all benefits," it was stressed, and both Napoleon and Madison "got just judgement from Heaven, defeat and ruin."[116] Some Americans even seemed to rejoice that "the invader had been humbled and the oppressed relieved" for they perceived that it was ultimately "the unrighteousness of the war"[117] which was resulting in disaster for the republic.

Scathing commentary on the American reaction to the British capture of Washington in 1814 and the flight of President Madison (Anne S.K. Brown Military Collection, Brown University Library, Providence, RI)

Though many Americans and Upper Canadians evidently felt in the spring of 1813 that it would "be found that the contest has been all for nothing," a New York report still predicted that the war, costing "thousands of lives and hundreds millions dollars in expense,"[118] would continue for at least two or three more years. A year later, however, rumours of peace began to be heard. In May 1814 Stephen Miles reported that many American papers expected an armistice shortly. "We have it on good authority," one commented, "that Madison wants peace. We have no doubts our Government having abandoned the retaliatory system; wise men calculate on it as a harbinger of an armistice and Peace – AMEN say we." A resident of Baltimore was reported to have observed in January 1814 that "if Great Britain would make peace upon any terms not absolutely degrading in the eyes of all parties,"[119] peace would be negotiated by August. In the spring of 1814 the American government was in severe financial difficulties and American troops were deserting in droves. Negotiations dragged on, however, and American conservatives continued to feel the "oppression of the administration."[120]

Throughout 1814 the British forces persisted in their vigorous prosecution of the war effort. That summer, fresh troops arrived at Montreal and Halifax. The British blockade of the American coast was tightened and in September British troops entered Washington. It was the end of the European conflict earlier in the year, however, that really marked the beginning of the end of the North American war.[121] In the spring of 1815 colonial newspapers finally announced that the war was over. "With exceeding great joy," it was proclaimed, "merciful Providence" had granted "the blessings of peace" with "so few sacrifices."[122]

For three years, many Upper Canadians had fought for survival, for their homes and their families, and some at least had fought for the right to live under the British flag. The War of 1812 had brought hardship to many and left bitterness in its wake. Yet, for most influential Upper Canadians, it reaffirmed their understanding of the United States and Great Britain and the colony's relationship to each. War with the United States had been thrust upon them. Upper Canadians had joined Great Britain in its noble battle against tyranny and oppression; yet they had refused to cut their ties with American friends. Indeed, many leaders of Upper Canada considered that their war against the United States was, in part, a defence of their federalist friends who themselves had been under attack by a despotic government.

Upper Canadians before and during the War of 1812 did not

Bruin become MEDIATOR or Negociation for PEACE.

Despite British and Russian attempts to open negotiations in 1813–14, the United States does not appear willing to take part (the Lilly Library, University of Indiana, Bloomington, Ind.)

condemn everything about the United States or all Americans. Certainly they were, as could only be expected, opposed to the policies of the Madison administration. And they condemned all the worst aspects of a republican form of government which had permitted the democrats to retain control of the United States. However, all colonial leaders, including those in York, believed that the government in Washington did not speak for all Americans. Upper Canadians' accumulated knowledge of the United States and their continuing ties with many of its citizens led them to conclude that there were a substantial number of good as well as bad Americans. From across the border, they viewed the republic not with the closed mind of the eighteenth-century British conservative but with the discriminating eye of British-North Americans who had been forced, by the propinquity of their neighbours and by the nature of their own population, to recognize fine distinctions in American political and social life. Their ties to the United States, however, had developed from more than a defensive reaction. Colonial leaders, by political and personal inclination, chose to rely on the American federalists for news and information and for an explanation of the common situation in which the two groups found themselves.

At the end of the war it seemed that Upper Canadian perceptions of the two great powers had changed very little. In the spring of 1815 readers of the colonial newspapers continued to follow American affairs with interest and the local editors continued to rely on the United States and particularly their federalist friends for most of their news. As Stephen Miles quite proudly acknowledged in June 1815, "he flatters himself for the arrangements he has made in procuring New York and Albany papers [so] that he will be able to publish Foreign and Domestic Intelligence earlier than it can be received from any other quarter."[123] For accounts in the newspapers confirmed that in 1815 the American people were still divided. Political and social upheaval, which were considered by some to be endemic to a republican form of government, still strained the fabric of the American nation. Prominent colonists were even aware that some federalists in New York and New England were actually considering secession from the Union.[124] In the short term, the alliance between the leaders of Upper Canada and the federalists in the United States was strengthened by their common response to the war. At its conclusion they continued to share a sense of community and purpose.

Nevertheless, in 1815 the ties of the Upper Canadian elite to the United States were already beginning to weaken. Unknown to both observers and participants, the federalists were doomed as a force in American political and social life. And while the American conservatives were in decline, Upper Canadian leaders were in the ascendancy. Increasingly, influential colonists, now secure in their positions, would rely more on the vital British connection and on their own native ingenuity than on the American federalists for support.

It is apparent, however, that the War of 1812 had also engendered a new sense of pride and self-worth among many Upper Canadians. For three years they had fought beside the British troops in defence of the king and their constitution. For three years they had shared a righteous cause. Consciously, if for many only vicariously, they had shared the battles and the hardships and the triumphs. The War of 1812 had forced Upper Canadians to look outside the limited environment of their local town or village. By their militia service, and through newspapers, official dispatches, military reports, and in the taverns and on the streets, the colonists had kept in touch with events in all parts of the province. Together, Upper Canadians came to believe, they had vanquished the forces of tyranny and oppression. Out of the war there arose a sense of community, an awareness of being Upper Canadian, which encompassed all settlers. The War of 1812 came to be considered by many as the colony's rite of passage into young adulthood.

PART TWO

2 A Map of the Located Districts in the Province of Upper Canada, 1813 (Special Collections, Douglas Library, Queen's University)

CHAPTER FIVE

Postwar Developments

An English visitor to the colony in 1817 remarked that "the last American War forms an important event in the history of Upper Canada." "It is continually referred to by the people," John Howison added in an account of his travels, who, "when alluding in a general way to the time in which any circumstance occurred, say that it happened before or after the war."[1] This is not surprising, for no Upper Canadian had been left untouched by the bitter conflict. To some the War of 1812 had brought unprecedented prosperity. There were many others who were left, however, with only painful memories of death and destruction. Few residents would willingly have repeated the experience. Yet no matter how resolutely Upper Canadians attempted to forget the past three years, the clock could not be turned back. The War of 1812 was an irrevocable watershed in colonial development. Within fifteen years of its end, Upper Canada was transformed from a string of scattered settlements on the frontier to a relatively well-established and prosperous province. More significantly, the war also came to symbolize the unity and loyalty of all residents of the new land and prompted the development of a new colonial consciousness, one which was distinctly Upper Canadian.[2]

The maturation of the colony did not of course occur overnight. In 1817 the colony seemed little different from what it had been fifteen years before. John Howison recalled that on his trip up the St Lawrence that year he found nothing remarkable – only "half cultivated fields, log-houses and extensive forests all around composed the monotonous scene." He continued, "we had seen nothing but rocks, forests and uninhabited islands, during the three days, everything appeared to indicate that we had passed the confines of civilization."[3] Just after the war, Upper Canada was still a number of tiny isolated settlements with a heterogeneous mixture of people and cultures led by small regionally based elites.

Yet it was clear to local residents that the colony had changed remarkably since the turn of the century and the postwar period promised even more accelerated growth. Within five years of the end of the war, a comparatively intricate system of land and water communications was established, linking Quebec to Niagara and joining the principal towns and villages of the province to each other and to their surrounding hinterlands. The plethora of new roads accommodated the introduction of regular stage coach services and this, together with the launching of steamships on the Great Lakes, greatly facilitated travel within the colony.[4] The rapid advancement in intracolonial communications was complemented by significant improvements in access out of the colony, whether south to the United States or east to Lower Canada and Great Britain.[5] Thus by the mid-1820s the physical isolation of life in the older communities of Upper Canada had largely disappeared; at the same time, new frontiers in the north and the west were opening up. Between 1815 and 1828 the population of the colony doubled, largely owing to the arrival of thousands of new immigrants.[6] Upper Canada's economy grew and became increasingly complex and diversified; and while new settlers perpetuated the pioneering spirit and lifestyle, a new maturity came to the older and more settled areas of the province.

In Kingston, Niagara, and York and in the rapidly expanding villages along the north shore of the St Lawrence and the Great Lakes, a myriad of social institutions sprang up after the war to meet the needs of the growing population. Among other things, schools, libraries, local theatre, and newspapers flourished in the 1820s.[7] The general economic growth prompted the formation of banks, development companies, and agricultural societies. Yet such developments did not necessarily promote harmony. The expanding economy and "the increasing mobility of the population" also imposed "heavy strains upon the social organization." By 1820 York and Kingston had been forced to establish local police forces; and prominent residents of various Upper Canadian communities felt increasingly compelled to support local bible and benevolent societies, formed to both aid and inadvertently control the growing number of indigents and ill-prepared immigrants in their midst.[8] By the mid-1820s residents of most of the towns and villages of Upper Canada enjoyed the amenities of a relatively sophisticated urban existence. And the loneliness and back-breaking hardships of a backwoods existence was being replaced by a much more open and diversified community life. By the end of the decade, Upper Canada was at last beginning to approach Lieutenant Governor Simcoe's dream of a relatively cohesive and integrated society.

Symbolic of this newly emerging maturity was the transformation of York from a small village isolated in the backwater of the colony to a bustling town whose influence came to permeate all aspects of provincial life. Within fifteen years of the end of the war, York had tripled in size and it had become a centre for trade and commerce.[9] More importantly, the capital had also become, in fact as well as in law, the centre of political life in the colony, a political life which was itself far more integrated and complex than had ever existed before.

At the popular level, increased literacy, coupled with a greater interest in and awareness of events throughout the colony, fostered a growing political consciousness among many residents. After 1815 settlers began to consider issues not only in the light of their immediate situation but also according to their perception of what was good for the colony as a whole. In the immediate postwar years, admittedly, the division between town and country and between popular and written cultures persisted. And initially the cultural and religious diversity of the colony was reinforced by the arrival of thousands of immigrants from various parts of Great Britain. Nonetheless, that process of integration and assimilation which the war had sparked among the colonists could not be arrested. Increased mobility after the war enabled and encouraged Upper Canadians to keep in touch, either personally or through the growing number of colonial newspapers, with individuals and events throughout the province. Gradually personal concerns began to be viewed within an overall provincial context. Upper Canadians from all walks of life and all parts of the colony increasingly came together to debate the political, social, and economic issues of the day in the light of differing political viewpoints, not regional or cultural ones. By 1828 Upper Canada was a society which took for granted its own basic unity and the shared concerns and purposes of its people. And inevitably colonists looked increasingly to the provincial capital for direction and guidance.

This is not to say that local elites did not continue to have considerable influence on Upper Canadians' lives or on the formation of colonial policy. Regional leadership groups remained very active in the postwar years, particularly in local, social, and economic affairs.[10] It was soon clear, however, that the growing complexity and integration of colonial life necessitated the implementation of broad, all-encompassing colonial policies – policies and programs that the prewar structure of regionally based elites was unable by its very nature to formulate. Moreover, as political power began to be divorced from the economic life of the colony, the influence of local leaders, whose power and authority had rested on the integration of political, social, and economic forces in any one area, began to give way to colony-wide, politically motivated leadership groups based in York. Gradually old political networks were extended and new ones were formed and soon new individuals began to come to the fore and replace those of the first generation.

This fundamental change in elite formation was not readily apparent in the years immediately after the war. A number of old faces still predominated in the 1816 session of the legislature. But it was also clear that the original guard of loyalists was fast disappearing. Robert Hamilton had died in 1809 and his partner Richard Cartwright had succumbed to illness six years later. In Kingston, George Okill Stuart[11] had taken over his father's place at St George's Church and Rev. John Strachan was now entrenched in York as chaplain of the garrison and rector of the local congregation. Over the next fifteen years, the number of unfamiliar faces increased. Between 1815 and 1828 a new generation of Upper Canadians with new ideas and new understandings of the needs of the colony and of its relations to Great Britain and to the United States took over the reins of government. They were an integral part of the new Upper Canada – one which looked confidently to the future and not merely to the past.

The initial prominence of most of these members of the new elites, like that of the loyalist leaders before them, rested on their conspicuous display of loyalty during the war. Such men as John Beverley Robinson, John Macaulay, Christopher Hagerman, Charles Jones, John Rolph, and Robert Nichol had all been militia officers during the War of 1812 and had distinguished themselves in the field.[12] For some, this service together with their proven ability and previous political connections was immediately recognized by the colonial officials, who appointed them to lucrative and influential administrative posts. Though a number of others received no immediate political recognition of their service, their participation in the war did gain them invaluable political support later. Particularly in the 1820s, the War of 1812 became an increasingly important symbol to many Upper Canadians of the colony's unity and loyalty to king and country. All the public figures who had fought in the war had the advantage of this growing myth. Members of the emerging leadership groups depended on more than their involvement in the war, however, to cement their influence in political affairs. Of equal if not greater importance was an individual's political and personal connections with the colonial executive, formal involvement in the government in York, and, for some, growing popular support.

The initial attraction of York for a select group of ambitious young men was the dual presence there of the seat of government and of their old teacher, Rev. John Strachan. John Beverley Robinson, attorney general of the colony, Christopher Hagerman and George Markland, members of both the legislative and executive councils, and Charles Jones, member of the House of Assembly, had all once been Strachan's students in Cornwall. Over the years a strong and enduring friendship had developed among the boys and between the students and their master, and when Strachan moved to York and began to have the ear of the colonial administration, he naturally encouraged many of his bright young students to join him.[13] A few like John Macaulay preferred to remain in the eastern district of Upper Canada; many others, however, including Robinson, Hagerman, and Jones went to the tiny capital where under the continuing influence of their old teacher they became part of the ruling tory elite. Sharing a belief in British conservative ideals and respect for authority and order, principles engrained during their school days, these men by the mid-1820s comprised the nucleus of what was to become known as the Family Compact.[14]

By the mid-1820s there were a number of other young men, however, who began to advocate quite different political ideals and policies. Initially the presence of John Rolph, Colonel Nichol, William Warren Baldwin and his son Robert, Barnabas and Marshal Bidwell, and other like-minded colonials went unnoticed in York, for they lacked those essential personal and political connections which had so quickly enhanced the influence of many of Strachan's students. And throughout the period this group of men never had the direct political power wielded by supporters of the executive. Nonetheless, from their seats in the House of Assembly, these well-spoken and able landowners and professionals were able to gain considerable political and press support from the growing number of colonists whose views were at odds with the executive's policies. In 1828 this very loose alliance of reformers[15] won, much to the consternation of the executive, a majority of seats in the House of Assembly and for the first time formed a viable opposition to the tory administration. What is ironic, though it was perhaps inevitable, is that at the same time political power in Upper Canada began to be centralized and to coalesce, there also emerged some basic political divisions which polarized the colony into two warring political camps.

This is not to conclude, as some historians have suggested, that by the mid-1820s there were two distinct political parties in Upper

Canada as we would understand them today. Both the tory elite and the reformers lacked the necessary organization and ideological cohesiveness to be considered political parties. Rather, they were very loosely aligned groups of individuals whose expectations of government and the development of the colony as a whole differed, often sharply. The members of what became the Family Compact were in the 1820s easily identifiable by their interpersonal relationships and for many by their direct association with the colonial executive. The tory elite shared a pro-British, anti-American bias which reflected their acceptance of common conservative values of order and tradition. Those who became the Reformers of the 1830s to a large degree lacked the outward cohesion which derived from shared boyhood experiences and ongoing personal relationships. They often publicly disagreed among themselves, in the House of Assembly and in the press. And in the 1820s they certainly had no predetermined policy for reform. Indeed, it was only as the reformers increasingly found themselves at odds with executive policies, and ironically as the government identified them as an "opposition faction," that shared concerns and viewpoints induced them to coalesce in a political alliance.

Upper Canadians of the 1820s did, nonetheless, recognize that there were two identifiable political groups in their government. Colloquially, the tories were almost always referred to as "the court party"; those in opposition were frequently dubbed the "country" or "people's" party or the "patriots." The very use of these terms, reminiscent of political debate in eighteenth-century England and in the thirteen colonies before and during the revolution, gives some indication of how Upper Canadians characterized their own politics.[16] To well-read and educated residents, familiar with both British and American history, the court party was associated with prerogative, with backward-looking traditions, and with strong ties to the executive and entrenched power. The use of such terms as "country" or "people's" or "patriots'" party was clearly intended to be derogatory by those who used them most. To the tories, the terms immediately evoked images of the revolution, of disloyalty and of a society where unrestrained democracy threatened to overwhelm the dictates of good government. The reformers, however, took pride in taking the people's side and in the independence and virtue implied by the term "country." And though "patriot" did evoke some questionable qualities, it also suggested that a number of Upper Canadians feared that their own situation in the 1820s was far too similar to that which had forced the Americans to rebel forty-five years before. The identification of both groups with certain historical events and circumstances was undoubtedly intended. Yet it is also clear that such political rhetoric and terminology had a specifically Upper Canadian significance which was firmly grounded in the particular and unique circumstances of the colony, as the evolving attitudes of the two leadership groups and their supporters reflected the many changes that were occurring in Upper Canadian society after the war.

The battles between the tories and reformers did not really erupt until after 1820; the fuse which ignited those bitter political debates and encouraged and heightened political consciousness among many Upper Canadians was lit, however, in the immediate postwar period. When Lieutenant Governor Gore opened the fourth session of the seventh Parliament of Upper Canada on 6 February 1816, he urged the legislators to give their attention to the future "growth, prosperity and happiness of the province." In the light of their experiences during the war, many anticipated that a "period of more rapid growth" was at hand. "From a recollection of the past," Allan MacLean, speaker of the House of Assembly, confidently predicted, the colony has "the brightest prospects of the future."[17] But by February 1816 the bubble had already burst. In the short term, the return of peace heralded not accelerated growth and prosperity but economic stagnation. Prices fell and specie became increasingly scarce. Upper Canadians, initially perplexed, soon became openly discontented as the economic situation worsened and was exacerbated by the postwar depression in Great Britian and the United States. For the first time, individuals from all parts of the colony joined in vocal and active opposition to the executive and many of its policies. The arrival of Robert Gourlay at the end of 1817 provided a convenient vehicle for this opposition, but it is apparent that the Englishman only gave focus and direction to sentiments already existing in the colony. It was really the growing maturity of the Upper Canadian community and the colonists' increasing appreciation of their common interests and concerns that provided the psychological and political environment necessary for broad colonial protest.

Throughout the 1820s the political lines which had been tentatively drawn during the Gourlay affair hardened. Questions concerning the rights of the House of Assembly, taxes, trade, and citizenship increasingly engaged Upper Canadians' attention and drew them to support either the tory elite or the reformers. The topics that provoked dissension were, for the most part, local colonial issues; the context of the debates was usually the views of the House of Assembly against those of the executive; it is apparent, however, that both the roots of many of the controversies and the terms of the postwar debates came from outside the colony and particularly from differing understandings of Great Britain and the United States and the colony's relationship to each. To understand the evolution of Upper Canadian ideology, it is therefore essential to appreciate its leaders' views of these two nations – views which superficially resembled those expressed before the war, but because of changing circumstances and personnel were in fact quite different.

CHAPTER SIX

Foundation Stone of Canada

On 3 June 1814 Rev. John Strachan preached a Thanksgiving Sermon to his congregation in York celebrating the deliverance of Great Britain from the devastating conflict in Europe. "Thankfully and devoutly," he declared, we "acknowledge the mercy and goodness of Almighty God; for protecting His Majesty and His dominions during the whole of this arduous contest; and for the signal and glorious victories obtained by its armies." "Our joy is full," he continued, "when we reflect that ... Great Britain has been chiefly instrumental, through the blessings of God, in bringing about the happy changes which we now contemplate." "Truly," she was "the preserver of the independence of Europe" and "the proclamation of peace," he declared, would triumphantly bring her to "a new era of glory." And though peace had yet to be won in North America, Strachan called on Upper Canadians to "rejoice." We have earned "the happiest time ... now rising upon us," he maintained. "We have shown that the same spirit animates the children of the Loyalists which inspired their fathers to put down treason and rebellion; and to stand up for the unity of the empire. We have given many proofs of our loyalty and affection for our gracious Sovereign; reverence for our laws and constitution, and devotion to our country."[1] It was only a matter of a short time, he concluded, before Britons in North America too would enjoy the blessings of peace and victory.

When the North American conflict did finally draw to a close six months later, Upper Canadians did indeed rejoice. "Happily," they too were now "preserved from subjection," and remained an "integral part of the greatest and most glorious Empire,"[2] Strachan proclaimed. But, he warned, victory must not encourage complacency. It was now the duty of all influential Upper Canadians to ensure that the distinctively British character and heritage of the colony, for which residents had sacrificed so much, be secured and strengthened. And in the years immediately after the War of 1812, Upper Canadians, as "dutiful and loyal subjects," continued in their various addresses and petitions to the crown to express their un-questioning allegiance to their sovereign and their gratitude for "the blessings entailed upon them and their posterity," most particularly for "the glorious Constitution of Great Britain."[3] As the decade came to a close, it became apparent, however, that the overwhelming sense of gratitude which the first loyalist settlers had felt towards the mother country was being increasingly qualified by a more impersonal and, at times, critical assessment of Great Britain. Though the formalized rhetoric and the rituals of allegiance persisted, the words began to take on different meanings and the symbols of the king and the constitution gained new and varied significance.

This is not to say that in the postwar period Upper Canadians lost interest in British affairs. Those bonds across the Atlantic which the war had revitalized were strengthened in the postwar years by the arrival of an increasing number of immigrants from all over the British Isles. Moreover, after 1815 more and more colonists began to make the trip home; British newspapers began to find a ready market in Upper Canada; and educated colonists, perhaps in large part in reaction to their growing awareness of the republic to the south, turned increasingly to Great Britain for inspiration.

Yet far from providing a unifying force within the colony (as so frequently has been presumed), Upper Canadians' continuing in-terest in British affairs and renewed consciousness of their depen-dence on the empire only served to exacerbate the already existing political divisions in the province. All influential Upper Canadians realized that the actual circumstances of the two lands were signif-icantly different. Nonetheless, the tory supporters of the colonial executive, particularly after the arrival of Lieutenant Governor Mait-land in 1818, interpreted the unfolding political and social situation at home as strong justification for their continued conservative stance in Upper Canada. In particular, they claimed that those same prin-ciples of a strong executive authority and proper subordination of the elected branches of government, that the British cabinet was committed to at home, could and should be applied in Upper Can-ada. The growing forces of reform in the colony placed quite a different interpretation on British affairs. Events in England in the postwar period, coupled with their reading of Lieutenant Governor Simcoe's policies twenty-five years earlier, led many in the House of Assembly to conclude that it was the executive power that had to be checked by a strengthened legislative branch. Moreover, they believed that the very image, not just the principles, of the British constitution had to be carefully guarded in Upper Canada. Bitter controversy arose in part from these divergent interpretations of events in Great Britain. Despite this, influential Upper Canadians between 1815 and 1828 agreed that the province was and must remain politically, culturally, and emotionally a British province. And as in the prewar years, it was the king who provided the one element of constancy and unity.

On 2 February 1821 Lieutenant Governor Maitland announced to the Upper Canadian legislature that "since the prorogation of Parliament ... we have had to deplore the final close of that long and glorious reign under which this country became incorporated with the British Empire." King George III was dead. Though the news was almost a year old, the lapse in time did not in any way detract from the sincerity of Maitland's and the government's tribute to the old king. "The demonstration of grief," Maitland noted, "at the death of our late Venerable Sovereign" had been "worthy of a Province first peopled by men who throughout a trying contest had preserved their loyalty to his sacred person under every sacrifice of interest and in defiance of every danger."[4]

Perhaps no single event in the postwar years better illustrated the colonists' continuing emotional bonds to the mother country, while at the same time implicitly acknowledging the beginning of a new and essentially different era. King George III had been a living link with the past. His reign joined the trials of the first loyalist settlers with the battles their sons had fought during the War of 1812. Though he had been retired from public life for many years, George III was the only king whom the great majority of Upper Canadians, both young and old in 1820, had ever known. He had been "our beloved sovereign," who had consciously maintained that vital "Parental relationship to a faithful people." Over his long reign there had been many "astonishing changes" in the history of the world and in Upper Canadians' lives in particular.[5] As the editors of the *Kingston Chronicle* (successor to the *Kingston Gazette*) commented in March on receipt of the news of his death, "while Kingdoms were convulsed and thrones hurled from their foundations ... the energy and undaunted perseverance of His Majesty's Councils [had] enabled him to ... defend the ark of the British constitution and the majesty of the British name ... The memory of his reign will always be cherished by Upper Canadians," editors Macaulay and Pringle concluded. It was "the epoch when His Majesty's government so liberally extended to them the benefits of a constitution which ... is inferior to none in the world."[6] But that glorious epoch had now passed. It was time for a new king, time for Upper Canadians to look to the future and not to the past.

The colonists' relationship with King George IV in the 1820s echoed their fathers' relationship with George III. Annually the militia was mustered to celebrate his birthday; sermons were preached; toasts were drunk, and formal addresses were sent to the sovereign to commemorate the day. Indeed, for many of the new generation of politicians, George IV had been their king in all but name for the last ten years of his father's reign. As the members of the House acknowleged in 1816, "the complete success of the grand struggle in Europe ... may be justly attributed to the auspices of His Royal Highness the Prince Regent." And it was really the direction and policies of the heir apparent that had lately guided the United Kingdom "to the summit of national prosperity."[7] Thus, when the prince regent finally ascended the throne in 1820, the ceremonies must have been somewhat anticlimactic. Upper Canadians already viewed him with feelings of "the most unfeigned duty and respect" and were "grateful to Divine Providence for selecting him to be the means of dispensing ... happiness to the World."[8]

It seemed, however, that George IV was not, and never would be, able to evoke the kind of personal commitment which the loyalists had given his father. The editors of the *Kingston Chronicle*, in a short paragraph announcing the succession, hoped that the new king "may long be preserved in health and happiness" so that he could "rule like his August Father in the heart of a dutiful and loyal people."[9] The relationship of the first Upper Canadians to their king had clearly been unique. Twice they had fought under his banner. Many had sacrificed their homes and families for his cause and in return he had been a very real father to them. In contrast, King George IV could only be a symbol of the empire, a rallying cry for loyalism and for the continuance of Upper Canada as a British colony.

Nonetheless, as the members of the House of Assembly stated in 1821, "the Province was mindful that it had received many signal benefits" from their sovereign and the empire. Without "the powerful assistance and the generosity afforded" by the mother country between 1812 and 1815, the colony would have fallen to her "powerful and unprincipled neighbour."[10] Great Britain was "the *foundation stone*" of Canada, Charles Fothergill wrote in *A Sketch of the State of Upper Canada* in 1822, and throughout the 1820s the colony continued to "depend upon the prudence and wisdom of *her* councils."[11] A full ten years after the war, the editor of the *United Empire Loyalist* and many others were still conscious of this unique relationship to the empire. The paper's New Year's Address concluded:

> Though Atlantic's angry billows roar;
> And far divide us, BRITAIN from thy shore,
> The voice of gratitude, shall be heard,
> For all thy benefits on us conferr'd.[12]

This continuing sense of appreciation of and gratitude to king and country was coupled in Upper Canadians' minds with an intense pride in their membership in the British Empire. Britain's successful stand against the forces of Napoleon had confirmed that she was mistress of the sea and "the first ... among the nations of the world."[13] And not only were the British adept at war. As an article in the *Niagara Spectator* in 1818 stated, "in that isle" more had been accomplished "for the glory of the species"[14] than in all the regions of the globe. "The principal claims of England to universal admiration," it was asserted, "are founded on her achievements in literature, in science and the arts and the prodigious variety in which she had poured forth the most glorious talents." It was "the sublime intellect of an *Englishmen*" that had realized a host of discoveries and accomplishments. "Who discovered the circulation of the blood?" it was asked, or "the lymphatic system?" or "invented logarithms?" All these and far more were the accomplishments of Englishmen. Newton, Blackstone, Burke, Priestley, and many others had "shed a blaze of purest glory on those sister isles, where the germ of almost every nobler attribute of human nature seems to have been deposited by Providence ... watered by the blood of martyred heroes and where the standard, erected by Freedom, still towers and shines along the rocky battlements of her hereditary home."[15] Such genius commanded reverence and it was little wonder that "true Canadians of British feelings" were determined not "to change their national character."[16] As British subjects, Upper Canadians shared in this heritage and basked in its reflected glory. They too were "in full possession of British laws and immunities" and had "a constitution nearly on an exact model of that of England."[17] It was not an impossible step for some, at least, to conclude that they who inherently possessed many of the qualities of the British people would soon share the prosperity and eminence of the parent state.

Upper Canadian admiration of Great Britain and her people encouraged leaders to look across the Atlantic for guidance and support, particularly in political affairs. Yet for even the most wealthy and influential residents, knowledge of the actual conditions and circumstances in Great Britain was somewhat limited. Of the rising younger generation, John Beverley Robinson was one of only a few who had made the pilgrimage home. By the end of the war Rev. John Strachan had not seen his native country in fifteen years and most native Upper Canadians would never take the long voyage across the Atlantic. The growing number of literate Upper Canadians and their leaders were still dependent on second- and third-hand information from newspapers, official reports, and personal correspondence for their information about Great Britain. Inevitably, many events "at home" lost much of their significance by the time the news eventually reached the colony. In most cases, it was, therefore, not the reality of life in Great Britain which was so important for Upper Canadians.

This was progressively true as Upper Canadians' self-confidence grew after 1815 and the colonists' gratitude to Great Britain became increasingly tempered by a belief that the province itself had played an active and vital role in preserving the colony within the empire. "During the early period of the war," the House of Assembly claimed in 1816, "it was the gallant defense ... by its own Militia, supported only by a very small portion of His Majesty's Regular Forces"[18] that had initially saved the colony. Upper Canadians, too, could talk of "the toils and dangers which we have surmounted, the fortitude and intrepidity which we have exhibited." Many in the 1820s undoubtedly did "look back on this war with the most lively satisfaction through their whole lives, from remembering the active part which they had taken in its vigorous defence and repairing its trepidations." The War of 1812 engendered a feeling of "mutual dependence"[19] not only between Upper Canadians and Britons in the rest of the empire but among the colonists themselves. And as the immediacy and reality of the colony's wartime experiences receded with the passing years, the role of the native Upper Canadian forces in the defence of their homes was magnified. In the 1820s and 1830s the War of 1812 became a Canadian victory with Upper Canadian heroes. By mid-century it formed the basis of an emerging Canadian nationalism.[20]

The mother country nonetheless remained a kind of ideal. She symbolized a way of life which many wished to emulate in North America. As the centre of a mighty empire, Britain was the giver of life and security; she also represented a power and eminence that Upper Canadians hoped one day to match. And such ambition could be realized, many Upper Canadians believed, if they were willing to learn from British experience and from her political and social affairs.

Between 1815 and 1828, it is clear, many Upper Canadians watched political and economic affairs in Great Britain with interest and at times with some concern. After the Napoleonic Wars, Britain entered into a period of economic and political dislocation as the nation readjusted both to peacetime conditions and to new social and political demands from all classes of people. In the immediate postwar period, a severe economic depression was exacerbated by four years of bad harvests and high prices for food stuffs. At the same time, massive demobilization and the introduction of new technological advances in industrial areas caused severe unemployment, low wages, and general dissatisfaction among the growing working class. As T.S. Ashton notes, "underemployed and underfed men were not over nice in theorizing as to the cause of their distress."[21] The subsequent destruction of machinery, marches on London and Manchester, food riots, and increasingly radical demands for reform terrified the government and resulted in even more severe repression. It was not until the mid-1820s that prosperity, political reforms, better food, more work, and increased wages began to relieve the social and political tension.

To Upper Canadians, Great Britain had seemed during the War of 1812 to be "the manufacturer, the banker and the merchant of the whole world." And in 1815 and 1816 the colonists, like many Britons at home, fully expected that the "return of universal peace" would be "the harbinger of plenty and happiness,"[22] both in the mother country and in her North American colonies. By 1817, however, it was becoming apparent that a suddenly stagnant economy was giving rise to "symptoms of distress ... in many parts of the United Kingdom." Initially the colonists were confident that the troubles in Britain would be only temporary. Yet "deep agricultural distress"[23] continued to touch all Britons and workers in the manufacturing sectors became increasingly demoralized. Between 1816 and 1822 Upper Canadian leaders were fearful (and, as shall be seen, with good cause) that the British government's efforts to alleviate economic distress at home would detrimentally affect her commitment to the colonies. But this was not their only concern. In the mother country, traditionally idealized as the land of liberty, tranquillity, and order, the radical reformers were proposing economic and political changes which explicitly challenged the policies of the constituted authority. Though many fully expected that "the undaunted spirit and persevering industry of the British people" would enable her "to rise superior to her present economic difficulties,"[24] for a time there was some question in Upper Canada as to whether the constitution would survive the struggle. This was a particularly important issue for many colonists for it directly influenced their own attempts to quell local discontent and to ensure that the constitution remained untarnished in North America.

On 4 January 1817 the "Post Boy" observed in his New Year's Message in the *Kingston Gazette* that "Great Britain is once more at peace, but opposition does not cease." He continued:

> While British subjects groan and sweat,
> Beneath new loads of foreign debts.
> The public debt the mighty weight
> Which moves the clockwork of the state,
> Increas'd by every war's expence,
> And growing yearly more immense,
> Make the machine now run so fast
> They feared 'twill break the wheels at last.

Only occasionally in the next two years did Stephen Miles and other Upper Canadian editors include reports of the economic discontent in Great Britain. It was expected that "Peace with Commerce in her hand" would soon "shed blessings on the lands of our fathers." John Macaulay and Robert Pringle, the editors of the *Kingston Chronicle*, reported in January 1819 that "the wise provisions of the legislature" had placed British "Financiers in the most flourishing conditions and no longer is heard the Croak of Faction, predicting ruin and national bankruptcy."[25] And though six months later the paper recounted that the British economy was still depressed, there seemed to be "no cause for alarm or despair."[26] Yet by autumn it was evident that the editors of the *Chronicle* had spoken too soon. "In many instances," it was acknowledged, "a turbulent and seditious spirit has manifested itself" in England. Indeed, the threat to law and order was surpassing "anything of the kind which has occurred since the period of the revolution in 1688." And by December 1819 popular agitations led by what were characterized as "a few malcontents"[27] were triggering a full constitutional crisis.

Most Upper Canadians watching the growing disorder in Britain seemed to have some sympathy for the plight of the disaffected there. "In Great Britain and Ireland," it was realized, "the people are exposed to unwanted difficulties and hardships."[28] Their taxes and poor rates were heavy and Britain's "immense debt ... the decreased sale of her manufacturers ... and the want of employment for a superabundant population" caused much distress, "particularly among the poorer classes." Furthermore, it was understood that some abuses had crept into the British constitution.[29] Some recognized that the

British House of Commons was "very imperfectly constituted, as representative of the people at large." Unlike the situation in Upper Canada, much of the land in England was not freehold and the voting rights of many had been severely curtailed by "the immense accumulation of wealth in a few hands." Even the conservative editors of the *Kingston Chronicle* had to acknowledge that those in the mother country advocating parliamentary reform had reasonable grounds to question whether "the ends of government have been better attained in England, in the present state of representation than in any other country."[30]

Yet the tory press in Upper Canada, in detailed news reports of events in Manchester and other British industrial towns and in weekly editorial comments, nonetheless deplored "that band of undisciplined demogogues" who were "openly exerting every nerve to render the lower classes of people discontented with their present form of government." "However laudible and patriotic their motives," the extreme activities of the radical reformers could not be condoned. "Whatever distress" the British people "may be labouring under," it was declared, "the plan of Reform proposed by Hunt and Cartwright, Woollen and Cobbett is unlikely to do much good."[31] Admittedly the "right of the people ... to meet and petition for the redress of grievances" was sacred. The actions of these so-called "champions of liberty"[32] revealed their true characters, however. The radical reformers "have apparently refrained from acts of violence," the editors of the *Kingston Chronicle* conceded; but it was charged that they really only "pretended to preserve order among their followers." In fact, it was generally believed that the agitators were "artfully endeavouring to influence the minds of the people against the existing government."[33]

To many leading Upper Canadians, the situation unfolding in Great Britain must have been very reminiscent of the circumstances which had precipitated the American Revolution forty years before. Certainly the rhetoric used by many Upper Canadian leaders was remarkably similar to the loyalist response to the American patriots. The radical reformers, like the patriots, were "mere organizers of faction and leaders of a rabble." Far from being meetings to discuss legitimate concerns and grievances, the gatherings at Manchester, like those in the thirteen colonies in the 1770s, had "degenerated into licentiousness and anarchy."[34] By early 1820 it was being argued in Upper Canada that these traitorous Englishmen "had entered into a diabolical conspiracy to destroy the King and Parliament." "By the circulation of blasphemous and seditious writings among the populace," they were sapping "the very foundations of morality and religion" and had opened "a door to dangerous innovations which might ultimately subvert the venerable fabric of the British Constitution."[35] With a "ruthless spirit of cruelty and lawless revenge," the "vile party" had transformed the understandable grievances of the British lower classes into "traitorous and seditious activities"[36] reminiscent of the turbulence and anarchy caused by the revolutionaries of France and America. Many Upper Canadians hoped that "the efforts of the disaffected will be subdued without any danger to the constitution."[37] But successive acts of violence and the need for military intervention to disperse the rioters were alarming.

As events unfolded in Great Britain in late 1819 and throughout 1820, the members of the tory elite centred particularly in York realized that there was much they could learn from the British situation. In February 1820 the editors of the two "government" papers, the *Kingston Chronicle* and the *Upper Canada Gazette*, applauded the actions of those "wise and good and virtuous men of all parties in the government" who, "forgetting their dissensions and sacrificing them upon the altar of their country," had rallied "around the throne in the hour of peril." And some Upper Canadians heartily approved the measures taken by the British government "to strengthen the hand of the Executive"[38] and to quell the disturbances.

As the military were deployed and the British government initiated policies to forestall the efforts of the revolutionaries, it seemed to North American observers that party spirit was gradually given way "to the irresistible impulse of patriotism." The vast majority of Britons, it was reported, were "happily, too well informed to be deceived by such pretended patriots as Hunt and his associates."[39] Most Britons were showing a "truly British feeling, a feeling which while it is eager to protect the liberty of the subjects from the encroachment of power, is alike anxious to prevent that liberty from degenerating into licentiousness and anarchy." Many Upper Canadians were saddened that the actions of the military "while executing the orders of the civil power" had, despite "their utmost forbearance,"[40] resulted in injury to a number of innocent people. However, considering the "disposition of the reformers," the editors of the *Kingston Chronicle* concluded, "we are content to purchase peace and tranquility even by *such sacrifices* as these." For "the banners of laws and the constitution" must "finally wave triumphant over the flags of the disaffected and all the other insignias of sedition."[41]

News of the political agitation in Great Britain in 1819 and 1820 and of the actions of Parliament in quelling the discontent came to Upper Canada at a very opportune time. In 1820 colonial leaders had themselves been experiencing the unsettling effects of a disgruntled populace. While Cobbett and Hunt were raising questions about the essential nature and underlying traditions of the British constitution and form of government at home, Robert Gourlay had been asking similar questions in Upper Canada. To influential Upper Canadians in 1820, the parallels between the two situations were striking. Like the British government, the colonial administration in 1817 had hoped to ignore the unrest, confident that most settlers were loyal and content. But it was soon clear that, like those of the radical reformers at home, Gourlay's suggestions threatened the very fabric of Upper Canadian society. Prominent Upper Canadians quite naturally looked across the Atlantic for models of how best to deal with the situation. And many colonial leaders must have believed that their response to Gourlay was implicitly strengthened and in part legitimized by the policies of the British government.

In October and November 1817 Robert Gourlay addressed the resident landowners of Upper Canada. "I am a British farmer and have visited the Province to ascertain what advantages it possesses in an Agricultural point of view," he announced in both the *Kingston Gazette* and the *Niagara Gleaner*. After three months in the colony, he was "convinced that these are great, far superior indeed to what the British have ever held out." What was needed, he asserted, to facilitate the colony's development was the arrival of large numbers of "suitable" settlers from Great Britain.[42] Gourlay therefore proposed to compile a statistical account of Upper Canada for distribution in England to encourage such immigration. As Gourlay moved about the colony in the winter and spring of 1818, his suggestions for reform became more explicit. Increasingly, he began to criticize both members of the government and their policies. Indeed, by February 1818 it was clear that Gourlay was no longer interested in merely promoting immigration to the colony. He was determined to reform radically the administration and the immigration and settlement policies of the new colony.

"The Canadian people are favoured beyond the lot of their fellow subjects at home," Gourlay asserted in his second and third addresses to Upper Canadians. But the caprice of a tyrannical executive and the general ignorance of her people meant that Upper Canadians "could no longer boast of freedom." "Gentlemen," he proclaimed in February 1818, "the constitution of the province is in danger and all the blessings of social compact are running to waste." The root of the problem, Gourlay believed, was the administration's abuse of its executive powers and the failure of the elected legislature to assert "the strength and spirit of its constituents." At public meetings held throughout the province, Gourlay repeatedly condemned the policies of the local administration and exhorted the elected members of the House of Assembly and the population at large to assert their rights in order to withstand the domination of the tyrannical executive. Upper Canadians, Gourlay declared, should demand "an immediate Parliamentary inquiry" into their situation.[43] Failing this, he advocated that delegates be chosen from across the colony to attend a provincial convention which would draw up a petition to the prince regent for redress of their grievances.

Though "not naturally inclined to take part in political discussions," a "Traveller" noted in 1817 that the addresses of Mr. Gourlay "have lately awakened" Upper Canadians' "attention."[44] The *Kingston Gazette* and the *Niagara Spectator* both provided a public forum for his viewpoints, printing his addresses and his letters usually in their entirety. Most Upper Canadians who read or heard of Gourlay's original suggestion for a colonial survey evidently welcomed the idea. "The wise, patriotic and humane motives which activated that worthy man to his present laborious undertaking," a "Canadian Farmer" wrote to the *Kingston Gazette*, "are beyond the power of praise." "I trust," he declared, that "Mr. Gourlay will meet with the support and encouragement which he justly merits."[45] For the first three or four months of Gourlay's residence, respectable yeomen farmers, clearly upset by the economic depression and the dislocation that had accompanied the peace, met in small groups throughout the colony to draw up answers to Gourlay's questionnaire.

Not all Upper Canadians, however, approved of Gourlay's endeavours and many more soon began to regret their original support of the man and his mission. Some took exception to his championing of American immigration. Others were appalled by his outspoken criticism and what was considered to be his unwarranted personal abuse of certain individuals in York and Kingston. The supporters of the colonial administration, in particular, came to believe that Gourlay's activities jeopardized the very foundations of Upper Canadian society. Like Hunt and Cobbett in England, he was conspiring against constituted authority, encouraging the tyranny of the people, and, at a very personal level, threatening the continued prominence of many of the tory elite.

Gourlay was often called "an artful adventurer"; he was a demagogue, "a dangerous incendiary" who "fostered public commotion and disaffection" and deluded the people.[46] A few Upper Canadians disparagingly referred to his "Republican principles." Others identified him with Justice Thorpe and his attempts before the war to overthrow the government. Most, however, accepted Gourlay's self-proclaimed association with such British reformers as Wilkes, Chalmers, and Hunt. John Simpson of Augusta openly charged the Englishman: "you appeal to the ignorant, rouse the inanimate and insidiously promulgate suppositious oppressions ... you disseminate your poison that you may enjoy the consummation of Rebellious destruction."[47] Upper Canadians were warned to "stand upon your guard." "Let us watch" Gourlay's pursuits "with an attentive and jealous eye,"[48] declared one concerned colonist. Otherwise, it was implied, Upper Canada would be torn by that same civil discontent which prevailed in Great Britain and had resulted in the successful revolution in America. Despite such warnings, however, popular support for Gourlay and his ideas seemed to grow.

In the spring of 1818 the threat that Gourlay posed to the political life of the colony was undoubtedly heightened in the minds of the colonial executive by the apparent intransigence of the House of Assembly. Only a month after Gourlay's second address was published, the members of the House confronted the Legislative Council over the question of the supply bill. Claiming "the high considerations, privileges, and immunities of British subjects," the House unanimously asserted that they alone should determine how revenue that they had voted should be used. In an address to the prince regent, the elected members declared their determination "to preserve inviolate their Civil and Constitutional Rights in their fullest amplification." Like the House of Commons in Great Britain, it was maintained, the House of Assembly should and did have the power over money bills. But at present, the members continued, "Their constitutional rights and privileges have been vitally assailed by the Resolutions of the Honourable the Legislative Council."[49] Their determination notwithstanding, Administrator Samuel Smith prorogued the House with no supply bill passed. Political life in Upper Canada seemed to be in chaos and Gourlay's persistent calls over the next six months for reform only added to the tension.

In an attempt to still Gourlay's voice and halt the growing unrest in the colony, Attorney General Robinson, in the summer of 1818, twice charged the Englishman with libel. But to the consternation of many, Gourlay was triumphantly acquitted in both Kingston and Brockville. "As soon as the verdict was delivered," Stephen Miles reported in August 1818, "an instantaneous and general burst of applause, which continued for some minutes, marked the state of the public's feelings on this interesting matter."[50] Also that summer delegates met in York to draw up an address to the prince regent.

Though the group was small and acted with restraint, the very presence of this extragovernmental body in the provincial capital alarmed even some of the members of the House of Assembly.[51]

Clearly Gourlay was doing "damage to the people"[52] and to the reputation of the province as a whole, and the colonial administration finally felt compelled to take strong measures to quell the unrest. In October 1818 the legislature, in response to the York convention and under the strong leadership of the new lieutenant governor, Peregrine Maitland, passed "An Act Preventing Certain Meetings in the Province." "This favored land was assigned to our fathers as a retreat for suffering loyalty," it was asserted during the debates. Upper Canada was "not a sanctuary for sedition," but rather a home for loyal Britains who had already twice fought and in some cases died for their king and constitution. The resolution of the House Assembly supporting the act stated that "the convention was highly derogatory and repugnant to the spirit of the Constitution of the Province and tends to disturb the public tranquility." The right of petition "is the birthright of British subjects"; but, it was argued, only the members of the House of Assembly were "the constitutional representatives of the People."[53] Many members of the House of Assembly clearly considered that they had a duty to perpetuate the mission of their loyalist fathers.

This "gagging act" was accompanied by renewed attempts by the executive to bring Gourlay himself under control. In December 1818 Gourlay was charged before the magistrates in Niagara under the old Sedition Act of 1804. After some time in jail, he was convicted and was given ten days to leave the colony. His refusal to do so earned him another eight months in jail. It was not until August 1819 that Gourlay finally crossed the border into New York.

By the beginning of 1820 some prominent citizens in Upper Canada came to believe that "the prevailing good sense and good principles of the great majority" of the colonists, like their British cousins, had dissipated "those appearances of disturbances and discontent"[54] in the province. Gourlay's "lies" and his "encouragement of party spirit" had aroused only a discontented few. And though certainly his attempts "to revolutionize this great and magnificent country" had proven a danger to public order and tranquillity, it was asserted, nonetheless, that now "the inhabitants of this happy country are in truth contented."[55]

The agitation that Gourlay had sparked was not completely quieted, however. Though in the short run Gourlay's expulsion did dampen the flames of dissent, the legacy of his activities and of the government's response to them remained. Gourlay had raised the political consciousness of many Upper Canadians. He had asked basic questions about the rights of Englishmen and he had opened the door to political dissent in Upper Canada. Moreover, as Gerald Craig has observed in his authoritative history of the colony, Gourlay "came to be regarded as a martyr"[56] whose image haunted the tory leadership. The growing forces of reform in the colony had only to mention his name to evoke memories of an autocratic government which would obviously take any measure to maintain its own position. Yet the tories in the 1820s refused to repudiate their actions. To members of the executive, he symbolized all that their fathers had fought against in 1776 and all that they were now determined to eradicate in Upper Canada. The Englishman, like other radical reformers in Great Britain, had posed an active threat to the order, the stability, and the very well-being of colonial society.

The legacy of the Gourlay affair, however, was far more important than merely the image of one man. The agitations of 1818 had raised fundamental questions about the actual application of the British constitution in its colonial setting, questions which had first been addressed more than twenty-five years earlier by Lieutenant Governor Simcoe, Richard Cartwright, Robert Hamilton, and other provincial leaders. What is particularly interesting is that in 1818 and 1819 and, indeed, for the next twenty years, the philosophical positions of the two generations were seemingly reversed. In the postwar years, it was the supporters of the colonial executive who asserted that the colony had been established under the *principles* of the British constitution. Ironically, the reformers, harking back to the words of that eighteenth-century conservative, John Graves Simcoe, argued that Upper Canada had been granted the very *image* of the British constitution. It was, however, the lessons that both groups had learned from watching British affairs after 1815, combined with their own experiences with Robert Gourlay, that provided the basis and often the terms of the constitutional debate which rocked the colony in the 1820s.

In his address to the Grand Jury of the Home District in 1827, Chief Justice William Campbell set out some of the basic assumptions that many members of the government made about the colony. Upper Canadians, he wrote, "have the happiness to live under that Constitution" which had "stood the test of ages, the shock of foreign conquest and domestic commotions and Revolutions during many centuries, from the time of our Saxon Ancestors to the present moment." The chief justice was careful to note, however, that that same constitution "cannot in terms be precisely adopted in the Province, but it easily can in *principle* and by analogy." Specifically, he believed that it was impossible to compare the present House of Commons in Great Britain with the House of Assembly in Upper Canada. Nonetheless, he and others argued that the idea of a balanced form of government and of society, taken from the principles of the British constitution, could and should be maintained in the colony. "The concerns and welfare of the colony," Campbell and other tories believed, were best served by the well-considered policies of a strong colonial executive, which ensured the establishment of a government and society in which all would willingly know and accept their positions and duties. Moreover, political parties and controversies had to be avoided if at all possible; government should be by a consensus founded on "unanimity between the two Houses of Parliament."[57]

In the postwar years most prominent Upper Canadians, regardless of political persuasion, would have accepted at least the basic premises of Justice Campbell's rhetoric. In 1820, for example, William Warren Baldwin, a noted reformer, humbly appealed to "the Free and Independent Electors of the Counties of York and Simcoe" for their support in the coming election in similar terms. "I profess to you an affectionate regard for British liberty and the British Constitution." Baldwin continued, "your Representative whoever he may be, should in the discharge of his duties, never forget that these two objects of his care are, one to the other, the best and only Bulwark, and that to preserve the latter pure, the first must be preserved unwounded." As an Englishman, living in a British colony happily possessing "a constitution which under Divine Providence has raised the Parent State to an unrivalled eminence in Freedom and glory," Baldwin and the other candidates swore to defend, maintain, and support "the Rights and Privileges" of their fellow subjects by upholding "the rights and traditions of the British constitution." Yet it was clear that "the blessings of the British constitution"[58] often meant something far different after 1815 than had been understood by the original settlers in the colony. Even among the new emerging elites of Upper Canada, there was little agreement on what these specific blessings actually were. Baldwin and other reformers did not accept Campbell's basic assumption that the executive branch of government had to predominate; moreover, they began to question the intrinsic benefit of political consensus and harmony.

All those who stood for political office between 1815 and 1828, like the vast majority of their predecessors before the war, undoubtedly placed a high premium on their impartiality and independence vis-a-vis any political group. "I hate parties," stated Peter Robinson in 1816, and in sentiments that were echoed by other candidates of the period, he asserted four years later that "I will make no boast to you of my independence: I trust you think me much above any unworthy attempt to court popularity."[59] By 1820 however, a number of colonists were beginning to have some doubts about the independence of their representatives. An article in the *Kingston Chronicle* implored Upper Canadians to take the matter of selecting their members seriously. They should "reflect" carefully before casting their vote. "Put one thing in the balance against the other," residents were urged, "and take the trouble to try to judge rightly."[60]

W.W. Baldwin's concerns, as expressed in his appeal to the independent electors of York in 1820, were much more explicit. "I know Gentlemen, that your good sense convinces you that it is not the duty of the Representative to oppose, through the spirit of faction, the fair, beneficial and legitimate objects of the Administration." But, he asserted, "the purest Administration requires a vigilant activity on the part of all its constitutional checks." Therefore, Baldwin pledged, if elected he would surrender his government office so as to be able to perform his duties without prejudice.[61] "Freeman" took the principle one step further when, in a broadside to the electors of York, he urged that John Beverley Robinson not be elected. "That he is a man of the first talents and ability in the Province, nobody can deny," "Freeman" acknowledged; yet, "holding the situation he does," he must of necessity be under "the influence of the Executive ... Gentlemen, you should keep in mind that the power of the executive is to be guarded with a jealous eye." On the day of the election, "Freeman" counselled Upper Canadians "to reserve" their votes for "some person free from GOVERNMENT INFLUENCE and in whose honour, honesty and integrity you may with safety confide."[62]

By the early 1820s a number of Upper Canadians including Baldwin, John Rolph, and Barnabas Bidwell had come to the conclusion that there had to be a clear division between the executive and the legislative branches of government in personnel as well as in jurisdiction. The House of Assembly, they believed, should be "the forum of the People's side." "Let our Representatives support our cause with firmness and perseverance," they declared, "and we will support them. This is a reciprocal duty. It is the true constitutional principle."[63] It was also considered essential that the members of the House of Assembly should be as independent as possible. Only in this way, "Ploughjogger" argued, would they "look to their constituents and not to the government for their reward." The Assembly, rather than acquiesce or automatically "work in common cause with the government," should be prepared if necessary "to withstand the Influence of the Executive."[64] By 1824 W.W. Baldwin's 1820 election pledge that he would be "independent of the Executive" had become one of the tenets of the new reform group in the House of Assembly.

Not surprisingly, John Beverley Robinson, Henry Boulton, and other members of the tory elite did not accept this interpretation. These men saw no inherent conflict between continuing in their appointed government offices and faithfully representing their constituents. As Henry Boulton in his appeal in 1820 argued, "I trust that same Integrity and Execution I have always manifested when serving my King will continue to animate and guide my conduct when defending, maintaining and supporting the Rights and Privileges of my Fellow Subjects." Surely, he believed, "they must be one and the same."[65]

These two conflicting perceptions of the duties of the members of the House of Assembly became more pronounced as the decade unfolded. In 1822 the editor of the *Kingston Chronicle* observed that "Fierce political contest and party excitements ... irritate the public mind."[66] All involved in the government at that time continued to deplore party spirit; its presence and influence could not be denied, however. By mid-decade political life in the colony was split between those who supported the "court party" and those who supported the "country" or "people's party."[67] And once again it was a supply bill which precipitated a full constitutional dispute over the role and duties of the House of Assembly. To the chagrin of the executive, the House in 1825, as it had done seven years earlier, refused to accept the legislation proposed by the Legislative Council. What had once been associated only with a republican form of government or more recently with politics in the mother country had now become an integral part of the political culture of the colony.

To "stigmatise the people as a *party*," the antigovernment forces exclaimed, was to subvert completely both the principles and the text of the British constitution. The members of the House were "friends of a free Constitution" and when they opposed various government measures out of consideration for the wishes of the people, they were merely doing their duty. Everyone knows, declared "Hampden" in 1825 in a thinly veiled reference to Rev. John Strachan and his associates in York, that "the little bigot in little York and his pupils, parasites and sycophants throughout this Province dislike the present House." But, he believed, "the people will not, upon that account, think their representatives unfaithful servants." It was unfortunate that it was "impossible for the servants of the people to do their duty without incurring the abuse and the hatred of all the partisans of power and all the minions of authority."[68] Yet in truth, the reformers charged, it was *these* men, Rev. John Strachan, Attorney General John Beverley Robinson, and other members of the executive, who were endeavouring "to excite party feelings" and "promote rancour and railing" among the "impudent and discontented faction."[69]

John Strachan and all other supporters of Maitland's administration considered such accusations ridiculous. According to their analysis, those who were obstructing the true workings of the government while "perpetually crying up reform and the maintenance and rights of the people" were really only concerned with "the overturning of the best constitution in the world" and causing "the ruin of the country." An anonymous contributor to the *Upper Canada Gazette*, undoubtedly alluding to the American patriots of 1776 and the current situation in Great Britain, scathingly commented in February 1825, "it has been always the case that those who intend to subvert good order in society began by making extraordinary pretensions of public virtue and crying up the necessity for reform."[70] "The ignorance, illiberality and presumption of more than two thirds of the members" of the House of Assembly, it was contended, had "clogged the wheels of government" and were "retarding the development of the colony." Like the Cobbetts in England, these obstructionists were attempting "to administer a kind of slow poison and to inflame the public mind and to bring the Government and its officers into contempt."[71] The so-called "patriots" were not "the voice of the people" but "whirligig Demogogues" who "wrangled about matters of minor importance" and could produce nothing but a "barren period of legislation."[72] The tory elite was nevertheless forced to acknowledge that the evils of political parties and factions, which threatened the proper workings of the British constitution in Great Britain, now also prevailed in Upper Canada. And as they looked about to discover what had given rise to such devastating developments, one of the factors which they blamed was the colonial press.

After 1815 the development of the Upper Canadian press reflected the gradual evolution and maturation of the society as a whole. Before the war only two journals had served the small population. By 1828 there were ten flourishing newspapers in the colony, and in comparison with the prewar publications they were sophisticated gazettes, providing the growing number of literate Upper Canadians with news, personal and professional advice, and, increasingly, political commentary on the issues of the day.[73]

Upper Canadians in the 1820s obviously prided themselves on their press. As in the mother country, "discussion in Upper Canada is free" and many considered that it was this freedom which was "the bulwark of our liberty and the surest defense of the helpless against the proud man's contumely and oppressive word." It was therefore only to be expected that colonial editors in the postwar period, in the "true tone and spirit of British freedom,"[74] would continually assert their impartiality and independence in relation to any faction or party. As the editor of the *Gore Gazette* declared in his opening issue, his newspaper, like others in the colony, "shall be conducted upon principles of the strictest impartiality, neither influenced by the feelings of party nor warped by any prejudices."[75] In addition, all colonial editors asserted their belief that the British government was the best, and professed an ardent attachment "to the principles upon which the institutions of the British Empire are founded." It was nevertheless their duty, most editors asserted, "from time to time to point out" with "candour and moderation" any instance of "political and moral delinquency" or any action they considered to be "improper." "The noblest distinction of a free people" was a liberal press which was both "unshackled and unawed."[76]

However, by 1820 it seemed to many Upper Canadians that the distinction between liberty of the press and licentiousness was all too often lost. "There are few subjects so generally treated," declared the editor of the *York Gazette*, and few subjects "so little understood."[77] There was no question that individual newspapers were becoming increasingly identified with various political factions in the colony. In support of the tory elite stood the *Kingston Chronicle*, the *Upper Canada Gazette*, and generally the *Gore Gazette*, the *Farmers Journal*, and the *Niagara Gleaner*. In opposition, though by no means united or even in agreement over many issues, were the three York papers, the *Colonial Advocate*, the *Canadian Freeman,* and the *Observer*, and the *Upper Canada Herald* in Kingston. And as political positions hardened throughout the 1820s, the press of Upper Canada became increasingly engaged in the heated and vitriolic war of words.

By the middle of the decade, the supporters of the colonial administration believed that it was the many reform newspapers in Upper Canada which, like their counterparts in the old country, were consciously fanning "the rage of contending factions." Freedom of the press, the editor of the *Kingston Chronicle* charged, had become "prostitution of the press."[78] The *Colonial Advocate*, the *Observer*, and the *Canadian Freeman* were particularly singled out as "originals in their way," each "having a method peculiar to themselves of manufacturing and giving currency to their literary counterfeits." Their editors,

Francis Collins, John Carey, and William Lyon Mackenzie, "were nothing but demagogues" without "principles, honour or decency."[79] It was charged that their "foul mass of falsehood, malignity and folly" had subverted the constitution that they claimed they were upholding "with the most gross and flagrant abuses of the liberty of the press."[80] "Like Robespierre and Danton," these demagogues "wanted nothing but power" and they used their presses for "diabolical purposes" of stirring discontent among the people and encouraging "the overthrow of the constituted authority."[81]

These were not the only culprits. The *Upper Canada Herald* in Kingston was accused of making "scandalous misrepresentations" and even the *Niagara Gleaner* sometimes came in for the executive's abuse.[82] These malcontents and political misfits, the tories charged, had converted "an Engine as beautiful as it is powerful intended to promote the causes of the virtue and morality and for the diffusion of general and useful information among mankind into a disgusting, loathsome vehicle, in which the worst passions and the most deleterious persons find a place for the purpose of distribution among the people under the specious appearance of Patriotism and in the disguise of Friendship."[83]

"We are not advocates for restraining the liberty of the press," the tory elite explained. "We are too sensible of the advantages which have resulted and are daily resulting to the civilized world, from the existence of an unshackled Press ... but we cannot be mistaken, when we say, that if instead of being employed in the propagation of truth and useful information, it had been devoted to the dissemination of falsehood and private scandals, its effects upon the minds and morals of mankind would have been as deteriorating and injurious as it now has been beneficial."[84] Such ill effects, the tories believed, were becoming all too evident in the colony now.

The opposition editors denied all charges of partiality and wrongdoing. Francis Collins of the *Canadian Freeman* and other like-minded reform politicians in the House saw no contradiction in "fearlessly advocating the people's rights" while being "respectful of their rulers." Indeed, they considered it their duty to encourage "free discussion of public measures of a representative and responsible government."[85] Thomson, Carey, Collins, and Mackenzie for once agreed that the *Kingston Chronicle* and the *Upper Canada Gazette* were "in the pay and the confidence of the government" and unquestioningly supported all "court policy." With scorn, they pointed to the attempts of the *Kingston Chronicle* and the *Upper Canada Gazette* to "excite dissatisfaction with our House of Assembly by misrepresentation and abuse." As one anonymous contributor to the *Upper Canada Herald* ironically commented in 1825, the abuse of the House by the *Kingston Chronicle* "is a good sign of their favour."[86]

By the mid-1820s articulate and influential Upper Canadians were espousing two fundamentally different approaches to government and to the application of the British constitution in Upper Canada. Both tories and reformers were committed to the maintenance of the British connection; but they were continually at odds in their understanding of what that really meant. It has been assumed by some that it was the daunting presence of the republic of the United States that influenced much of the political life in Upper Canada after 1815. Certainly, as shall be enlarged upon shortly, Upper Canadians' consciousness of the United States and of the apparent evils of democracy did have a profound impact on the ideas and policies of colonial leaders. It must be stressed, however, that the elites' interpretations of events and circumstances in Great Britain also had a significant influence on colonial political life. Both the tories and the reformers saw themselves working within a British context. And the political questions that both groups confronted in the first fifteen years after the War of 1812 and the varied solutions that they posed were in large part shaped by their knowledge of political developments in Great Britain. Tories and reformers saw different things as they looked across the Atlantic – they saw what they both needed to see and what they desperately wanted to see. And the controversy this provoked touched more than just the supply bill of 1825. It went to the very heart of what Upper Canadians hoped to build and perpetuate in this British colony in North America.

As Upper Canadians attempted to grapple with some of these basic questions of individual rights and duties and of how a government should actually work, the mother country was not their only point of reference. Though the colonists had successfully resisted the American military assault during the War of 1812, they could not and often did not attempt to resist the more persuasive and pervasive influence of American ideas and examples. After 1815, as amicable relations with their southern neighbours were resumed, American ideas once again had a significant impact on the understanding and viewpoints of the rising generation of Upper Canadians. And though the influence of American ideas on colonial development was often quite different from that exerted on the first generation of Upper Canadians, it was, nonetheless, as profound.

CHAPTER SEVEN

Brother Jonathan – the Sometime Ally

In November 1825 a short article in Kingston's *Upper Canada Herald* reprinted from the *New York Commercial Advertiser* noted the completion of the Erie Canal. To mark the momentous event, editor Hugh Thomson reported that "two British sloops of war, with the American colours on the foremast had fired salutes on the approach of the flotilla" of American steam boats which had just passed through the canal. In reply "to this gratifying compliment," the American crews had given three cheers and the band on board the *Lady Clinton* "had struck up *God Save the King*." "The air was no sooner ended," it was recounted, "than the compliment was returned by the British band playing *Yankee Doodle*." The report continued, "another circumstance connected with the demonstration of good feeling must not be omitted." On board the British sloop, the *Swallow*, "an elegant breakfast was given in honour of the occasion." There, "tastefully displayed," were "a series of elegant, appropriate drawings ... representing Britannia, Columbia, the eagle, the lion, an English and American sailor, Neptune, Liberty, the flags and shields of both nations ... all denoting good feelings, fellowship and union of sentiment."[1]

Who would have thought ten or eleven years earlier that the lion and the eagle would be able to meet and exchange "gratifying compliments" of good will? In 1815 the war between Great Britain, Upper Canada, and the United States had just ended and the Upper Canadian press was still relating "all those miseries ... unprecedented in modern times"[2] which the armies of the republic had visited on the colony. There was no question that the war had "left in its wake strong feelings of resentment against the American government and people."[3] And though Upper Canada and Britain had "won" the war, it was also clear that the United States had not really been defeated. In 1815 the American republic was still a large, dynamic, and expanding nation whose very existence presented a continuing threat to the security of the colony at large and to its unique political and social institutions. Informed Upper Canadians in the postwar years could not help but be intensely conscious of the vulnerability of their situation.

The legacy of distrust and, for some, active fear of the United States, did not, however, imply that Upper Canadians in the post-1815 period were "absolute in their unchanging hostility to the United States."[4] In the short term, shared experiences and common responses to the North American war strengthened those ties which had linked contiguous American and Upper Canadian communities. When the conflict was over, leading residents had quickly sought to reestablish those formal and informal contacts which were vital to the colony's well-being. Yet even though the close personal relationships of the prewar years were weakened by the passage of time (and of the first generation of postrevolutionary leaders), the new generation of Upper Canadians continued to be interested in events and personalities south of the border. The two lands and peoples still had a great deal in common. Colonial leaders still found that there was much they could learn from their American cousins, particularly those in the state of New York; and in the long run, the republic continued to provide Upper Canadians with a constant point of reference by which to gauge their own development and state of society.

Colonial perceptions of the United States after 1815 did seem to be far more polarized, however, than in the prewar period. All leading Upper Canadians still heartily disapproved of the many excesses in American society. At the same time, it was clear that the editor of the *Upper Canada Herald* was not alone in 1825 in his congratulations over the completion of the Erie Canal. Most colonists admired American economic achievements and even some of their national leaders. Nevertheless, the tory supporters of the colonial government increasingly saw and used the United States as an example of a nation beset by those political and social problems which they were constantly trying to avoid in Upper Canada. In particular, they tried to set the colony apart from its American and democratic heritage. The reformers, on the other hand, tended to view the United States in a more open and favourable light. Upper Canada, they contended, was a North American community and one could not, nor indeed should not, remain isolated behind an impenetrable barrier.

Despite the political and personal animosity which emerged from the war, geographical realities forced Upper Canadians after 1815 to maintain regular contact with their southern neighbours. As the editor of the *Gore Gazette* declared as late as 1827, "the principal channel of communication between this province and the mother country" was still "through the United States, from Liverpool via New York to the frontier."[5] The republic was Upper Canada's window on the world, and after the war influential colonists welcomed and encouraged any measure which facilitated communications north and south.

In 1817, for example, Stephen Miles suggested that a regular and authorized mail service be established between Kingston and Sacket's Harbour. "There is an extensive correspondence carried on between the inhabitants of the Midland District and other parts of the province and those of Albany, New York, etc.," he wrote. Therefore "we are well persuaded that the revenue arising from an establishment of this kind (besides the convenience accruing to individuals ...) would doubly compensate the two Governments for the expense they would be at in setting forth the undertaking." A year later, the Kingston editor announced with considerable approval that the steamship *Sophia* had begun to provide a regular ferry service between the two communities. "The people are to be congratulated," Miles declared, now that the trip was reduced to a comfortable three or four hours.[6] Similarly, residents of Niagara looked forward to the time when "the communications between Buffalo and Detroit will be as regular and almost as expeditious as it now is between Albany and New York."[7] Yet as leading Upper Canadians began to take advantage of the rapid expansion in transportation across the border and in the United States itself, they could not help but become aware that once again American developments were outstripping their own.

Robert Stanton, editor of the *United Empire Loyalist*, wrote in 1827 that, "until very recently," Upper Canada's "advancement has been but slow; and although the lands of the United States cannot be said to possess any natural advantages which those of Canada have not in common with them, yet, while the inestimable treasures which Canada possess have remained dormant, the States on our borders ... are making rapid strides to improvements." As they travelled through the United States or read American newspapers, influential Upper Canadians seemed to delight in American advancements, particularly in manufacturing and agriculture.[8] Yet as the gap between northern and southern development and prosperity widened, this public admiration became increasingly tinged with jealousy. It was clear that in comparison, colonial development was sadly lacking; and as a result provincial leaders once again prodded their fellow settlers to make increased efforts and particularly to use those American ideas and models most suited to Upper Canada.

After 1815 it was still "the very good improvements" being made in American agriculture that were most interesting and useful to Upper Canadians as a whole. In the United States, farming continued to be "the basis of their strength and prosperity"[9] and it was stressed that the same could and should be true north of the border. American improvements "should put to the blush our own farmers," one anonymous Upper Canadian wrote to the *Upper Canada Gazette* in 1820. The present "indifference in that respect is shameful,"[10] he continued. Attitudes expressed by an earlier generation of Upper Canadians were echoed in the frequent injunction that the colonists "should feel a spirit of emulation" when looking to the United States, "and not submit to be out done by our neighbours on the other side of the lake."[11] American examples and expertise had to be incorporated into the colonial way of life, the local press, public notices, and local speakers persistently asserted, if the Upper Canadian economy was to reach its full potential. If Upper Canadians did not heed this advice, it was implied, the colony would always be but a second-best alternative to the United States; one day it might completely succumb to its powerful neighbour.

Apart from the numerous improvements in agricultural techniques, what was perhaps most dismaying and at the same time exciting to many Upper Canadians were the tremendous strides the Americans were making in the improvement of inland water communications. The republic's prosperity was being significantly enhanced by the rapid completion of numerous canals and waterways which also posed a direct threat to the prosperity and economic security of the traditional St Lawrence trading routes. In March 1817 an anonymous resident wrote to the *Kingston Gazette*, "I want you should write to John Bull and tell him that the American Government are actually raising money to cut a Canal through the high land between Lake Erie and the waters that fall to the Atlantic." "Pray look to the consequences," he warned, "and consider what Jonathan is about – they could not fight us, now they mean to starve us for want of water."[12] Such an alarmist reaction was not, however, really indicative of the general Upper Canadian response to the building of canals in the United States.

Most influential colonists, including the supporters of the government, considered that the Americans and particularly those in the state of New York merited "great praise for the enterprise and ability displayed" in their internal improvements. The canals "cannot fail to excite the interest of the Canadian population," for, the editor of the *Kingston Chronicle* remarked in 1822, they were "stupendous proofs of American enterprise" and "highly honourable to the growing energies and enterprises of our neighbours in the United States."[13] George Keefer, an entrepreneur from the Niagara region, observed in his address to the inhabitants of Upper and Lower Canada proposing the building of the Welland Canal that "the extraordinary exertions which our neighbours the Americans have made and which they continue with celebrated perseverance for the improvement of their internal navigation point out to those who wish well to this country not only the importance of the subject, but the necessity which exists for similar exertions ourselves."[14] Upper Canadians must show that "same spirit of enterprise" found in the United States. The Grand Erie Canal in particular, a number of residents believed, should be "our precedent throughout."[15] For as William Morris, the representative for Lanark, asked the House of Assembly in 1826, "Who that has travelled the long line of the Erie Canal, and witnessed the immediate effects of that stupendous work, on the large sections of wilderness through which it passes, where it has caused the 'wilderness to blossom as a rose' and exhibits to the view one continued line of prosperous and beautiful villages, starting into existence ... and spreading commerce and wealth throughout the country, can doubt for a moment the propriety of straining every nerve to forward such a work?"[16]

The Farmers Journal asserted that "the natural facilities possessed by this Province for such improvements are beyond comparison superior to those of our neighbours." The government, in particular, "wished to see canals intersecting every portion of this Province." But "unless some efforts are speedily resorted to," William Merritt, the chairman of the Welland Canal Company warned, Upper Canadians would lose any hope of rivalling the growing republic, either commercially or socially. He was appalled "to think of the apathy and indifference that has hitherto prevailed amongst us" and he called on the colonists to exert themselves and "contribute to the speedy and successful completion"[17] of this first of many glorious projects. "I verily believe," Merritt declared at the ground-breaking ceremony of the building of the Welland Canal in 1824, this "to be as great a national object to the Province as the Erie Canal to the State of New York."[18]

Between 1815 and 1828 Upper Canadians unquestionably both admired and envied the rapid economic and physical development of the United States. And as they consciously drew on American expertise to enhance their own development, colonial leaders looked for the key which could explain the republic's continuing success. The United States, it was widely believed, possessed very few natural advantages of land or climate; her progress could certainly not be attributed to the republican form of government. True, the United States had been settled far longer than had the British colony, but its startling advances were evident even in those areas most newly opened up. Some in Upper Canada suggested that the answer lay in the willingness of all Americans to work long and hard; others, however, believed that this explanation was too broad. To many Upper Canadian tories and reformers, the republic's success depended specifically on the peculiar character of the Yankees – those residents of New York and the New England states which had once been the heartland of the federalists.

The Yankees seemed a "moral and religious people," a people very much like themselves, and the majority of Upper Canadians considered themselves "the friends and admirers of Jonathan." "The Americans are a brave, industrious and acute people,"[19] one colonial commentator observed. Another asserted, "they are the Scotch of America," having "all the Scotch hardihood ... and a good share of the Scotch forebearance." In 1826 one contributor to the *Kingston Gazette* was effusive in his praise. The Americans "are chiefly remarkable abroad for their great good sense, their industry, their plain dealing, their equitable temper, their perseverance, their sound practical morality, cool courage and variety of resources, after the overthrow of any hope whatever." "The true Yankee is never discouraged," for he possessed "the faculty of alleviating present uneasiness by looking to the future."[20] Many Upper Canadians particularly admired the "enterprising spirit" of the Yankee farmer. "It makes him forget the laws that regulate the progress of improvement ... and conduct everything on a scale which would perhaps be premature many centuries hence." And most Upper Canadians seemed to be "gratified at their prosperity."[21]

This specific approval of the Yankees crystallized in the colonists' admiration and respect for the one individual who many believed was the quintessential Yankee – the governor of New York, De Witt Clinton. Clinton had been active in New York and national politics for much of his life. Though recognized as a republican throughout his career, it was clear to many Upper Canadians that his policies were not radically democratic in the Jeffersonian tradition. Before the war, Clinton, like many others in New York and New England, had opposed the embargo; in 1812 he had unsuccessfully contested the presidential election against James Madison; and in the postwar years he successfully led the apparently more moderate wing of the republicans, to the consternation of the more radical Van Buren faction. In fact, it was clear to many that Clinton's tenure as governor, from 1817 to his death, largely rested on the active support of a great number of former federalists.[22]

To many Upper Canadians Clinton seemed to embody all the best qualities of a good politician, diplomat, and businessman. This "scholar and statesman"[23] was eloquent, apparently honest, and totally committed to the betterment of the people of New York. His speeches were "luminous and comprehensive" and long extracts were often republished in colonial newspapers for the local residents' edification.[24] He was an upholder of justice and the law and throughout his career "promoted the ends of religion and philanthropy, to increase the happiness of his fellow man." Moreover, it was Clinton, many colonists believed, who had been instrumental in the building of the Erie Canal.[25] Indeed, Clinton incorporated all those qualities of the best Yankees. As the *Farmers Journal* declared on his death, "his genius was his own – grand and peculiar" and his passing in 1828 left not only New Yorkers but also Upper Canadians "deeply stricken with a sense of great loss."[26]

Upper Canadian perceptions of the Yankees and especially of De Witt Clinton between 1815 and 1828 were reminiscent of the attitude of many colonial leaders towards the federalists before the War of 1812. In part, the special relationship which residents after 1815 implicitly claimed with their neighbours in New York was undoubtedly a legacy of the strong ties which the previous generation had maintained. It must also be remembered that New York was still Upper Canada's closest neighbour; it was the American state with which the colonists had most contact and were most familiar. Indeed, it might be argued that to many Upper Canadians it was almost as though residents in New York were never considered part of that amorphous whole called the United States. Certainly most Yankees did not seem tainted by their Americanness.

Colonial approbation of "good" Americans did not blind a number of leading Upper Canadians, however, to the many faults that were to be found among most of the people of that nation. After the War of 1812, the colonists' admiration for their neighbours and their accomplishments was "dampened by disgust, at the envy, hatred and jealousy with which the majority of their people regarded our parent state." Though hardworking and enterprising, a great many Americans had also grown "vain and ambitious."[27] One contributor to the *Kingston Chronicle* applauded this overt national pride. "I submit to you ... that the blowing and puffing of the Americans in praise of their country are much more tolerable than the discontented croaking of others." Most, however, considered it "inordinate" and were offended by the American proclivity "to think no country equal to their own."[28] Prominent Upper Canadians particularly objected to the American claims of victory during the War of 1812. Frequently it was noted with some incredulity that even in those many instances when the American forces had been soundly defeated, their journalists had transformed these losses into glorious victories.[29] Obviously such "self-conceit" led to "wonderful impertinence" and arrogance and it encouraged "gross licentiousness"[30] in the American press. Actually, some Upper Canadians pointed out, the Americans "give no indication of genius and make no approach to the heroic, either in their morality or character." As one disgruntled tory asserted in the *Kingston Chronicle* in 1820, they "are but recent offshoots ... from England"; that, he declared, should be "their chief boast for many generations to come." And undoubtedly exasperated by other colonists' constant praise of the United States and its citizens, this commentator, ever mindful of the superiority of the British people, concluded that "considering their numbers, indeed, and the favourable circumstances in which they have been placed, they have yet done marvellously little to assert the honour of such a descent or to show that their English blood had been excited or refined by their republican training and institutions."[31]

This Upper Canadian ambivalence towards Americans generally also reflected the colonists' attitude towards many American accomplishments. There is no question that most admired the economic progress in the United States and believed that models from south of the border could point the way for Upper Canadian development. Among primarily the tory elite, however, there was the concern that the essential British and conservative nature of the colony which set it apart from the republic would be compromised by too heavy a reliance on American techniques. The editor of the *Upper Canada Gazette* felt compelled to assert on a number of occasions that the colony had nothing to be ashamed of. For example, in 1823, with the passage of the canal bill, Robert Stanton wrote, "even friend Jonathan would *stare* and cry *tarnation*, who would have thought it." Stanton continued somewhat defensively, "it is very possible to show Jonathan that the same spirit which gave him such a drubbing at Lundy's and at Queenston can rival and surpass him when directed at more honourable objects than throat cutting."[32] Upper Canada, it was continually asserted, could and would be "equal to any in the

United States." And though in 1827 Stanton acknowledged that the United States was still relatively more advanced, "now, however," he believed, "with us the prospect brightens and our valuable resources are about to be called into requisition."[33]

The constant comparisons that some of the local newspapers made between the colony and the republic, therefore, engendered considerable resentment among a number of the supporters of the colonial administration. A "Briton" scathingly wrote in January 1825, "if we are to immitate them in all their *whims*, there will be no end to changes among ourselves." Responding to the sugggestion that for the convenience and competitiveness of colonial businessmen, Upper Canada should adopt the American standardization of weights and measures, he asked, "instead of leading the public mind step by step by these and many other innuendoes and comparisons, why not make a bold push at once and recommend the government and the constitution of the state of New York as a *uniform standard*?" He continued, "in short, Mr. Editor, I dislike this continual harping about the State of New York ... Let us look to ourselves and govern ourselves and let our uniform standard be regulated by that of the land of our fathers – Old England." Comparisons between New York and Upper Canada were, he believed, "perfectly absurd."[34]

The favourable references to De Witt Clinton also sometimes met with opposition, particularly when some residents unfavourably compared Lieutenant Governor Maitland to the governor of New York. Robert Gourlay, in 1819, pointedly suggested that Upper Canadians would be much more advanced if led by this great American. "Must we shut our eyes to the splendour of Clinton and Monroe?" he asked from the Niagara jail. "Must we throw aside *their* speeches, charged with the balmy and illuminating light of truth and civilization ... blazing in eloquence, to bedim our eyes with staring on the blank and heart sickening records of provincial weakness?" "Oh god!" he exclaimed, "comparisons are odious."[35] Many leading Upper Canadians were evidently horrified at Gourlay's presumption. Upper Canada had nothing to envy in the United States, it was asserted, neither "the splendor of Clinton or Monroe" nor the "flowery eloquence of Adams."[36] Charles Stuart of Kingston asked in the *Chronicle* if Gourlay would "have us blinded by the obvious comparisons which rank Monroe and Clinton above the pure and elevated mind with which the gracious providence of God has blessed us?"[37] "Would he make us subjects of that Government, which had so recently sanctioned the murder of two of our fellow subjects? Would he make us the soldiers of Jackson?" Indeed, "far from envying the United States," the editor of the *Kingston Chronicle* declared, "we should be sorry to imagine that a parallel ... should be found amongst us."[38]

A number of residents in the 1820s continued to think that parallels, particularly with the state of New York, did exist. Some reformers, increasingly disenchanted with the policies of their own government and with its apparently tyrannical disregard for the Assembly, frequently compared their situation with what they understood existed south of the border. In 1824 William Lyon Mackenzie, editor of the *Colonial Advocate*, declared: "Look at New York, look at its machinery, its manufacturers, its canals, its Ontario glass works ... look at De Witt Clinton compare him with Sir Peregrine Maitland – the latter in enjoyment of a princely salary; the former wasting the best years of his life improving the resources of his country without fee or reward."[39] Government in the United States was cheap and all citizens, Mackenzie asserted, had an influence on its decisions. The supporters of the lieutenant governor were quick to reply. The tories alleged that Mackenzie and all who agreed with him showed a want of "independent principles" and an "indifference to the truth." "None but a licentious democrat," Robert Stanton declared, "could have made such an unwarranted attack on the universally respected and most worthy Representative of our Sovereign in this colony."[40]

Despite such bitter exchanges, it is clear that throughout the 1820s the gulf between the tories' and the reformers' understanding of the United States was not as yet unbridgeable. In his early years in the colony, Mackenzie carefully qualified his advocacy of the American system. While he "congratulated the United States on their flourishing condition," he believed that it was, nonetheless, "our duty to be warned by their follies ... to examine closely their peculiar excellencies and to imitate in so far as we may those improvements in general ... whereof their experience has demonstrated to us the safe and useful practical effects."[41] Few in the colony would have denied "the citizens of the neighbouring republic the merits of a clear perception of their own interest, a persevering industry in their pursuit and attainment of that interest, and a strong desire to secure to themselves the benefits arising from the advantages which nature has so bountifully bestowed upon them." Upper Canadians, tory and reformer alike, all conceded that "from the experiences of the people of the United States, those in Canada may derive many permanent advantages."[42] All agreed that it was only political and social models which were suspect and to be relied on only sparingly.

"The advocates of Republican Government," Mr Justice Campbell declared in his address to the Grand Jury of the Home District in 1822, "are furnished with specious arguments in support of their favourite system." "But these arguments," he pointed out, "derive all their force from the flattering and delusive effect they have on the mind of the multitude who are least capable of detecting their fallacy." In the ancient republics, "the fate of the most illustrious individuals was dependent on the wild caprice of the mob ... And even now, this mode of administering Justice" persisted in many modern republics. The use of trial by jury in the United States, an advantage which the Americans had derived "from the British Constitution," did moderate "the caprice of the mob." Yet, Campbell asserted, there was still "one material defect incident to all Republics." This was "the want of that permanence or duration, so essential to the progressive improvement and perfection of any human institution." The British, and hence the Upper Canadian constitution, was "the tried and perfected production of many ages." The constitution of the United States was not. "It is a well known historical fact," Campbell declared, "that republics are most perfect at their commencement and invariably fall off and degenerate, until by internal discord, corruption and anarchy ... they end in the most intolerable Despotism, or become an easy prey to some neighbouring power." Campbell concluded that "The universality of the fact furnishes sufficient grounds for attributing the evil of some radical and insurmountable defect in the system itself."[43]

Between 1815 and 1828 many in Upper Canada shared Justice Campbell's distrust of the political system of the United States. This did not mean, however, that Upper Canadians could or wanted to ignore political developments south of the border. As residents became increasingly preoccupied with their own internal politics, newspaper coverage of American affairs did decrease. Frequently colonial editors in the 1820s noted that the American papers were "barren of information which would be interesting to the Canadian reader."[44] Nonetheless, it was realized that all too often decisions made in Washington had a direct impact on colonial life. And Upper Canadians in the postwar years continued to be fascinated by political affairs in the United States. Some undoubtedly watched fully expecting to see the inevitable decline and disintegration of the nation. Others looked on with a sense of excitement as the republic thrust forward into the nineteenth century.

Upper Canadians primarily kept in touch with American affairs through their local newspapers. Annually colonial editors reprinted, often in their entirety, the presidental addresses concerning the state of the nation. In addition, local journals frequently included reports of major policy statements and of the proceedings of Congress, particularly when these related to America's relations with Great Britain and the North American colonies.[45] Reflecting their readers' special interest in New York, the Upper Canadian press often printed excerpts from Governor Clinton's speeches and accounts of the debates in the state legislature. Moreover, every four years, the colonial newspapers included accounts of the presidential election (though it was only the Jackson campaigns of 1824 and 1828 which prompted extensive reports).[46]

To interested observers in Upper Canada, politics seemed to pervade all aspects of American life. It was "a favorite topic of conversation with any American"; and though some Upper Canadians judged that "as a people" the Americans were "politically knowledgeable," most considered that they were too easily swayed "by the emotionalism of political parties and factions."[47] As one Kingston resident observed, the typical American allowed "himself to be dazzled by the galaxy and epithets by which his orators and newspaper scribblers endeavour to persuade their supporters that they are the greatest, the most refined, the most enlightened and the most moral people on earth."[48] It was this tendency, many believed, which had directly led to what had been for the United States the disastrous War of 1812. "In defiance of the law and the national prosperity," the editor of the *Niagara Gleaner* declared in 1817, the republican government had plunged its country "into the vortex of the French Revolutionary insanity."[49] Yet even defeat had not stilled the "hot electioneering rage." In 1817 the "Post Boy" observed in his New Year's Address in the *Kingston Gazette*:

> Their partisans with libels fight,
> And *Feds* and *Demos* rail and write;
> Damn their opponents, one and all
> And dip their party pens in gall.[50]

For the next ten years, Upper Canadians read in their newspapers of the "system of personal abuse and general violence which marked the course"[51] of many of the congressional sessions. In the "madness of party," Americans, it seemed, would do "anything ... intemperate and disgraceful."[52] Republicanism condoned party and faction and encouraged bitter political controversy; and, inevitably, it destroyed the harmony and order of society. Upper Canadians wanted no part of such a system. Yet it would seem that this general condemnation of political life in the United States and particularly of the republican form of government was largely rhetorical. Reports in the colonial press and in private correspondence indicate that many Upper Canadians also had a keen appreciation of circumstances unfolding south of the border and bold political judgments were often qualified when specific situations were being considered.

By 1817 many realized that "the *Federalist* party in the United States had declined in popularity." The editor of the *Niagara Spectator* among others believed that conservative Americans were "disposed to give up their opposition and unite with the administration," because the government had "adopted the principles of the Federalists."[53] By January 1818 the "Post Boy" of the *Kingston Gazette* reported that "*Demos* and *Feds* now shake hands with each other, / and follow MONROE as their leader and brother."[54] By the end of the year it appeared that there were only a few official federalists left in Congress. Yet, as an excerpt from the *National Intelligencer*, reprinted in the *Upper Canada Gazette* in December 1819, reported, "It should rather say that they are nearly all federalists. For the democrats have embraced most of the federalist sentiments and the basis of the others have been removed."[55] Influential Upper Canadians and many of their associates in New York and the New England states welcomed the "era of good feeling" of the Monroe administration and its endorsement of federalist ideas. Indeed, by 1820 many Upper Canadians accepted as fact that political parties in the United States were "out of fashion."[56] To some it appeared that that nation had at last achieved some state of political equilibrium and stability.

This apparent appreciation, and for some qualified approval, of American political life after 1820 also came to include many of its national leaders. De Witt Clinton had always been admired; ironically, by the mid-1820s such former presidents as John Adams and Thomas Jefferson were redeemed and resurrected to the state of "venerable patriots."[57] Some of the colonial press gave considerable coverage to their deaths in 1826 which coincided with the fiftieth anniversary of the Declaration of Independence. "The names of the distinguished patriots and statesmen," declared the editor of the *Niagara Gleaner* "will be gratefully remembered by the people of the United States." President Adams in particular was considered "one of the earliest and ablest and most fearless champions of his country's freedom" and "the land will mourn his passing."[58]

The political tranquillity which seemed to descend on the American political scene in the early 1820s did not blind Upper Canadians, however, to the strife which many continued to consider was endemic to republicanism. In part, the prevalent disorder could be attributed to the small criminal element which plagued all societies. The largest part of the problem in the United States, however, was believed to be the inevitable result of its political institutions which not only condoned but encouraged social strife.

On 5 January 1817 "A Dreadful Fact," a rather lengthy article in the *York Gazette*, was reprinted from the *Connecticut Courant*. "A great part of the news now stirring is the news of felonious deeds, of forgery, robbery, theft, arson and almost every species of villanous crime," it read. The article reported that crime in the United States had increased 300 per cent in the past four years. The author attributed most of this activity to the War of 1812. Various corps of troops which had been raised during the war continued after 1814 to pillage and to destroy property. Yet this was only a symptom of a far greater problem. The commentator believed that respect for law and order was generally diminishing in the United States. "In short," he declared, "the young republic has but a few more lessons to learn before she will bear a comparison with the most corrupted state in Europe." The evidence seemed overwhelming to Upper Canadians that crime was rife in the United States. News from south of the border regularly included reports of murder, robbery, arson, counterfeiting, and a host of other illegal activities.[59] Even in the north, traditionally viewed as the home of order, residents were not safe. In the spring of 1827 both Yankees and Upper Canadians were shocked by the abduction of William Morgan.[60] The most sensational crimes, however, seemed to be confined to the south, though even seemingly isolated incidents there touched all in the United States and sometimes threatened international peace. One incident in Florida shortly after the war brought this point graphically home to colonial leaders.

In 1817 two British merchants, Robert Amister and Alexander Arbuthnot, were tried for espionage by the commander of the American army in Florida.[61] After their speedy conviction, General Andrew Jackson had the two summarily executed though the court had recommended only their expulsion from the area. Initially Jackson's action seemed to be but one insignificant incident of war on the Florida frontier. But as the news reached the public press in London, New York, and Upper Canada, it became a *cause célèbre* and for a short time the United States and Great Britain appeared to be on the brink of war. Though the international crisis soon passed, Upper Canadians and many in New York State and New England continued to be preoccupied by the matter. "The dreadful butcheries of General Jackson"[62] only reaffirmed for both Upper Canadians and discontented Americans the evils which were permitted under a republican form of government. And not only were such atrocities condoned but the Amister-Arbuthnot affair highlighted the growing divisions between northern and southern states – divisions which had originally been evident in the prewar controversies between the federalists and the republicans and which now had the potential to destroy the moral and political fibre of the nation.

"Humanity must shudder," declared "Scrutator," in the *Upper Canada Gazette*, "at the recital of this atrocious trial and result." General Jackson had arbitrarily "dashed his pen through the [original] sentence of the court martial"[63] and had ordered the executions. Influential Upper Canadians, heavily dependent on American sources for their information, readily accepted the judgments passed by their associates in New York and New England who themselves had learned of the affair with "mingled emotions of astonishment and horror."[64] The trial had obviously been a "mockery" "against which the laws of nations and the customs" of the United States "positively protest."[65] How could General Jackson, it was asked, "a lawyer, a judge, not approve the proceedings of the court?" His actions were "marked with arrogance, injustice and cruelty." "Would that we could hide that whole transaction in impenetrable darkness," stated one article from the *Nations Messenger* reprinted in the *Kingston Chronicle*; "it is one certainly calculated to tarnish the pages of our history." Upper Canadian and American critics both considered it "the duty of every friend of justice and every lover of his country" to condemn, as a public disgrace, "such arbitrary and unlawful proceedings."[66] "It was MURDER," they declared, and "all right-minded Americans"[67] were horrified.

Leading Upper Canadians judged that because of Jackson's butcheries "a faint stain is fixed upon the national character of our American neighbours." "It remains with their Congress now in session," some asserted, "to declare whether it should be indelible or show to an observing world that 'laurelled power' shall not prevent the murderers from being brought to justice." Pressure by many Americans that the general be "brought to justice" was disregarded by the government, however. The administration seemed determined "to protect General Jackson."[68]

To Upper Canadian observers in early 1819 it appeared that once again the American government and its people were bitterly divided. And as had been the case ten years earlier, the enemies of justice had prevailed. Indeed, Upper Canadians expressed little surprise when, five years later, General Jackson ran for the presidency. Though he had "trampled on the constitution and the laws" and many in New York and New England vehemently opposed the election of a man who was clearly "not fit to be the ruler of a free people,"[69] his eventual success in 1828 seemed to many in the north inevitable. Was not the United States the "land of Democrats and confused Politics?" Jackson, "politically educated in the school of Jefferson,"[70] had a method and style that were ably suited to succeed in that perverted form of republican government. In 1828 there was some Upper Canadian sympathy for many in the north; but the colonists also realized that the focus of power in the United States had shifted decisively to the south and west.

Upper Canadian leaders did not attribute the growing political divisions between the north and the south merely to the rise of General Jackson. Its roots, the colonists realized, were far deeper and more insidious than that. Jackson's success was understandable in a society where lawlessness was encouraged even if not officially condoned. Far more significant, however, was the American government's acceptance of the institution of slavery. It had not only precipitated the persistent power struggle between the north and the south, it was also a continual degradation of the nation as a whole.

Slavery is "disgraceful to civilized man,"[71] cried the editor of the Kingston Gazette in 1817. The colonists had themselves abolished the practice before the turn of the century and they now proudly supported "the employment of the national arms" by Great Britain "against the piratical state of Barbery compelling them to abolish Christian slavery."[72] It is not surprising, therefore, that they followed the debates south of the border on the admittance of new slave states to the union with considerable interest.

From the beginning it was evident that, as the Kingston Gazette observed on 22 December 1820, "neither of the opposing sides" of the issue was "willing to yield." Most in the north actively and publicly opposed the spread of slavery and particularly the admittance of Missouri to the union as a slave state.[73] Slavery was "a curse," many Americans believed. It was "an abomination in the sight of God" and a "foul reproach to a Christian nation."[74] Others charged that it was "for the mere selfish gratification of those who were too indolent to work."[75] The representatives of the southern states, the former strongholds of the republican party, insisted vehemently, however, that Missouri be admitted. They argued that the state constitutions were "not contrary to the spirit of the federal constitution" and must therefore be accepted. It was asserted that "CHRIST HIMSELF GAVE A SANCTION TO SLAVERY."[76]

The eventual settlement of the question in 1821 and the admittance of Missouri into the union did little to halt the debate.[77] To many residents of the United States, the decision was a "mortification." "In vain," they cried, "shall we hereafter appeal to our Constitution, our laws and our moral and religious pretensions as evidence that we are a free, just and humane nation." Surely "our conduct give the lie to our professions and our acts proclaim us to be political hypocrites." For some, it seemed that *the freedom of our country has been sacrificed in the house of its friends.*" To Upper Canadian editors, relying heavily on American self-criticism, it was "indeed a satire upon true liberty and equal rights and fixes an eternal disgrace on the whole republic." As the editor of the *Kingston Chronicle* observed, "the decision ... affords a striking proof of the controlling influence of the slave holding states over those in which slavery is prohibited."[78]

While the "wordy war" raged in Congress, Upper Canadians also followed the debates on slavery in the New York legislature. The available evidence suggested that the vast majority in that state was vehemently opposed to the practice and had actively resisted the admission of Missouri into the union. At the end of 1821 this was confirmed in the state's new constitution which prohibited the practice of slavery.[79] Though having "no penchant for democracy" and questioning the "ultra democratic tendencies"[80] of the document, even conservative Upper Canadians heartily approved New York's stand on the issue. Nevertheless, in other parts of the union "the wicked practise" persisted. Reports of racial violence and abuse of slaves[81] frequently appeared in the colonial press throughout the 1820s. Truly, as the editor of the *Colonial Advocate* remarked, slavery had "become the greatest curse of republicanism."[82]

Throughout the postwar years, Upper Canadians undoubtedly looked south with some sense of superiority. Though party politics seemed to have lost some of their bitter divisiveness in the United States, it was clear to interested colonists that those problems from which many had fled in 1784 persisted. Crime was rife. Slavery poisoned not only those directly involved but all American society. Despite the best intentions and efforts of good Americans, public virtue, a quality which leading Upper Canadians considered essential to good government and society, appeared to be fast disappearing in the United States. Without the stabilizing influence and example afforded by the British constitution, it was deemed unlikely that this disintegration of civilized society could be arrested. Nonetheless, events south of the border were also a warning to Upper Canadians. Though many believed that similar developments would not happen in the British colony, this would only be the case if residents remained true to their constitution and British traditions.

Varying colonial perceptions of the United States had a profound impact on the development of the colony and on the evolving beliefs of its leaders. All prominent Upper Canadians were determined to maintain Upper Canada as a British colony. Conservative leaders in the province were adamant that only this prevented the province from inadvertently falling into American ways, particularly in political or social matters. Some tories even went so far as to try to close the border to all American influences. The reformers refused to accept such a bitter and paranoid reaction. Though there was much to condemn in the United States, they believed that there was also much to approve. They saw no reason why preserving the British roots of Upper Canada could not be compatible with developing closer economic and social ties with the United States and with using American examples to enhance colonial development.

These differences in outlook intensified during the 1820s. Varying views of the United States impinged increasingly on local debates concerning taxation, trade, and citizenship. For although these controversies were carried on within the context of Upper Canada's Britishness, the Americanness of the colony and its people could not be denied.

CHAPTER EIGHT

The Fear of Abandonment

On 13 June 1815 the *Kingston Gazette* reported the arrival of the first American ships into Liverpool harbour since the outbreak of the War of 1812. "This first effect of the restoration of amity between the two countries designed by nature's habit and mutual interest to maintain uninterrupted the relations of peace was hailed with great delight by the great number of spectators," noted the excerpt from the *Mercantile Advertiser*. The news undoubtedly delighted Upper Canadians as well. The resumption of trade between Great Britain and the United States confirmed far more than any treaty or proclamation could have done that peace was really at hand. Only now, many Upper Canadians believed, could they begin to look to the future with some confidence.

Few could ever forget, however, the essential vulnerability of their situation. In 1815 Upper Canada continued to live in the shadow of the two great powers. The colony was still a small British province perched on the shoulders of a powerful and expanding American giant. Like their predecessors, Upper Canadians in the postwar period relied on both Britain and the United States for their prosperity and well-being. More importantly, the colony's security and development continued to depend on the maintenance of peace between the two. As the tenor of that relationship fluctuated between diplomatic cordiality and open distrust, so did the colonists' concern for their very survival. At the same time, their understanding of the republic to the south led a number of colonists to fear that they might yet be overwhelmed without warning. And this time it was realized that Great Britain might not come to their aid. The mother country's commitment to the young colony seemed to be weakening in the postwar years, and a number of residents believed that "the British needed as much watching as did the Americans."[1]

Various colonial attempts to grapple with the everchanging international situation were significantly coloured by Upper Canadians' diverse perceptions and expectations of their own relationship to the two powers. Though clearly harbouring misgivings, the tories, publicly at least, continued to place their trust in the empire throughout the 1820s. Only if this vital connection was maintained and strengthened, they believed, could Upper Canada retain its essential Britishness and ward off the imperialistic designs of the United States. On the other hand, various reformers and antigovernment groups across the colony began to suggest that the existing connection with Great Britain was only retarding colonial development. Growing public criticism of the imperial relationship and repeated calls for closer economic ties with the United States aroused such men as John Strachan and John Beverley Robinson to a vehement defence of the status quo. Anything else, tories believed, was an open invitation for the Americans to invade and was simultaneously a convenient justification for the British to leave them.

In 1815 Upper Canadians' most pressing concern was whether the peace so recently restored between the two English-speaking nations would, in fact, last. The Treaty of Ghent had stopped the fighting; it had left many issues unresolved, however. At the end of the war, for example, the international boundary between the United States and British North America was still undefined. No agreement had been reached on the number of warships or fortifications the two powers would be able to maintain on the Great Lakes. Moreover, the peace had certainly not dispelled the hearty distrust the two governments felt for each other. Particularly in the light of this last factor, influential Upper Canadians believed that it was essential that the remaining questions be quickly resolved; they knew only too well how easily difficulties could erupt between neighbouring countries.

"It ought to be the wish of every government," declared the editor of the *Kingston Chronicle* in 1821, "to have its lines clearly defined to avoid its servants falling into error."[2] For years Upper Canadians had followed closely the work of the joint commission which had been established to determine the boundary between the republic and the British colonies. All had originally hoped that the question "could be speedily adjusted";[3] but the negotiations had dragged on. First the British and then the Americans had brought new claims to the commission; and some residents had expressed fears that they might suddenly find themselves living in a neighbouring jurisdiction. It was seven years after the two parties had first sat down at the table before the *Kingston Chronicle* could report that the boundary, along the St Lawrence and the lower Great Lakes, had been finally decided "with fairness and impartiality." And obviously conscious of American enterprise, the report concluded somewhat ruefully that the lands assigned to the United States "will doubtless soon be disposed of ... and become settled and well cultivated. We fear ours will remain for some time longer the waste lands of the Crown, and continue to be the resort of squatters and smugglers."[4]

The intentions of the governments on both sides of the border to reach an amicable understanding did not prevent a few Americans and Upper Canadians from continuing to take advantage of the peculiar geographical circumstances of the region. As had occurred in the years before the war, relatively serious tensions periodically erupted, particularly in those areas around Kingston and Niagara. British soldiers continued to see the open border as an invitation to desert and the attempts of superiors to retrieve their men met with renewed animosity from American residents.[5] Occasionally customs officers on one side of the boundary impounded their neighbours' vessels, citing the traditional claim of infringement of national trading regulations. Counterfeit American dollars often found their way to Upper Canada and counterfeit Halifax currency appeared in New York. And smuggling remained a constant problem for officials on both sides of the border.[6]

In arguments reminiscent of those put forward before 1812, influential Upper Canadians and Americans living along the border deplored such "unpleasant occurrences."[7] "The subjects of the two nations," it was reasserted, had "the strongest possible incentives to reciprocal good offices and durable friendships."[8] If at all possible, any cause for rupture between their governments should be avoided. The matter was especially pressing for Upper Canadians. Though many had friends and business associates in the United States, the memory of the war was still fresh in their minds and it was believed that the American government would welcome any excuse to invade.

The editor of the *Upper Canada Gazette* was one of the first to voice this concern explicitly. Only two years after the end of the war Robert Horne commented that "the government of the United States is using with utmost diligence the leisure afforded by peace to provide for the vigorous prosecution of war." In fact, it appeared that only "the want of another war in Europe"[9] was discouraging the Americans from mounting another military offensive against Upper Canada. Upper Canadians had already been "exposed to the ravings of a powerful and inveterate foe." "Twice had the American standard been planted in Upper Canada."[10] Let not "the remembrance of these awful events die with us, nor pass away as a tale that is told," the settlers were exhorted. That experience was "the inheritance of our children, to the last posterity, instructing them ... to withstand the aggressions of wicked ambition."[11] Many prominent colonists after 1815 found it difficult to accept that the republic had ceased its imperialist designs and given up its interest in the British North American colonies. For the moment, however, most of America's attention was directed not to the north but to the Spanish colonies in the south.

In September 1815 an excerpt from the *National Intelligencer* informed the readers of the *Kingston Gazette* that the United States was at war with Spain. Though many Americans and some Upper Canadians initially questioned the accuracy of the report, by the end of 1816 various accounts confirmed the American invasion of the Floridas.[12] For the next two years, Upper Canadians watched with fascination and some apprehensiveness as the Americans advanced south. A number of colonists judged that this campaign "endangered all European colonies in North America." As the editors of the *Kingston Chronicle* remarked, no one knew when "this grasping people would sit down contented with the territory they have obtained."[13] Other residents were reassured, however, by these latest military exploits. The American action in the Floridas strongly suggested that "both the motive and means for the conquest of Canada are daily decreasing. It is the South ... where their strength, or at least certain political strength is advancing." A number of Upper Canadians concluded, therefore, that "the North American colonies had little ... to fear." They were "secure and we may safely labour for their growth."[14]

The situation was soon complicated, however, by the rapidly deteriorating relationship between Great Britain and the United States. Repeatedly the two governments claimed that "a most friendly understanding existed" between them. Stephen Miles noted in 1818 that there was "mutual expectation that the Peace will be a lasting one."[15] The execution of Arbuthnot and Amister by General Jackson in 1819 and the apparent growth of anti-British sentiment among the American people, however, threatened to compromise the existing harmony. A "Loyalist," writing to the *Upper Canada Gazette* in April 1819, was decidedly "anxious for the safety of the Province." "An invasion was imminent," he believed. Though four months later the *Niagara Spectator* reported that "there will be no war on account of Arbuthnot and Ambister,"[16] Upper Canadian concern for the colony's security persisted. Early in 1820 the *Kingston Chronicle* reported that President Monroe had called for the expansion of the American navy, and at the end of that year Macaulay warned that "appropriations of money so extensive for the construction of military works, though professedly with a view to defensive operations merely, are not to be regarded with indifference by the local inhabitants of these Colonies, especially when coupled with the present state of our fortifications." He continued, "war is indeed, we would fair hope, a very distant possibility, but as the President himself intimates, it is a possible event."[17] British and American interests continued to come "into collision"[18] throughout the next few years. Tensions arose over shipping on the Great Lakes, jurisdiction over the St Lawrence and trading rights to the West Indies. Of far greater concern to many Upper Canadians in the early 1820s, however, was the growing anti-British feeling which emanated from south of the border.

"The most remarkable modern instances of indiscriminate national hostility is to be found in that implacable hatred which the Americans bear to the British," observed one Upper Canadian in 1819. It seemed to dismayed observers that the American government and "people hate England with all their hearts and souls and strength." Some colonists attributed this growing animosity to the natural antipathy which often develops between members of a family. The editors of the *Kingston Chronicle* noted in June 1821 that "it is a very true and a very trite observation that when members of a family happen to quarrel, the animosity they feel towards each other is much more inveterate than it should have been had no relationship existed between the parties."[19] Most, however, believed that this "feeling of detestation" was consciously being "fostered by various writers in the United States."[20] Particularly offensive to the tory elite were the writings of Robert Walsh of Philadelphia who, as one colonist put it, seemed to collect "all the nasty trash which he can find against Great Britain"[21] to include in his newspaper, the *National Gazette*. Upper Canadians objected most, however, to his recently published pamphlet, *An Appeal From the Judgement of Great Britain, Respecting the United States of America*, which was widely circulated in Upper Canada.

The *Appeal*, originally intended to be the first part of a two-part publication, was a detailed account of British-American relations from the beginning of the seventeenth century to the end of the War of Independence. In an attempt to refute some of the apparent aspersions which had been cast upon the American character by some British journalists (including contributors to the *Edinburgh Review* and the *Quarterly Review*), the pamphlet illustrated at some length how it had been the British and not the Americans who were to blame for any animosity between the two peoples.

"You are pleased to be offended with England," John Strachan replied to Walsh in the *Kingston Chronicle* on 1 January 1820, "but I divine not motives." "It is not my intention," he declared, "to add fuel to the flames; I will endeavour to extinguish it, while I present you, as a melancholy example of perverted talents – talents capable of the noblest efforts, but which are now employed in pandering to vice and sowing the seeds of future discord and misery."[22] In this first of fourteen letters responding to the *Appeal*, Strachan, writing as "Scrutator," agreed with Walsh that "national antipathies are to be deprecated." "But," he continued, "I accuse you of acting in opposition to this maxim, and of having most wantonly offended against humanity and religion in the work which we are now examining." Point by point, "Scrutator" refuted Walsh's claims of British injustice to the United States and, in the process, presented what many tories considered to be some of the essential differences between the United States and Great Britain.

Frequently relying on information gleaned from various American commentators, Strachan contended that, among other things, "the representation of the people" in government was "purer" in Great Britain than it was in the United States. "The defects of the former," he wrote, "have been produced by time and neither by the vices or corruption of men." Echoing an opinion that many prominent Upper Canadians had formed over the years, Strachan declared that in the United States, the defects "are the consequences of corrupt laws, made for the purpose of aiding the determination of the ruling faction to trample upon its opponents."[23] In another letter, Strachan compared "the dreadful butcheries of Generals Jackson and Coffee"[24] with the measured and just treatment that the British government afforded aliens and natives. And to compare the English attitude towards the slave trade with the American history of inaction, Strachan declared, was a "blatant distortion of the facts."[25] "To me," he wrote, "it has always been a matter of grief to see two nations connected by so many ties eagerly collecting motives of hatred one against the other." But with such works as Walsh's *Appeal* and American determination "to have no friends among the British,"[26] animosity was, he believed, inevitable. Strachan was clearly proud to be British and was not willing to acquiesce quietly in aspersions cast on the British character.

Strachan was certainly not alone in his condemnation of Walsh and of the other American journalists who encouraged hatred of Great Britain. The editors of the *Kingston Chronicle* highly recommended the "Scrutator" letters to their readers; "Crito" was appalled by the "malignant slanders"[27] put forward by Walsh. Other colonists bitterly denounced the "style of calumnious reflections on that Great and noble ... British nation and character"[28] prevalent south of the border. Moreover, Strachan's extensive use of such American commentators as the late Dr Timothy Dwight, president of Yale College, Mr Carey of New York, and Dr Jeremy Belknap, author of the *History of New Hampshire*, implicitly demonstrated to Upper Canadians that a number of Americans shared their viewpoints.[29] Even a review of the *Appeal* taken from the *National Intelligencer* and published in the *Kingston Chronicle* in February 1820 regretted this "desire to cultivate hostile feeling to Great Britain." Walsh was seen to be "a renegade."[30] Nevertheless, many Upper Canadians feared that the anti-British sentiments which he and others in positions of influence generated would encourage an eventual confrontation between the two powers.

If only *"Old England* on the eastern and *New England* on western side of the Atlantic understand their true interests and cordially unite in the grand system of politics for the steady support of national freedom," wrote the editor of the *Upper Canada Gazette* in 1824, "there is not a corner of the earth that will not be eventually blessed by the cordial reconciliation and future harmony subsisting in the great English family, whose children and whose language, laws and institutions are destined to cover so wide an expanse of the civilized world."[31] Indeed, by 1824 it did seem that the so-called "war of ink" between American, Upper Canadian, and British journalists had become "less acrimonious."[32] Some American newspapers were even actually beginning to adopt a pro-British stance. But many tories were sceptical about their sincerity. "The United States," John Stuart declared in 1824, "are *among* the most formidable rivals of this country and must in time become the *most formidable*. There is certainly no power less friendly to the interests of Great Britain." Others continued to believe, as Rev. John Strachan stated in an address at Woolwich that same year, that "the United States will, the first opportunity force these provinces into one union with themselves and against"[33] Great Britain. Two years later, reports confirmed that the United States was once again fortifying its northern border. A number still continued to hope, according to the editor of the *United Empire Loyalist* in 1826, that "the two nations, connected by political institutions, differing but in *name*, possessed of the same religious faith, speaking the same language, mingling daily in the most confidential relations in business and those relations cemented by personal attachment might move on together without severing those ties by the sabre." But the threat that an ever-expanding neighbour posed to Upper Canadians' security, merely by its presence, could never be completely discounted.[34] Throughout the entire period, from the end of the War of 1812 to 1828, this threat coloured all Upper Canadians' perceptions, not only of their relationship with the republic but also of their association with the empire. For many in the colony believed that their surest defence against American aggression was the maintenance of a strong British connection. Some wondered, though, if Great Britain was still willing to meet those commitments that she had made to the first loyalist settlers.

"There are persons" in Great Britain, observed an article from the *Colonial Journal* reprinted in the *Kingston Gazette* in 1818, "who hold forth the doctrine that the North American colonies are insecure ... They pretend that these possessions must soon be overrun by the United States and they infer that Great Britain would be wise in giving preference to establishments elsewhere."[35] Upper Canadians had been apprehensive about the intentions of the British government for some time. In the spring of 1815 the British had withdrawn a large number of regular troops from the colony. Soon fortifications had begun to fall into disrepair and the flow of British capital into British North America had decreased substantially. As the mother country became increasingly preoccupied with her own growing economic and social problems, North American affairs seemed to be forgotten. It was, however, the proposal originally put forward in 1815 to move the colonial capital from York to Kingston which crystallized many colonists' fears of abandonment. Even the most ardently loyal subjects felt betrayed by what they considered to be "the Prelude of delivering Upper Canada into the hands of our enemies."[36]

"The glory obtained in Europe by Great Britain seems to have blinded her to her true interests with America," argued Strachan in a memorandum on the matter.[37] The present ministry seemed more than willing to make concessions to the United States, regardless of the fact that these were "highly prejudicial to many loyal and meritorious subjects and injurious to the Colonial system." The proposed removal of the seat of government to Kingston was, he asserted, one such impolitic concession. "I can easily conceive that in England, the change of the seat of government of Upper Canada is considered a matter of no consequence," he wrote; many in the colony, however, saw it as "proof of ulterior motives, tending to sever the Colony from the Parent State." Though Strachan acknowledged that this was probably not the intention, for British officials "erroneously" supposed "that Kingston is more inland than York," he predicted that at least "the Government at Washington will naturally consider it a preliminary step to the abandonment of Upper Canada"; and to the

Americans, "who were continually plotting directly or indirectly the expulsion of the British from North America," such action would be more than welcome.

Strachan hastened to state that he was not questioning the right of the mother country to make such a decision. "When the interests of the Parent State and those of a particular colony are opposed, the colony ought to yield," he declared. But such acquiescence did have limits. This particular issue was a local matter and ought to be left to the colonial administration; certainly, Strachan asserted, no sacrifice should be made "that renders the colony useless or its inhabitants miserable." The right of the British government to make such a decision had to be qualified by her duty to the colonists in North America. In the past, Great Britain had given "the strongest pledge of protection" to those who "in declaring for the unity of the Empire had hazarded their lives and lost their property." Upper Canadians were "therefore connected with England by the nearest and dearest ties, and it is not easy to name any sum of money when their claims for protection are considered that can justify the desertion by Great Britain." "Every principle of honour and good faith" demanded continued British support for "protection and obedience are reciprocal."

If allowed to go forward, Strachan predicted, the present proposal "will prove a stamp act in its consequences." "The hearts of the Loyal will be shut – they will no longer repose confident in a Government preparing to desert them – nor can they help detesting a capricious measure which puts a whole province to trouble and distress, blasts the hopes and prospects of hundreds, ruins the whole internal arrangements of the country and hazards the most valuable colonial possessions of the Crown to save an officer the occasional trouble of riding one hundred miles." Without question, Strachan declared, this would be "the severest punishment" for the "tried loyalty and devotion" of British North Americans.

Strachan's arguments for the retention of York as the colonial capital are perhaps the most comprehensive statement of the tory elite's attitude towards their relationship with Great Britain. It should be remembered, however, that Strachan's memorandum was prompted not just by his concern for the colony at large but also by his own immediate personal interests. If the capital was moved to Kingston, he wrote to a friend, all his plans for the religious and moral instruction of the people would be lost.[38] Perhaps more importantly, both for Strachan and for many of his associates in York, the move would cause them considerable personal expense and hardship. And though many Kingstonians undoubtedly welcomed the proposal,[39] other tories realized that moving the seat of government would decrease their hard-won influence and destroy the relatively sophisticated and closed social world which had been so painstakingly established in York.

The local concerns and implicit conflicts (particularly between Kingston and York) notwithstanding, most tories throughout the colony shared Strachan's basic apprehensiveness about the growing anticolonial sentiment in Great Britain. The "ignorance of the Lords of Parliament as to the condition and even the geographical location"[40] of Upper Canada continually astonished colonial leaders. The needs of the North American colonies seemed clearly of secondary importance in London and many in the mother country were even questioning "the benefits, if any, from the possession of the Canadas."[41] There were many indications that the British government would be willing to surrender the colony without protest to the United States. Upper Canadians were aware that not all Englishmen shared this view; they nonetheless deeply resented the general attitude of apathy and indifference.

The suggestion that "the period is not too distant when [Upper Canada] will fall from the parent state" particularly offended colonial leaders. "We consider ourselves British subjects," declared a defiant "A.B." "It was impossible" that our residents "could feel a wish to connect themselves with any other country."[42] In the late war, had not "the Canadas, amidst all the disadvantages, made good the defence of their country against all the good efforts of the Americans?" "Neither force nor flattery," it was declared, "on the part of the American goverment to overcome the resistance"[43] had proven successful; nor would it in the future.

Both influential Upper Canadians and their few supporters in Great Britain asserted that Upper Canada was not to be regarded as a millstone to be cast off by the British with impunity. Though all were aware of the tremendous progress south of the border, they would have agreed with the writer in the *Quarterly Review* (quoted in the *Upper Canada Gazette*) who asked, "why should Canada ... not attain the same comparative strength?" With adequate support and encouragement, Upper Canada would soon be able to feed herself and have a surplus for sale. It was even predicted that in a few years the North American colonies could be producing a surplus of fish and timber to supply the West Indies.[44] Far from being a burden, this loyal colony could be an economic asset to the empire. Even in their present state, supporters of the colony both in North America and in Great Britain declared, Upper Canada's membership in the empire directly enhanced its might and power.

"The Canadas," the article reprinted from the *Quarterly Review* in 1821 stated, "should with the utmost diligence, be cherished and fortified" if for no other reason than that they were "the bridle of the United States."[45] It would be "the height of madness," a number of loyal subjects declared, "to think of relinquishing our colony to the Americans."[46] Without the colonies in North America, the United States could and would challenge the prominence and prosperity of the whole British Empire. For even if the British "retired from Canada" on the pretext of economy, they would "still have to contend for the West Indies."[47] An article in the *United Empire Loyalist* in 1826 was most explicit. "If Canada and the other provinces must merge, as everyone knows with the American republic," editor Robert Stanton declared, "it is quite clear the Americans will gain and that England will lose ... The evil to England will be far more serious and important than any advantage she could hope for in getting rid of the expense incurred by the possession of them." Rather than ignore their possessions in North America, it was argued that the British should give them their "timely attention."[48] In particular, military and financial support should be continued and the colony's development generally encouraged.

Between 1815 and 1828 there was considerable controversy within the colony itself, however, over how imperial attention and aid should be applied. An increasing number of Upper Canadians were unhappy with the present relationship and were not loath to criticize British colonial policy openly. Only the tory supporters of the colonial administration remained careful to keep their concern private. Though John Strachan's memorandum on the moving of the provincial capital and his often critical comments on colonial policies were undoubtedly common knowledge and the subject of conversation in many Upper Canadian homes, they were rarely published or mentioned in public. With the ominous threat posed by the United States always in mind, these men considered it essential to emphasize publicly their loyalty and their willing support for imperial policies. The United States, it was feared, would perceive anything else as a sign of weakness. What could prove more hazardous was that the British government might consider any internal discontent as confirmation of the argument that the colony should be abandoned quickly. A pivotal issue which highlighted the growing differences in outlook among various colonists was the question of trade and commerce.

In November 1815 the *Kingston Gazette* printed an "Important British Order in Council." "From the date of this order," it read, "there shall be paid on the importation into this Kingdom from the Territories of the United States of America ... the same duties of customs that are payable on such goods ... when imported on British ships."[49] Recognizing the importance of American trade to the whole area's development, Upper Canadians after 1815 quickly resumed economic relations with the United States. "The trade carried on between our country and the Canadian provinces is already considerable and is rapidly growing," noted De Witt Clinton in his 1817 message to the New York legislature. After the war, the St Lawrence and the lower Great Lakes waterways continued to provide the primary outlet for all surplus goods produced on both sides of the border. "This trade is indeed profitable to many of our citizens who engage in it," Clinton told his government; but he concluded, "it is much more so to the British."[50] There were a number of Upper Canadians, however, and particularly some in the Kingston area, who questioned the benefits to be gained from this commercial traffic. Some felt that American merchants and entrepreneurs were invading colonial markets; hard-earned money, rather than enhancing the development of the province, was flowing south. As a result, it was argued, the agricultural and commercial development of Upper Canada was being retarded rather than encouraged.

"I am a Tanner and Courier by trade," wrote one concerned resident to the editor of the *Kingston Gazette* in December 1815. "I have a large stock of leather on hand but can find no sale for it owing to the quantity brought in by the Americans, who, from the low price of labour, are enabled to sell cheaper than we can." It was not fair, he declared, "that those very people who but the other day would have cut our throats" should be allowed such privileges. "Ought this not to rouse the attention of the government and to call forth the energies of the legislature, if any it possesses, to put a stop to this evil?"[51]

Many tradesmen and merchants in the Kingston area obviously shared the tanner's concern, for three months later the "Merchants, Traders, Carriers and Mariners" of the area petitioned the provincial parliament. "It is with the deepest regret that we see the internal agricultural trade of this country daily diminishing and the country drained of its specie by the great influx of articles for sale from the United States," the petition stated. Surely, the petitioners declared, "it is a general rule in all countries that agriculture, commerce, inland trade and carrying goods, wares and merchandize from port to port on their own shores is confined as much as possible to subjects of their own." Yet this did not seem to be the case in Upper Canada. In addition to invading Upper Canadian markets, the Americans were also beginning to monopolize the carrying trade. Therefore the petition requested that the legislature take measures to ensure that, among other things, "all goods ... brought from the United States ... be dutiable in like manner as British goods are dutiable in the United States."[52] In addition, it urged that Upper Canadians be granted exclusive rights to the carrying trade between Prescott and Queenston. This was "of the highest importance to the country,"[53] it was stressed, not to mention being financially beneficial to individual traders and farmers in the area.

Many in eastern Upper Canada argued that Upper Canadians had to be placed "on an equal footing with the United States."[54] "It is well known," commented "Candidus" in the *Kingston Gazette*, "that the citizens of the United States when they visit us are suffered to enjoy many advantages which they are unwilling to allow British subjects in their turn when in their territories." Though most Upper Canadians were not in favour of taxation or increased duties, many considered it only prudent "to retaliate when American restrictions on our commerce are laid on us ... It is a true maxim that one nation should never exclude another from trading with it except from very good reasons."[55] The present situation seemed to present a very good reason indeed.

Yet there were some in the Kingston area who did not agree. "I have been very much pleased and gratified," declared "True Briton" in February 1816, "to see our markets so well supplied with all kinds of provisions and the town so well stocked with various kinds of manufacturers ... I hope that we should, since the ratification of the *Treaty of Commerce* enjoy not only all the comforts, but even the luxuries of life, at a much cheaper rate than we have ever hitherto done." "True Briton" reasoned that "if the Americans were cut off from intercourse with us, our markets will be badly supplied and we shall again be obliged to pay the same extravagant prices for our grain and hay for our cattle, and provisions for our families." Surely "there is not an inhabitant in this place but will purchase from him who sells the cheapest."[56] Others in the area agreed. The exclusion of American produce would "grind the faces of the poor," they argued. It would "give rise to smugglers and galley slaves, to customs and monopolies, to pirates and excitement." In truth, it would be "a tyrannical exertion of authority"[57] which would eventually lead to the ruin of both countries. Supporters of a free and open market conceded that the Americans did demand money for their goods; but, they noted, "a substitute which is quite as convenient in the transactions of life is left in its place." The way for Upper Canadians "to have money aplenty," it was asserted, was "to produce a plenty of the articles to bring money in."[58] Monopoly, in any form, should never be sanctioned; "it is preposterous as it is unreasonable."[59]

In 1815 and 1816 the question of free trade was really only a concern in the Kingston area (and was but another example of that persistent localism which had characterized colonial life and politics in the years before the war). Residents in York and in the western sections of the colony seemed, in the short term, to be indifferent to the matter. Even within Kingston itself, Stephen Miles noted at the end of April 1816, the debate, for the moment at least, was "entirely laid aside."[60] But as the province matured and its economy became more integrated and diversified, the issue began to take on a broader colonial significance. Between 1818 and 1820 farmers and manufacturers throughout the colony increasingly demanded protection from the American producers. At the same time, other Upper Canadians asserted that high custom duties generally "furnished some inducement or apology for smuggling";[61] and rather than increasing provincial revenues and the prosperity of the colony, tariffs tended only to impoverish many and to turn them against the government. As the colonial debate primarily between consumers and producers broadened towards the end of the decade it was complicated by the economic power struggle being waged between Great Britain and the United States. By 1818 Upper Canadians suddenly found themselves caught in the middle of this bitter struggle. And well aware that their own economic well-being depended directly on the economic agreements that must eventually be reached between the United States and Great Britain, the colonists watched anxiously as the two nations jockeyed for position.

In 1815, as Great Britain resumed her peacetime patterns of trade, the Americans found themselves increasingly excluded from European markets and from the extensive carrying trade that they had developed over the previous five years. In consequence, American markets had become glutted; prices had fallen and unemployment had increased.[62] Many officials in the United States believed that the only way to alleviate this growing economic distress was to force American goods back into the international markets. As a result, the American administration proposed in 1817 that a new Navigation Act be approved which would exclude British ships from American ports. Rufus King, a senator from Massachusetts, explained this action in a speech to the Senate, reprinted in full in the *Upper Canada Gazette*. "The British ... had enacted the ancient and exclusive system of trade and navigation." Clearly they had "a strong desire to acquire by restriction and exclusion a disproportionate share of the general commerce of the world." In contrast, he continued, the commercial system of the United States "is an open one – our ports and our commerce are free to all – we neither possess, nor desire to possess colonies." British political and economic policies were, however, forcing their hands. "In self defense and to protect the legitimate resources of our own country," many Americans considered that it was necessary "to restrict our ports to British vessels." This measure, King declared, was not intended "to be unfriendly to England." "England is a great, illustrious nation" and "we are the powerful descendants of England, desiring perpetual friendships." But, he asserted, "either the intercourse must be reciprocally beneficial, or it must not be suffered to exist."[63]

For the next few years, Great Britain and the United States imposed restrictions on each other's trade. Though the commerce of both suffered, customs duties were systematically raised and, at times, each government even placed a partial embargo on goods coming from the other nation. The government of Upper Canada, reluctantly caught in the crossfire, concluded that the activities of the American government were a conscious attempt "to break down our colonial system." The only thing to do, they believed, was to meet "Congress half way in fettering the commercial intercourse between the two countries."[64] Thus, partly in response to local pressure and partly in support of imperial policy, the legislature passed a new intercourse bill in 1820 placing higher duties on American goods entering the province. Its supporters argued that in the light of British-American relations there was little choice in the matter.

A number of Upper Canadians suggested, however, that "the provisions of the new bill may be justly questioned." The editors of the *Kingston Chronicle* categorically stated that "we cannot approve of any measures intending to leave the rest of the community at their mercy with regards to the price of the necessities of life."[65] The Kingston editors and a number of others in the region, expressing their overriding concern for the economic development of the colony and undoubtedly for that of their own particular region as well, considered the 1820 intercourse bill "unwise and impolitic."[66] This hasty and inconsiderate legislation, it was argued, "would provide powerful temptations for smuggling" and would inevitably cause "a sharp increase in the price of our consumer goods." Rather than "assist or enrich" the farmer, the bill would "injure and impoverish the Province."[67]

Luckily the international crisis quickly passed. In 1822 British restrictions on American trade with the West Indies were modified and American ports were reopened to British and Upper Canadian goods. At the same time, the economic depression which had gripped the colony since the end of the War of 1812 finally began to lift. The colonists' economic problems were not over, however, for in the years after the war British North Americans, like their republican cousins to the south, had also experienced the constricting effects of the British imperial system. In 1815 the British parliament had tightened the Corn Laws and effectively curtailed Upper Canadian exports to the mother country. Four years later, officials in London, in an attempt to alleviate economic distress at home, had proposed higher duties on colonial timber entering the British market. Increasingly, concern about trade with the United States was submerged in what was considered a far more fundamental problem – relations with Great Britain. By the end of the decade, a few articulate colonists actually began to challenge the existing economic connections and restrictions that bound Upper Canada to the British Empire.

It was with some consternation that Macaulay and Pringle of the *Kingston Chronicle* commented in 1819, after learning of the proposed changes in timber duties, "it would completely put a stop to this trade" from Upper Canada. Though confident that "no change in the system will be adopted ... without mature consideration," they nonetheless followed the debates in the British parliament on the issue carefully. It soon became apparent that there were a number of Englishmen who shared the colonists' concern and opposed the proposal, fearing that it would "seriously affect the shipping interests of Great Britain."[68] The *Chronicle* expressed some hope, therefore, that if Upper Canadians would "make known their wishes and sentiments"[69] to the imperial authorities, this would convince the British goverment of the folly of its position. Many leading Upper Canadians in the early 1820s were nevertheless careful never to criticize imperial policies directly, despite their obvious concern.

"We have already received so many favours," it was declared, that criticism would be churlish. The British government had spent "vast sums of money and ... these will not in all likelihood be diminished."[70] Moreover, it was reluctantly judged, in all conscience "we cannot indeed expect that the interests of Canada should be preferred to those of the Mother Country." The editors of the *Kingston Chronicle* commented that "should the imperial parliament find any alteration in the timber duties productive of benefits to the Empire at large, though detrimental to us in particular, we have no just grounds to complain." Most tories, publicly at least, remained confident, however, that Parliament "will always be disposed to yield us assistance and encouragement when not inconsistent with more important national interests."[71] And, it was argued, "as our means increase, we shall become able to avail ourselves of the great privilege which we enjoy in trading to all our sister colonies as well as to Great Britain."[72]

Despite this spirited pro-British offensive, a number of Upper Canadians began to call on the British to initiate "a more liberal policy to the colonies."[73] While individual colonists were forced to pay higher duties on imports both from the United States and from other parts of the empire, the antigovernment press observed that the Americans seemed to be prospering as never before. To rectify the situation, a few Upper Canadians in the early 1820s suggested, as Richard Cartwright had done thirty years earlier, that the colony completely open its commercial borders with the United States. Colonel Robert Nichol, a member of the House of Assembly representing Norfolk County, first raised the matter in the colonial legislature in the fall of 1822, ironically though perhaps appropriately advocating that duties imposed on tea brought into the colony be dismantled. Six months later, the House of Assembly recommended that the duty be lifted;[74] the restrictions and monopoly of the East India Company remained, however, and Upper Canadians, unlike their American friends, were forced to continue to pay what many considered to be exorbitant prices for the commodity. Three years later, the few "friends of free trade,"[75] with increasing support in the House of Assembly and throughout the colony, felt obliged to take the issue one step further.

In the spring of 1825 Hugh Thomson of the *Upper Canada Herald* wrote that "at present, we cannot compete" with the United States. "In addition to the natural disadvantages of our interior situation and remoteness from the ocean, the want of free trade amounts to an effectual prohibition of exports from the Province."[76] In fact, he and others argued, "til Canada is placed on an equal footing with the United States with respect to trade and commerce, it is in vain to hope that she will become populous, rich or prosperous."[77] At the root of the problem, a number of Upper Canadians (many of whom supported constitutional reform) alleged, was "the old system of colonial monopoly." It compelled "the colonists to consume British manufacturers and at the same time disabled them from paying for them, by excluding their staple produce from the markets of the Mother Country." To a number of residents, "this state of colonial disability and impoverishment" appeared "more grievous when contrasted to the superior commercial advantages enjoyed by our neighbours." Potentially far more disastrous, however, was the impact that this tremendous difference in economic development and apparent personal wealth could have on the attitude of the colonists towards

Britain. Only those who were blind, some members of the House declared, could not "see that these colonial restrictions naturally and necessarily tend to weaken the attachment of the colonists to the Mother Country and to generate a secret wish for separation and independence."[78]

Supporters of the Maitland administration were appalled by the call for free trade and by the general discontent in the colony. "We ought to be grateful to that noble nation to whom we owe allegiance and who have so kindly watched over our interests,"[79] cried the editor of the *Niagara Gleaner* in 1825. These "spend thrifts and idle fellows" who advocated free trade obviously did not understand "the great privileges" Upper Canada enjoyed "over every Foreign Country." The inhabitants of Canada, "a small part of the British Empire ... could not expect to induce the British Government to break the sacred engagements and alter the *machine* of Government to accommodate us – it would be the height of presumption in us to propose such a measure." The editor argued that "if we enjoy all the privileges of British subjects, we ought also cheerfully to submit to some disadvantages, if disadvantages they are."[80] "Much that we consider really absurd has been written in the Province concerning the freedom of trade," maintained the *Kingston Chronicle*. Truly, "those croakers in and out of Parliament ought to blush" at their misguided assumptions. Already faced with controversy over the supply bill and as shall be seen mounting opposition to the proposed naturalization bill, the tories not surprisingly believed that in advocating free trade a dangerous few were consciously attempting "to embarrass the British government" by creating factions and disseminating falsehoods. More insidiously, a number of reform-minded free traders were trying to "instill into the minds of the people how much they were injured by our connection with Great Britain, insinuating that we would be better off if we were to depend or connect with the United States."[81]

As the decade drew to a close, extensive changes in imperial trading policies and the opening of new markets for Upper Canadian goods dampened the agitation for free trade. Nevertheless, the growing political discontent in the colony and the mounting opposition of the reformers to a number of executive policies prompted the tories to continue to defend the existing imperial relationship and stress the numerous benefits Upper Canadians received from the mother country. Increasingly on the defensive, they clearly felt the need to assert the Britishness of the province. Great Britain and Upper Canada, they constantly reminded the colonists, are "the giver and the receiver of benefits." The British parliament's "only considerations with respect to Canada have been to increase its prosperity and to attach it to England by the bonds of interest and affection."[82]

No colonial leader in the 1820s denied the importance of the imperial connection to Upper Canada's future development. All were Britons, living in a British colony, and their interests were irrevocably tied to those of the mother country. Some prominent Upper Canadians, however, could never forget that they also lived in a North American province. The example presented by the United States encouraged these men to challenge various imperial policies which they felt were retarding the development of the colony. Colonial prosperity and progress could only be enhanced by closer economic ties with the republic, and Upper Canadians, it was argued, should take advantage of their proximity. If this opportunity was not grasped, it was feared, the strong ties which traditionally had bound many colonists to the mother country would be weakened by political and economic unrest.

As for the tory elite, their predominant fear of the United States led them to oppose any fundamental change in the colonial relationship, though clearly many were concerned about the detrimental effect some British policies were having on the colony. Yet the proximity of the United States discouraged these men from fully and publicly expressing those concerns. Britain's commitment to her North American colonies was precarious enough, it was believed, without jeopardizing it any further by appearing to be ungrateful. To John Strachan, John Beverley Robinson, and other members of the tory elite, any colonial discontent with the existing association would only suggest to Parliament that Upper Canadians would welcome, or at least be willing to accept, a severing of colonial ties. And only that special relationship continued to protect Upper Canada from the imperialistic designs of the United States.

The apparent indifference of the mother country, particularly in the first years after the War of 1812, was, nonetheless, disheartening even to the most pro-British Upper Canadian. Indeed, it seemed, especially during periods of economic dislocation, that Great Britain was not only willing to abandon the colony but that she was actively aiding the development of the United States. For though refusing to encourage emigration to British North America, many in England were encouraging Britons to move to the American republic. Upper Canadians, who considered that emigration was vital to their future development, understandably felt betrayed.

Two years before the war, "William Penn" had written in the *Kingston*

Gazette that "the wealth, strength and importance of a nation was in proportion to its quantum of labour." Although by 1810 the population of the colony had increased significantly, "Penn" urged that emigration from *all* sources should continue to be encouraged. "In this point of view," he had written, "every additional labourer is a valuable acquisition. While idle vagrants are discountenanced, actual settlers coming hither with a view of permanent residence and bringing with them habits of enterprise and industry, adapted to agricultural, mercantile and mechanical or liberal pursuits ... are entitled to encouragement." Care had to be taken "to harmonize and consolidate our whole population into one congenial mass of good subjects under a good government." He concluded, however, that "the prosperity of a nation is composed of the individual prosperity of its inhabitants; and prosperous individuals according to a well known principle of human nature are generally loyal subjects."[83]

The need for people to clear the land and generally to add to the prosperity of the colony was even more pressing after the War of 1812. But the experience of many colonial leaders over the previous three years caused them to question the wisdom of admitting settlers indiscriminately and particularly of allowing unlimited numbers of Americans into the colony, as had been the previous practice. "The danger of the promiscuous introduction of settlers from the United States," Robert Baldwin commented in 1818, had been most severely felt during the war.[84] It was acknowledged that a number of American settlers, unwilling to fight for the British, had quite rightly left the colony. Many colonial leaders believed, however, that many others had remained "concealed in the country" and kept up "a communication ... with the enemy."[85] "In several districts," Baldwin reported in a letter to a friend, "where they were the majority, or supposed to be so, rebellion was organized"; and "but for the prompt energy of a few," he noted, the London district in particular would have succumbed to the American forces.[86] At the root of these difficulties, some influential colonists argued, was obviously "the encouragement which had been given to Americans in the first distribution of the Lands, by which the country had in it characters always doubtful and most often dangerous."[87]

In 1815 a number of provincial leaders were determined to ensure that a similar state of affairs would never again arise. Under the direction of the imperial authorities, Lieutenant Governor Gore ordered local magistrates in October 1815 not to administer the oath of allegiance to any new American arrivals,[88] thereby prohibiting them from legally holding land in the colony and, it was anticipated, effectively curtailing any further American immigration. Many co-

lonial officials considered this was "a measure of imperious necessity,"[89] and long overdue. Even with the memories of war still fresh
in their minds, not all Upper Canadians supported this policy, however. Residents in the western districts of the province in particular
argued that American farmers should be encouraged to come to
Upper Canada. The new policy was ill-informed, they charged, for
it threatened not only the future of the Niagara region but also the
development of the colony as a whole. And despite frequent official
condemnation, and charges that these were merely "the selfish views
of some land grant speculators," William Dickson, a member of the
Legislative Council, Colonel Nichol, and others in the Niagara region
persistently agitated in York for the suspension of the discriminatory
policy.[90]

The question of immigration in general and the admittance of
American settlers in particular was brought to the attention of the
colonial population at large by Robert Gourlay in 1817 and 1818.
In his first address to the resident landowners of Upper Canada,
Gourlay had called for "an enlarged and liberal connection between
Canada and Great Britain." "The government never can give too
much encouragement to the growth of this colony by a liberal system
of emigration," he wrote. He deplored "the state of ignorance" of
many Englishmen about Upper Canada, which had resulted in the
arrival of "chiefly poor men driven from home by despair." "Canada," Gourlay declared, "is worthy of something better than the mere
guidance of the blind and the lame." The Englishman called on
Upper Canadians to "advertise the excellence of the raw materials
which Nature has so lavishly" provided them. Able British farmers,
"presently sickened with disappointed despair," had to be persuaded
to come to the colony. "England alone," he wrote, "could give fifty
thousand people annually" and indeed "it is absolutely necessary
even for the domestic comfort" of the mother country "that a vent
should be immediately opened for her increasing population." "Why
should not this stream be diverted in the woods of Canada ... rather
than to the States of America?"[91] he asked. It was then that Gourlay
had proposed to compile his *Statistical Account of Upper Canada*.

Gourlay's suggestions struck a responsive chord in the minds of
many in Upper Canada. Since the end of the War of 1812, they had
watched with growing frustration the tide of British emigration flow
to the United States. Reports had frequently appeared in the colonial
press of the arrival of British settlers at New York, Philadelphia, and
Boston. Often, farmers had arrived in Quebec or Montreal, only to
reembark immediately for the United States.[92] Gourlay's second address, however, lost him a good deal of the support which so shortly

before he had won. For not only was he highly critical of the colonial administration, he also advocated that the province be opened to American settlers. Fully three-quarters of the province were Americans, he argued, and "these men [had] stood foremost in the battle defending British rights." "How in the name of God," he demanded, "could all this have happened, had the law been impolitic? – had people from the United States been unworthy of its adoption?" Picking up on arguments that some residents of the Niagara area had already put forward, Gourlay reiterated "that there were unprincipled villains in Canada was indeed proven by the war." "But who were they?" he asked, "and from whence did they come? Has it been shown that the majority were American? Is it not true that the basest of all were European born?"[93] Loyalty, he maintained, could and should be determined by performance and not by an accident of birth. Only "a liberal system of emigration," including the encouragement of American as well as British settlers to Upper Canada, would satisfy the colony's pressing need for people. And in answer to the often expressed concern that the loyalty of the American residents would always be suspect, Gourlay and his supporters argued that without the economic prosperity that these new arrivals would create, the loyalty of *all* Upper Canadians would be weakened.

Most prominent Upper Canadians were clearly "astonished" to find Gourlay "an advocate of the admission of American settlers" and his second address was greeted by many "with sentiments of surprise as well as regret." It was readily conceded, even by the most ardent defender of king and constitution, that extensive immigration was vital to the development of the province. Leaders in the colony were not willing, however, to compromise that essential British nature of Upper Canada by repeating what they believed to be the mistake of their fathers in admitting Americans, whose natural allegiance must be to the United States. "The loyalty which has once secured this country" would only lose strength, it was asserted, "by the acquisition of so many republicans."[94] Moreover, ever conscious of the expansionist tendencies of the United States, certain colonial leaders declared that "we are living and cultivating our fields in the face of an active and a powerful enemy, who has heretofore shown but little delicacy in scrupling at the basest means to attain his ends." Those "ambitious and arrogant people" south of the border, Charles Fothergill warned residents of Port Hope in 1818, "are thirsting for your blood." Their eye "is steadily fixed upon the unsuspecting lamb, even the lamb of Canada." "The day is not far distant," he believed, "when they will once more assail your domestic sanctuaries with all the tumults and horrors of war." If American settlers were admitted indiscriminately, the colony's "subjugation under the yoke of noisy and unprincipled democracy"[95] would be all the easier. The only viable solution to the colony's need for settlers was to attract British emigrants to Upper Canada. These people might not have all the skills and expertise of the American Yankee. They did, nevertheless, possess that invaluable asset of being Britons; they had grown up with and could be expected to accept the importance of British traditions and institutions.

After the war, however, Great Britain seemed unwilling to encourage her surplus population to settle in Upper Canada. Certainly the British seemed "friendly to emigration in general."[96] The editors of the *Kingston Chronicle* in January 1820 commented that "we observe every exertion being made to direct the stream of emigration ... into various channels, *viz* towards the Cape of Good Hope, New South Wales, the Red River and the western territories of the United States. We see the press teeming with pamphlets and newspaper paragraphs depicting these several countries as so many modern Canaans, abounding with milk and honey."[97] But as one colonist ruefully noted a year later, many Englishmen appeared to entertain "certain objections to the North American colonies in particular." The principal objection seemed to be that Upper Canada would eventually become part of the United States. Even if this was not the case, others in the old country were arguing that the colony was not worthy of any extensive aid and encouragement. As a result, one colonist remarked, "Canada, is being left without a friend to bring her into notice."[98]

Upper Canadians realized that part of the problem was the nature of the publicity available through the British press. Colonial critics particularly objected to "the exaggerated and even false accounts ... respecting the *superior* advantages of emigration to the United States," and especially to those about such settlements as that founded by Morris Birkbeck in Illinois, which were luring emigrants with "false premises." These attitudes, it was charged, "have done and still continue to do much injury, not only to His Majesty's colonies, by robbing them of many useful citizens but also the individuals themselves, who are thereby trepanned to become the subjects of a Power the avowed enemy of their native country."[99] A number of Upper Canadians were also aware, however, that they were themselves at least partly responsible for the problem. "Hitherto," remarked the editors of the *Kingston Chronicle*, the matter of British immigration "has been treated with apathy and indifference" by colonial officials, "as if the country had little or no interest in the business." "Few amongst us hold out the hand to welcome the newcomers," it was noted; yet

This caricature of 1832 reflects the longstanding Upper Canadian view of the many middle-class immigrants who arrived completely unprepared for frontier life (C-41067, Public Archives of Canada)

American agents and land jobbers "often with their artful misrepresentations" actively enticed immigrants "by the finest promises to seek their homes in the territories" of the republic. "Not only is no encouragement given to Emigrants to remain among us," but "some of our *fellow subjects* at Quebec have [even] gone about to advise them to go over to people the wilds of Illinois or seek employment in Pittsburgh."[100] It was reported that still other potential emigrants, confused and discouraged by the inefficiencies and false rumours resulting from imperial and colonial bungling, "were induced not to proceed at all." If such bad management and indifference continued, Upper Canadians must expect immigrants to go elsewhere. "Give the emigrant moderate encouragement and he will remain with us; neglect him and he will fly to those arms which are open to receive him."[101]

Shortly after the end of the war, therefore, some concerned Upper Canadians initiated a program to counteract this neglect and to encourage and actively assist immigration to the colony. Private emigrant societies were formed. The government was called on to provide ongoing support, for "without the cooperation of the Government," it was asserted, "no private society can be possessed of the requisite information." Moreover, Macaulay and Pringle recommended that the government and the community unite their efforts. "Whilst the one takes upon itself the care of supplying information, let the other ... be prepared to meet some of the demands which must necessarily be made upon them."[102] In addition, though many in the colony had vehemently objected to Gourlay's activities in 1818, it was acknowledged that his suggestion that a statistical account be compiled to inform Britons of the advantages of Upper Canada was in fact sound. As one interested observer declared in 1821, "the principal thing wanted" to enhance the colony's growth was "information."[103]

Thus at the end of 1819 the editors of the *Kingston Chronicle* hoped "that some friend to the Province possessed of leisure and ability to execute the work ... will be found patriotic enough to give to the inhabitants of the mother country a fair and impartial account of this part of His Majesty's Dominion." "Until this is done," it was contended, "we may never look to see Canada rise to that degree of importance which her natural advantages might warrant and her latent resources, when fully developed would ensure."[104] It was with considerable approval, therefore, that the editors of the *Kingston Chronicle* noted at the beginning of 1820 the publication of Charles Stuart's *Emigrant's Guide* and a year later of John Howison's *Sketches*. These accounts were considered generally "fair and impartial." While they extolled the advantages of emigration to Upper Canada, Macaulay and Pringle commented, "we do not think that any person who may be induced to make an attentive perusal of the volume in question and to transfer himself ... to the fertile plains of Upper Canada will have any cause to complain of being disappointed or being misled." The *Kingston Chronicle* noted that particularly the *Emigrant's Guide* "tells the Emigrant ... that he must weigh well the hardships of settlement before he quits his native soil." He must realize that the earth would not "produce her fruits spontaneously, but on the contrary, it is only by patient and persevering industry that he can succeed."[105]

By the mid-1820s it appeared that Upper Canadian efforts were beginning to be successful. Emigrants were arriving in the hundreds; new lands were being opened up and old lands were being improved. Indeed, even the mother country now seemed anxious to encourage people to move to Upper Canada. In 1824 the editor of the *Niagara Gleaner* was "much gratified to find that this province, so long neglected with respect to internal improvements, has at last attracted the attention of the monied gentlemen of England."[106] A year later the editor of the *Kingston Chronicle* defended the formation of the Canada Land Company, judging it "a very favourable presage to this Province." And despite the reservations of a few, most colonial leaders welcomed the "money and settlers that were beginning to come to Upper Canada."[107]

The preoccupation in the 1820s with promoting British emigration to the colony did not alleviate the colonists' anxiety that Upper Canada might be inundated with British paupers and indigents. As early as 1820 the *Kingston Chronicle* had remarked, "certain it is that too great a proportion of the emigrants are in indigent circumstances that when they reach their lots, they are incapable of performing the task of settlement." Europeans with more capital had to be encouraged to join the throng of emigrants, for these men would help "furnish employment for its poorer classes of people"[108] while themselves realizing a great profit. On the whole many contended that "emigration upon a small and moderate scale, in a gradual and steady stream would unquestionably prove beneficial." As the editor of the *Upper Canada Gazette* warned in 1827, "if INDISCRIMINATE emigration is encouraged, we can foresee in it nought but distress and ruin."[109]

Some influential residents, however, discounted these concerns and campaigned for a completely open-door policy with respect to emigration. Once again looking south, it was pointed out that the United States was completely "indebted for their present prosperity to an extensive and indiscriminate Emigration." Upper Canada should therefore also open its doors to all who wished to come. As Christopher Hagerman reminded the House of Assembly in 1821, "Emigration to this Province has increased the wealth and prosperity of the country."[110] Two years later, Robert Baldwin was far more explicit. "If thousands of emigrants were to come, even naked and in distress, still they should be encouraged." Some in the House even began to object to the administration's policies intended to induce men of wealth to come to Upper Canada. "The want of men of capital, education and independent means," acknowledged Robert Nichols in 1824, "was a great evil to the Colony." He nonetheless strongly objected to granting whole townships to individuals, fearing "it would establish an aristocracy."[111] What was most needed, claimed Nichol, Baldwin, and many others in the House (many of whom were reformers), was "population" – people to clear the land, to work the soil; people who by their very presence would make Upper Canada prosperous.

It was soon apparent that the debate over emigration went far beyond whether all Britons, regardless of means, should be admitted into the colony. By the mid-1820s some members of the House of Assembly were once again raising the question of admitting American settlers. Throughout the period, men like John Strachan, John Beverley Robinson, and other members of the ruling elite continued to support the exclusionary policies of 1815. To ensure that Upper Canada remained a British colony and to secure the province against American domination, they believed that it was essential that only Britons be permitted to take up land in Upper Canada. The Baldwins, John Rolph, Hugh Thomson, and other supporters of reform in the House of Assembly considered this policy shortsighted and actually harmful to the future development of the colony. Though in no way condoning the political and social divisions which persisted in the United States, they saw no good reason why American expertise in the form of hardy Yankee immigrants should not further the province's progress.

These sharply differing perceptions of the needs of the colony affected far more than the question of whether American immigrants should be admitted to Upper Canada. In the 1820s colonial leaders found themselves confronted with the problem of deciding who actually had the right to call himself an Upper Canadian and of determining in particular the legal status of those thousands of American settlers already in the colony. The controversy over immigration policy quickly merged into a growing concern over "aliens." Inevitably the arguments that both the tories and the reformers presented on the first matter composed an integral part of their

For Emigration

THE PARTING HOUR.

Published in London in the early 1820s, this sketch depicts those immigrants whom all Upper Canadians abhorred, the riff-raff of Britain (C-4987, Public Archives of Canada)

response to the second; the question of aliens also formed a continuing backdrop to the periodic constitutional crises of the period and did much to widen the gulf between the tories and the reformers. The naturalization bill, or alien bill as it was more often called, became perhaps the most significant political issue in Upper Canada in the 1820s. And at its resolution in 1828, it was clear exactly how important the differing Upper Canadian perceptions of the United States and of Great Britain were to political affairs in the colony.

CHAPTER NINE

Who Is an Upper Canadian?

"By law, the issue of natural born subjects born out of the King's allegiance, of Parents not in the service of Powers at emnity with Great Britain are considered as natural born subjects,"[1] the chief justice of Upper Canada, W.D. Powell, wrote to Lieutenant Governor Gore in January 1817. In the chief justice's considered opinion, all those Americans and their children who had settled in the colony before the War of 1812 and had taken the oath of allegiance retained the rights of British-born citizens, regardless of the fact that they had previously sworn allegiance to the United States. Doubts expressed by various Upper Canadians about "the Loyal distinction"[2] of these individuals notwithstanding, the chief justice believed that the statute and common law were clear on the issue.

Lieutenant Governor Gore and many other prominent Upper Canadians did not welcome such conclusions. There had been considerable concern about the loyalty of the American settlers in the colony from the very beginning; and after the war it was frequently wondered if any American could be trusted. Surely "the Americans should always be considered Aliens," Rev. John Strachan stated. They "should be declared incapable of holding landed property or of having any share in government." The security and well-being of the colony demanded, as far as men like John Strachan were concerned, that it be freed "of the depravity of the American character" and from "the contamination of the United States."[3] To permit anyone whose allegiance to the empire was questionable to retain the rights of British subjects was a betrayal of all those principles and beliefs for which loyal colonists had twice fought, and for which many had died.

Over the next ten years, colonial leaders were increasingly preoccupied by this question of who was or could become an Upper Canadian. Though the immediate threat of invasion had receded, many continued to believe that the United States was still actively interested in annexing the northern colony. This concern was compounded by the apparent unwillingness of the mother country to provide the colony with sufficient military or economic support to defend itself. To cope at least in part with the situation, the provincial government curtailed future American immigration and made determined efforts throughout the 1820s to attract European settlers. Yet this did not resolve the existing problem created by the thousands of American-Upper Canadians already resident in the colony. Though it was generally acknowledged that many of these settlers had readily defended their homes in 1812, the colonial government continued to be apprehensive that the enemy was in their very midst.

There were a number of Upper Canadians who, as the 1820s unfolded, did not share and actively began to challenge the administration's attitudes towards American settlers. Loyalty, the reformers contended, was not necessarily determined by an accident of birth. Indeed, it was essential for the many American-born Upper Canadians or former residents of the republic and for their defenders in the House of Assembly to believe that loyalty could also by shown by actions and by hard work. Their self respect, their future and, they asserted, the prosperity of the colony depended on such an interpretation. It was one, however, which was not readily accepted by the tories around them.

The question of who actually was a loyal Upper Canadian had preoccupied a number of the colony's earliest residents; the founding fathers would have been horrified, however, at the way in which the matter erupted into the public arena in 1818. Robert Gourlay argued that the colony had to be reopened to immigration from the United States and he cited two interrelated factors in support of his proposal. Under British law, any individual could change his allegiance while maintaining his British-born status; and those American settlers in the colony had already demonstrated their commitment to the king and the British Empire by their active involvement in the War of 1812.

"By the war," Gourlay declared, "the gallantry" of all residents "was proved" and "an important and pleasant truth was established." It was clearly evident that "the settlers from the United States were to be depended upon as loyal and faithful subjects" and they had earned the right to consider themselves British subjects. Much more to the point now, however, Gourlay argued, was that under British law these Upper Canadians were already British subjects, even though most of them had remained in the United States after 1783. If this was not the case, then "a full half of the adult population of Upper Canada had perjured themselves" by taking the oath of allegiance to both the United States and the British crown, and they "may be fairly put to death whenever they cross the American frontier." Moreover, if the law was not interpreted in this way it would have to be concluded that "the British government has been stealing men from all the nations of the earth for the last four-score years."

Particularly "in this part of the world," Gourlay contended in his second address to Upper Canadians, this issue of citizenship had to be resolved quickly and finally. "Here, for many hundreds of miles, two nations, sprung from the same stock, speaking the same language, governed by the same laws, ruled by the same customs, assimilated by the same manners and connected in a thousand ways, by the endearing ties of relationships, are closely in contact." "Good God!" he exclaimed, "is the narrow boundary between two such christian nations to flame with eternal hate? Is the independent spirit of man to be confined by the accident of birth? Are we to have no law by which in safety, we may change our abode?"[4]

Some colonial leaders did, however, wish to close the border between the United States and Upper Canada. They believed that "Gourlay's doctrine of changing allegiance" was "highly dangerous to the uninformed." If at all possible, Americans *should* be "confined" to their republic;[5] otherwise it was feared that their presence would contaminate the colony with political and social principles which were antithetical to the British constitution. Though in a strict legal sense, influential Upper Canadians were forced to accept the Englishman's interpretation of the rights of Americans already in Upper Canada, they were not willing to accept Gourlay's proposals for further American immigration; nor did they allow the chief justice's interpretation of naturalization to go unchallenged for long.

Three years after Gourlay had been banished from the colony, the electors of Lennox and Addington, in a petition to the House of Assembly, called for the nullification of the election of the former attorney general of Massachusetts and former master of the Ernest Town school, Barnabas Bidwell, on the ground that he was not eligible to run for office. To represent the electors of the county or, indeed, even to vote, Bidwell had to be a loyal and natural-born subject of Great Britain within the meaning of British law, it was argued. And many in the riding and all the tory supporters of the colonial administration vehemently asserted throughout the next three years that this condition was fulfilled neither by Barnabas Bidwell nor by his son, Marshall, who attempted to succeed him.

"It is utterly impossible," declared Attorney General Robinson, the leading supporter of the petition in the House of Assembly, "that Mr. Bidwell could be a natural-born citizen ... Immediately after the independence of the United States, [Bidwell] voluntarily went forward and abjured all allegiance to the British Crown, took the oath of allegiance to the United States and accepted a high office under that government." Soon after that, Bidwell and his fellow subjects had met loyal Britons "as aliens in war." Surely, "if aliens in war," the attorney general declared, "they must be aliens in peace." "Was it to be supposed that the citizens of the United States who involved Great Britain in war and the people of this province in ruin, as soon as their backs were washed of the blood of our fellow subjects, should be allowed to cross the river and enjoy all the privileges of British subjects?" he asked. "No, it would be preposterous to think it."[6]

Echoing sentiments expressed earlier by his mentor, John Strachan, Robinson asserted that "Americans have always been treated as aliens by the government" and he defied any member to point out "one instance in which they were entitled to the privilege of natural-born subjects." Simcoe's proclamation of 1792 had expressly invited only such persons "whose loyalty and good conduct in the country which they resided, entitled them to encouragement."[7] Certainly it did not apply to Barnabas Bidwell, a well-known republican and a criminal in his former home; equally, Robinson argued two years later, it could not apply to his son Marshall. If Barnabas Bidwell was a natural-born subject, the supporters of the original petition declared, then, logically, "Jefferson, Madison, and Monroe, and all those who fought against us in the last war might come in, hold land and enjoy the rights of British subjects." Indeed, "the door would be let open to all," it was scornfully suggested, "from the President down to the common executioner."[8]

Again and again throughout the debates in the House of Assembly and in the local press, the tory elite appealed to the loyalist heritage of Upper Canada to support their case. Those "who had so notably retained their loyalty during the Revolutionary War" were asked "to reflect a moment upon the suffering their predecessors underwent in supporting the cause of their sovereign." They had been forced to flee "from a lawless and rebellious nation ... which afforded no supply to their craving wants." "Put your hands on your hearts," one tory supporter in the House exhorted his associates, and "say that they would be willing that a person who instead of demonstrating the same loyalty and attachment to his King, remained in the revolted colonies, enjoying his property, and perhaps the very property which belongs to some of those subjects ... should come to this province and be entitled to the same privileges and immunities that they are?"[9] If such was the case, Christopher Hagerman asserted, "this Province could no longer be considered a safe retreat for loyal people who left that country and came here for an asylum." Moreover, if a stand was not taken now, "the very men who had committed treason and destroyed the constitution" in the original thirteen colonies "might continue the same treasonous practices here and perhaps with equal success." They "would shortly overturn the sober and the loyal and sever one of the proudest branches of the free."[10]

The vehemence of the government's arguments reflected both its total commitment to the tory vision of the colony and its overriding fear of possible American domination. To maintain a true British colony, it was believed, its residents must be unquestioningly and totally committed to preserving British institutions. That such men as Barnabas Bidwell should with impunity claim to be British subjects and actually expect to take an active part in framing the colony's laws was considered to be incredible. "This house should consider well this question," Hagerman warned, "and decide that Mr. Bidwell should not retain his seat; otherwise, they would be putting aliens on a footing with British subjects and affording all the advantages of the British constitution to the very men who, by their treason and rebellion endeavoured to subvert it."[11]

It was, therefore, with considerable satisfaction that the editors of the *Kingston Chronicle* reported after the first vote on the issue in January 1822 that "Truth *has* indeed prevailed ... the righteous cause prospered, for Barnabas Bidwell, that '*distinguished* citizen of Massachusetts' has been ousted from his seat." Nonetheless, Macaulay and Pringle remained concerned and with very good reason. "While we congratulate the *honest* part of the community on the grand triumph of the cause of correct principles and sound morals," they wrote, "we cannot nor indeed are we anxious to disguise our regret in seeing that it was a majority of *one* only that saved the Province from appalling disgrace and its House of Assembly from indelible pollution." In fact, the House, fundamentally divided on the issue, had refused to determine whether Bidwell and all other Americans resident in Upper Canada possessed the rights and privileges of natural-born subjects. The decision of early 1822 had been grounded specifically on Bidwell's supposed "moral delinquency,"[12] not whether, in law, he was a British subject.

The following year, Barnabas's son, young Marshall Bidwell, stood for election for Lennox and Addington and his candidacy was also immediately challenged by some in the district. As had occurred a year earlier, the growing group of reformers in the House of Assembly, including Robert Nichol, John Rolph, and William Baldwin, once more rose to a Bidwell's defence. "By the treaty of 1783," these men argued, "the subject was not deprived of the right of claiming allegiance and protection of the British government."[13] Citing extensively British statute and common law, they asserted that "American-British subjects born before the treaty and their sons and grandsons, retained their rights as natural subjects." "Naturalization due and vested by birthright cannot by any separation of the Crown be taken away," and even though Bidwell and many other settlers had once been American citizens, "upon their return," it was reasoned, "their American allegiance would cease."[14]

Bidwell's supporters could not accept Attorney General Robinson's interpretation of Simcoe's Proclamation of 1792 and the first act of the provincial parliament concerning residence in the colony. The reformers believed that many Americans had been drawn to the colony by the express invitation of the British government. By coming to Upper Canada, they had merely "returned to the British fold and renewed their allegiance." If this was not the case, William Baldwin asked, "how did it happen that so many grants of land were made them, without their going through the necessary qualifications? And was it the intention of the government that these persons would not be entitled to vote at elections or sit as members of the House of Assembly?" Surely the Americans had all come to this province "on the good faith of this government, and to tell them now that they must forever remain aliens would be a mockery of the legislation." It was against the principles of any British government, it was argued, "to seduce persons into her colony to improve and enjoy lands and take those lands from them afterwards."[15]

Moreover, the reformers contended, using arguments put forward by Robert Gourlay four years earlier, loyalty had little to do with place of birth. As John Wilson, the member for Wentworth, noted in the 1823 debates of the House, such Americans as Jefferson, Monroe, and Madison were not the only revolutionaries to be feared. Was not Tom Paine, "a man whose life was devoted to anarchy and rebellion," a British subject? Though "abhored by the British Government" and "by the majority of the British nation, the sworn enemy of Kings; yet this man with all his vices returned to England ... and was received by the Government as a British subject." "Surely," Wilson demanded, "if a man of his demoniac principles was allowed the privileges of a British subject, this house could not deny that right to Mr. Bidwell. The law that protected the rights of one must protect the rights of the other."[16]

The point at issue was clearly much broader than the isolated case of Barnabas or Marshall Bidwell. "If they disenfranchised the present member for being an alien," it was asked, "what would be the result? the disenfranchisement of thousands – a catastrophe too melancholy to think of." It would mean that "every person who did not withdraw from the United States according to the stipulation of the treaty was in the same predicament, and also the persons who came to this Province from that country since." Therefore "the House should be very cautious in giving their opinions."[17]

Many of Bidwell's supporters went so far as to advocate that all "Americans ought to be considered as strong sheep returning to the fold, and instead of driving them off, we ought to hail with rejoicing their return, receive them with open arms and order the fatted calf to be killed and make merry."[18] Those who opposed the petition of the Lennox and Addington electors saw no threat either in the large numbers of American settlers in the colony or in admitting additional Yankees. In fact, most believed that without the expertise and capital of such settlers, Upper Canada would remain a poor struggling dependent of an increasingly reluctant Great Britain.

To the colonists who watched the debates in the House of Assembly in 1822 and 1823, it must have been clear that "a more interesting question was never agitated than that which has lately been started."[19] In fact, it is likely that many American-Upper Canadians were perplexed and concerned about the matter. As one resident of Kingston noted in 1823, "heretofore, they have ... not only considered themselves, but have been uniformly considered and treated ... as subjects with respect both to the enjoyment of rights and the performances of duties." Any change in their status, this contributor to the *Upper Canada Herald* asserted, "would be a breach of public faith." There were others in the colony, however, who believed that such sentiments were sadly mistaken. An anonymous government supporter asked, "Shall the guest, who is admitted to the feast, prescribe the dishes to which he has not contributed? Shall we, who have sought out for ourselves through the wilderness with the greatest difficulties and exertions, a new home having lost all which we once considered our patrimony, yield up to interlopers an equal claim with ourselves to the highest offices in our Government? Shall one put poison to the vial that it may the more speedily spread through the system?" And he continued, "I am not one of those who think the U E spirit extinct. Let those who imagine themselves fettered or restricted in the display of their energies disgorge their local allegiance, and return to the land of liberty and independence."[20]

In April 1823 the members of the House finally decided that "Marshall S. Bidwell, so far as allegiance, was and is eligible to a seat in the house."[21] The issue was far from resolved, however, for a year later the Court of King's Bench in England reversed its earlier interpretation of the rights of Americans within the empire. Henceforth any settler in British territories who was or had been a subject of the United States, regardless of parentage or allegiance prior to 1783, was to be considered an alien and had no right to inherit property in Great Britain. This decision obviously had serious implications for the majority of residents in Upper Canada. Legally, it suggested that fully four-fifths of the Upper Canadian population was unable to hold land, to vote, or to exercise any of the rights and privileges of British subjects. If this was the case, all colonial leaders, regardless of political persuasion, realized, it would do irreparable harm both to the political stability and the future development of the colony. Quickly attempts were made to rectify the situation; yet no consensus could be reached. Indeed, the issue only engendered increasingly bitter controversy as Upper Canadians were forced to be "explicit about their definition of loyalty."[22] By 1828 the gulf between the reformers and the tory elite had widened to the point where Upper Canadians seemed irrevocably divided.

In November 1825 Lieutenant Governor Maitland sent an address to the House of Assembly. "Whatever difference of opinion may have formerly prevailed with respect to the civil rights of persons ... who had once been Citizens of the United States," he wrote, "the solemn decision of the question in the mother country, whose laws we have adopted, leaves no room for doubt." At present, "the inhabitants of the Province are exposed to the inconvenience of finding those rights denied which they have hitherto enjoyed." Among other things, most land titles were now questionable and many residents no longer had the right to vote and to participate in government. Many "are equally by law exposed to the danger of being regarded as aliens." Therefore, having received "His Majesty's express sanction to assent to an enactment which may afford relief to such persons as are now in the Province," the lieutenant governor called on the House to give its "early and attentive consideration"[23] to the matter.

The bill that the colonial administration presented to the House for consideration proposed that those persons who had emigrated from the United States after 1783 and were, therefore, not "naturalized as British subjects by an Act of Parliament" could, after seven years' uninterrupted residence, take an oath of allegiance in open court and, after registration, be affirmed and declared "His Majesty's natural born subjects to all intents, constructions and purposes, as if they and everyone of them had been born within the Province."[24] The members of the House of Assembly appreciated that some measures had to be taken. Many believed, however, that the administration's proposals were not the answer. And as a result, as Francis Collins of the *Canadian Freeman* observed in 1825, "a very great ferment exists throughout the country on this subject."[25]

"The question is purely a legal and constitutional one," declared the supporters of the colonial executive. The sole intention of the British government and of the proposed Naturalization Act was to confirm for those individuals referred to in the Court of King's Bench decision "full and unquestionable enjoyment of their property and political rights."[26] "Without this aid," wrote the editor of the *Kingston Chronicle*, "however meritorious the party, the inflexibility of the venerable Laws of England can admit no change of this kind in the settlers' political condition."[27] In the House of Assembly, at town meetings, and in the tory press, the colonial executive assured Upper Canadians that "the provisions of the bill would not take away their rights, but they were to confer and more perfectly to secure to those persons the rights and privileges so long enjoyed, which without the bill, might be jeopardized."[28]

Underlying this solicitous concern for the welfare of a large number of Upper Canadians was, however, the tory elite's continuing doubts about the loyalty of many of the American settlers, a concern which only intensified as opposition to the bill increased. The bill, as it was explicitly pointed out, did not apply to "U.E. Loyalists, nor men of American origin who retained their allegiance to the British Empire and who *fought* and *bled* in its support."[29] These "gallant and faithful United Empire Loyalists" had "stood the test in the day which had tried men's souls." Their "privileges ... had been purchased ... by the sacrifice of the blood and property from whom it is now our boast to have descended." It was stressed that these men had never forfeited "their title to the rights of British subjects."[30] The bill, the tories explained, only applied to those who were formerly citizens of the United States of America, "persons who if asked before they emigrated hither ... would have said they were American-born, and that they lived in allegiance to the United States ... persons who deserted the Union of the Empire and espoused the Union of the States." "Catharus" wrote in the *Kingston Chronicle* that "the aliens were those after having fought against their King, or became citizens of the United States and even held offices in those states, have emigrated to this country." The fact that many had subsequently fought in the War of 1812 in defence of the colony did not change their status. "In the eyes of the Law," they were "aliens." Generally, it was asserted, "naturalization, though it may be merited by achievements in the field, can never be gained by fighting," however gallantly. It was "a boon that can only constitutionally be conferred by act of Parliament."[31] Surely, the tory leaders commented, "any man in Canada, who is at heart a true British subject, may take the oath with a clear conscience."[32]

To the colonial administration the issue was indeed crystal clear. Upper Canadians, as members of the empire, had to accept the dictates of the British parliament and courts. The British government, in its generosity, was willing to confer the privileges of British birth and "the rights of free citizens, under a happy, free and envied Constitution,"[33] on those who at one time had revolted against the king. Moreover, Parliament, in an unprecedented move, had given the colonial government the authority to draw up its own remedial provisions. Upper Canadians should, therefore, be grateful. And though some could understand the frustration of the majority of Upper Canadians and their reluctance to admit that they were aliens, American-Upper Canadians should take the oath to ensure that there could be no future misunderstandings.

The majority in the House of Assembly and an increasing number of residents throughout the colony did not see the proposed naturalization bill in this light. With growing incredulity, they demanded to know "who are those persons to be styled Aliens? Surely not those who have brought Upper Canada to display its value to the Imperial Government by bringing a wilderness to blossom as the rose; and certainly it could not be those, or the sons of those who in danger rushed to our standard and repelled the Invaders from our shores." Was it "not cruel and unjust," the reformers asked, "to stigmatize so loyal a Province by acknowledging a large portion of its inhabitants Aliens ... who had so long and faithfully sustained the character of British subjects?" Charles Fothergill, once editor of the *Upper Canada Gazette* but in this matter a fervid opponent of government policy, was only one of many who stated categorically that I am "proud to rank myself amongst those who feel a just and an honest indignation at the idea of disenfranchising and alienating full three fourths of the most loyal inhabitants of the Province without whose aid in the dark hour of danger and distress, we could not have been now here to question their just right." The bill proposed was "treasonous against the people of the country."[34] Its provisions were "odious, contained a political lie and were utterly disgraceful to the people." Clearly it was intended "to deprive of their rights loyal subjects of His Majesty, men who have for thirty years exercised the rights of Britons."[35]

Specifically, the antigovernment editors and the reformers in the

House of Assembly, citing among other things Simcoe's "celebrated Proclamations of 1792" and Jay's Treaty of 1794, argued once again that the settlers in question had arrived in Upper Canada "by the invitation"[36] of the colonial and imperial governments. Echoing the position that had been taken in Bidwell's defence, Fothergill asked the House whether any man really doubted that the original enactments had expressly encouraged these settlers to move north. Upper Canada was chiefly indebted to the United States for the population it had now and its American settlers were still "amongst the most useful, industrious and loyal subjects of His Majesty."[37] And certainly the question of alienage "had not been stated when the services of the people were required."[38]

More important, it was asserted that the late war had conclusively proven the steadfast loyalty of *all* residents in Upper Canada and particularly the loyalty of those thousands of former Americans who had chosen Upper Canada as their home. The close proximity of the United States and "the relative situation" of that country vis-as)vis the colony, had "put their fidelity to the test in a degree rarely experienced in any other country."[39] Many American-Upper Canadians, like their loyalist compatriots, "could say that during the last war, they had lost a father or a son, in defence of the Country." They were rightfully proud of their loyalty and the reformers refused "to torture them by calling them Aliens." "What was Patriotism?" they queried, "but a love of one Country in preference to all others." Surely "these people possessed it." Fothergill asked, "Could the House then say to them away with all your losses, you are Aliens, and must register yourself as such?" He proclaimed that "sooner should his tongue cleave to his mouth and the pen fall from his hand than he should consent to visit such a degradation on the people."[40]

The reformers in the House of Assembly publicly wondered whether indeed the whole issue had not been manufactured by the colonial administration. In 1825 Francis Collins of the *Canadian Freeman* suggested that "the Alien Question has been nothing but a snare – a hidden trap with which to destroy the civil rights of the American emigrants in the colony – an apple of discord, with which first to divide the people and then rule them with an iron rod."[41] These Upper Canadians could not believe "that the British Monarch, great, generous, glorious and magnanimous as he is, or that the British ministry, so wise and liberal as they are ... could stoop by any means, and ignominious shift, cavil, trick or political sophistry or chicane to entrap, deceive, disqualify, disenfranchise and alienate the best of settlers and of subjects without whose aid ... we could not have been now here to talk of their heroic deeds?" "Sir!" Fothergill exclaimed in 1825, "it is monstrous, inconceivable, impossible."[42]

For the most part, "public opinion" seemed to "acquit His Excellency and the home government of any danger against the liberty of the people." Some, in fact, in language reminiscent of that used by the American patriots in the early 1770s, went so far as to wonder whether the instructions of the imperial authorities had "ever been submitted to His Majesty?"[43] As the controversy became more heated throughout 1826 and 1827, the reformers became increasingly convinced that the whole issue had been fabricated "by the ministerial party in order to deprive the American emigrants of the elective franchise."[44] "A great deal has been said," they noted, "about republican principles, republican prepossessions, and republican prejudice"; but the great danger to the future well-being of the colony, they believed, emanated from the policies of its own government. The executive's naturalization bill of 1825 was an attempt "to oppress the people."[45] Many reformers believed that "some trick is about to be played by ... a few deep and designing politicians who have long nestled about the Colonial Executive"; they were men who "like the fable of the snake and the country men, the moment they have been warmed into existence by the fruits of the toils and the industry of the American emigrant farmers – the early pioneers of our forests – turned round upon their benefactors and shed upon them the deadly poison of political malice."[46] In an attempt to maintain political power, it was charged that the present authorities were intending to force this "most odious and unpopular measure" upon the people. And in so doing the supporters of the Maitland administration had "abused the trust and confidence reposed in it and dishonoured the British name and character." It was the executive, not the reformers or American-born residents, who had "raised a spirit of discord, disillusion and strife in the colony," a situation which some warned "might prove ruinous in the end to British interests in this quarter of the Globe." For, the reformers observed, "misrule and official corruption" were causing "the interests of the country to be neglected."[47]

The threat to the integrity and internal security of the colony, the reformers asserted time and again, came not from the United States or from the American settlers resident in Upper Canada but from the colonial executive. John Rolph, member for the County of Middlesex, asked, "will not those who come here and have property become attached to us, to a government in the welfare of which they have a deep and personal interest?" He declared, "it is only when a man's political rights are endangered that the seeds of distrust and discontent arise in his bosom; and judging from the past policy of this country and its present state, I think there is no danger to be apprehended from the Americans." The settlers had come, he and others believed, "to subdue, not our government but our forests; to overcome, not our authorities, civil and military, but our wastes, our desolate places." "Nothing," the reformers proclaimed, "can be more contemptible in any nation, than to manifest in times of peace, a jealousy of other friendly governments."[48] The colonial executive was autocratic and its ministers corrupt. Therefore, in 1827, the reformers proposed to "again address His Majesty to submit the case of the people to the Imperial Legislature to provide the remedy required." Only the sovereign and the British parliament, they believed, could be trusted to uphold the principles of the British constitution and to enact measures in the best interests of the colony as a whole. As Fothergill stated, "a bill passed in England would be satisfactory, but the one presently under consideration would never meet the approbation of the people if passed by this House."[49]

To many reformers, the executive's policy with regard to the naturalization bill illustrated all too clearly the extent to which the principles of the British constitution had been perverted in Upper Canada. During the early 1820s the government had attempted to subvert the authority of the House of Assembly and to overthrow the tradition of a balanced form of government. Now the tories were trying to deny Upper Canadians those basic rights and privileges which all Britons were guaranteed under the constitution. The American Revolution had shown what could result when a corrupt and tyrannical government tried to oppress the people. The reformers in the late 1820s were obviously fearful that similar consequences might occur in Upper Canada. For they believed it was only if Upper Canadians could maintain the constitutional rights which they had first been granted and for which they had fought, that the colony would remain a loyal member of the British Empire.

The concerted opposition to the naturalization bill shocked and appalled the colonial administration and its supporters. With their belief in the need for a strong executive and their fear of political factions and dissent, the tories construed opposition to their authority and to their proposals as a challenge to the very foundations of Upper Canadian society. Surely, they declared, "the oath is one which no true British subject would scruple to take once a week if any good object could be obtained by doing so."[50] The bill itself had "in it nothing degrading, nothing oppressive, nothing that can hurt the feelings or wound the pride of the most scrupulous individuals."

It was only a "remedial measure" and great care had been taken "that no one should be deprived, by its passing of any privilege he held before."[51] "If there be any injustice or illiberality in it all," a "True Born Upper Canadian," writing in the *Kingston Chronicle* in 1827, maintained, "it is to those only and their children who at a well known period emigrated to this country under the full assurance of the protection of the British government, as a reward for their loyalty and affection and who are now to be deprived of their birth-right by the inundation of those very persons whose fathers to a man revolted against their benefactors in another land."[52] It was obvious that those who opposed the bill and refused to take the oath of allegiance were not, nor wished to be considered, "true Britons." This agitation against the generosity of the crown could only be interpreted, many members of the executive concluded, as "a refusal to foreswear their American allegiance."[53]

This response was not surprising, for the administration believed that many settlers had arrived with little or no intention of denying their loyalty to the United States. Most had come, John Beverley Robinson declared "because they could no longer remain where they were," or to improve their condition.[54] At best, it was believed, "only one-fourth, in any probability had heard of Simcoe's proclamations." And to the claim "that but for the bravery of Americans in the late war, this colony would have fallen prey to the United States," one Upper Canadian retorted, "it was not true and he did not like to see such things reported to the country in fine eloquent speeches."[55] "Catharus" did admit that a number of American settlers in 1812 had "served under our colours." But he wondered, somewhat rhetorically, "was this the effect of principle, loyalty, or of circumstances?" Could they have kept property or remained in the country and acted otherwise, he asked. "Could they have avoided fighting when drawn up in line with British soldiers and the loyal tories of the old school?"[56] In the end, it was repeatedly declared that regardless of their intentions, these Americans were still aliens within the meaning of British law.

The tory elite considered that to resolve the present legal dilemma by passing an act simply declaring all residents of the colony to be British subjects, as was being proposed by the opposition, was out of the question. The menacing presence of the United States and the tories' constant fear of the insidious influence of republicanism and unfettered democracy on Upper Canadian society made this impossible. As "Vindex" noted, "Like a virgin, pure, chaste, and holy, conscious of her intensive excellency of character and fond of her unsullied reputation – England deigns not to accept the professed affections of a heart, already in part devoted to a proud rival. She will have none worship at the altar of her loyalty, who cannot bring the precious incense of an undivided affection. Let us therefore show ourselves worthy of the protection and the adoption of such a Country." "To admit the doctrine of double allegiance" would be disastrous.[57] The tories believed that only "British laws, British legislation and British principles" should gain ascendancy in the colony. In addition, they asserted, "we wish positive subjects ... devoted to the British crown; those who are not so, we desire not to see elected to make laws for us in our assembly."[58] And "many trembled and dreaded the very idea of [more] Americans coming into the Province."[59]

It was clear to the administration that there were already a number of Americans in Upper Canada "who would like to put on their allegiance and put it off as they would a great coat, and have half a dozen changes of it to suit their interests."[60] Would not men such as these expect "to say in the time of danger, 'I do not want to remain here any longer, I wish to join the enemy who have invaded the country in which I was born'?" "That danger (to say nothing of the absurdity of a distinct class of people)," it was believed, could "prove fatal"[61] to the colony. Moreover, there were obviously others in the province "who with their mouths full of loyalty and patriotism care not a farthing for either King or people." They "would as soon have Canada under the Turks or Ashantees, as under the British rule." They were "men who are fattening on the best of the land, living under the protection of our laws and partaking of all the blessings we enjoy but who are ready to betray us to any enemy who would make fair terms with them ... our Government cannot desire subjects of that description."[62]

The conservative leaders of Upper Canada particularly feared those "individuals who have long enough lived in the Province, without at any time possessing the least spark of British feeling" and who were "increasing in their endeavours to maintain a republican ascendancy in the colony, and to stifle and put down affections and attachments to the British Empire." Some people, they asserted, "seem to forget that this is a British colony, and talk as if they wished it should not be such." But, it was declared, "this is not a nursery for enemies to Britain or radicals of any kind, not a plantation peopled for the purpose of increasing hereafter the wealth and strength of the United States; but it is an asylum for Britons and a nursery for loyal men, and as such our Government is willing to naturalize all foreigners here who regard her and love our institutions."[63] It is unlikely that anyone actually believed that the majority of American settlers fell into this category. Nonetheless, it was suggested that "one of the most beneficial effects of the law will be to bring" the dissident elements "into public view, and to distinguish them from the loyal part of the population."[64]

The growing opposition to the proposed naturalization bill demonstrated to the tories the degree to which subversive, democratic elements had already invaded Upper Canada. "Tis quite pleasant to hear such men talk of loyalty to the King," commented "Catharus," somewhat sarcastically, "men who are not only aliens, but who refuse to be naturalized – aliens who scorn to be made British subjects in the only legal manner in which it can be done." Obviously "we can never expect that even favours and kindness will make men educated in republican principles ... ever become loyally attached to our government and laws." "No sir," "Catharus" wrote, "they wish the American character and party here to stand out in bold relief" and "we may as well throw ourselves into the arms of the United States."[65]

Despite the determined efforts of the tories to restrict citizenship in Upper Canada to the British-born, loyalists, and those Americans who would take an oath of allegiance, the naturalization bill finally passed in 1828 reflected both the demographic realities of the situation and, to a large degree, the arguments put forward by the reformers. Responding to the representation made by the House of Assembly in 1827 and the numerous petitions of ordinary Upper Canadians, the British parliament had decided that the colonial government's initial proposals were repugnant to British policy. The Naturalization Act given royal assent in May 1828 declared that all American-Upper Canadians resident in Upper Canada before 1820 were British subjects and possessed all the rights and privileges of natural-born subjects. Those who had arrived subsequently could, after seven years' residence, take the oath of allegiance and become naturalized. The act acknowledged both the historic development and the unique circumstances of Upper Canada. Demographically, as well as physically and economically, the colony was a North American and an Anglo-American community. In part, at least, the reformers had won their point. The question of new American immigration remained, however.

Far from supporting a bill which "intended to frighten Americans out of the colony, or from coming to settle here,"[66] many members of the House of Assembly had throughout the 1820s actively advocated that American immigrants be encouraged to come to Upper Canada. Only American settlers, they believed, knew best how to prosper on this North American frontier. "Shut the door on Americans? No," said John Rolph, one of those who could not sanction such a thing. "Let all who love the blessings of a limited monarchy come hither and help us to cultivate the wilderness and improve the soil."[67] For "while Michigan and every other corner of the United States are fast filling with people, the colony remains a comparative desert" and under the present policy will continue in "a puny and feeble state." Members of the House, therefore, applauded the "enlightened mind and liberal policies" of former Lieutenant Governor Simcoe and recommended that his "wise and beneficial"[68] attitude prevail.

The reformers experienced little difficulty in reconciling the admission of more Americans and the recognition that those already in the colony were British subjects with the continued presence of Upper Canada in the British Empire. The American presence and the British connection were, they asserted, complementary. Certainly many reformers were apprehensive of the power of the United States. They shared, though perhaps not to the same degree, the tory's view of the imperialistic tendencies of the American government; and they too disapproved of many of the political and social consequences of republicanism. Most in the House, however, felt the best way to defend the colony against any future aggression by the United States or gradual American influence was to ensure the colony's future growth and prosperity. The only way this could be done was to add to Upper Canada's population.

To the tories, the passage and approval of the naturalization bill was a partial defeat. Between 1821, when they had first challenged Bidwell's election, and 1828, when the issue was finally resolved, they had fought adamantly for their vision of the colony. To John Beverley Robinson, John Strachan, and other supporters of the local executive, Upper Canada was, and should remain, a bastion of British power and influence in North America. Its institutions, its laws, its traditions, and, obviously, its people, they believed, must clearly reflect and actively support this. Though many tories did admire some developments in the United States, their understanding of the nature of republicanism and of the expansionist tendencies of the American government far overshadowed any admiration they expressed. Indeed, to be British, it was contended, was to be not American. The two systems of government and the two societies were antithetical and usually operated to radically different ends. There was no room in Upper Canada, the tories asserted, for anyone or any idea which overtly or even implicitly challenged the British constitution as they understood it. The very presence of so many former American citizens and the growing opposition to government policies indicated that American and thus anti-British ideas and sentiments were already too prevalent.

The controversy over the Bidwells and naturalization was another of those issues emerging in the 1820s that graphically illustrated the growing ideological split in Upper Canada. Like the supply bill controversies of 1817 and 1825, it was largely a battle between the court and the country parties. Yet the naturalization bill precipitated far more than a political dispute between the executive and some members of the Assembly. As one historian has suggested, the alien question forced Upper Canadian leaders to articulate fully their "concept of loyalty." For both the tories and the reformers, loyalty formed "the basis not only of political legitimacy but also of acceptance into the society of the province." And over the years, loyalty, and particularly what it meant to be a loyal Upper Canadian, came to mean different things to the two groups. The tories "used loyalty as both the means to distinguish those of loyalist origin from the American latecomers and as the means to differentiate those who supported the political status quo, and those who did not."[69] To the reformers, loyalty had little to do with who arrived first in the colony or with political dissent. Rather, loyalty was evident through an individual's actions, through his defence of the constitution, and through his commitment to the colony. Thus, while the tories used the War of 1812 to illustrate the numerous problems arising from indiscriminately admitting Americans to the colony, the reformers increasingly considered the three years of conflict as proof of the allegiance of all those who had actually taken part. Moreover, after 1815 the tories felt that American settlers continued to threaten the colony and undermine residents' commitment to the empire. The reformers, on the other hand, believed that only with the economic prosperity that these settlers could bring to colonial life would the commitment of all Upper Canadians to the mother country remain strong. Perhaps more importantly, the tories considered all political and social opposition to the policies of those in government evidence of disloyalty; the reformers believed that opposition, if in defence of the British constitution, was not only the right but the duty of every loyal subject.

This divergence in perspective evolved primarily in response to political and social developments in the colony after 1815, though its roots extended back to the time of the first arrival of the loyalists. It is evident, however, that the two notions of loyalty were also shaped by the differing understanding that the tories and the reformers had of unfolding events in Great Britain and the United States after the war. After watching developments in England, the tories were sympathetic to the attitude that the British government had taken towards radical reform and were determined that such subversive radical activities not be permitted to develop in Upper Canada. They also looked with disdain on the destructive effect that opposition and political factions had on society in the United States. For their part, the reformers were much more concerned about the effect that a corrupt and tyrannical government could have on society. They too were committed to ensuring that Upper Canada remained a part of the empire. The threat, they believed, however, was not primarily from external factors – from the United States, from republicanism, or from radical reform. Rather, it emanated from the internal oppression being imposed by the Upper Canadian government. Upper Canada, they asserted, had to learn from the lessons of both the political upheavals in Great Britain and the events leading up to the American Revolution. Upper Canadians had to be vigilant; they had to ensure that the colonists were not forced into rebellion by the ill-considered policies of their government. More important, they had to be true to the very image of that constitution which was the source of those rights and privileges that had originally been granted to them, while at the same time taking advantage of all that the North American environment and the examples provided by the United States could offer for their future development. Only then would Upper Canadians, by choice, become and remain loyal and true subjects of the British crown.

The decision on the naturalization bill did solve the immediate problem of who, in law, was an Upper Canadian. It did not, however, reconcile the divergent opinions that existed in the colony concerning who was loyal and who was not. Indeed, the controversy brought the political and ideological divisions between the tories and the reformers into sharp relief. And over the next ten years, the gulf that separated the two sides only widened.

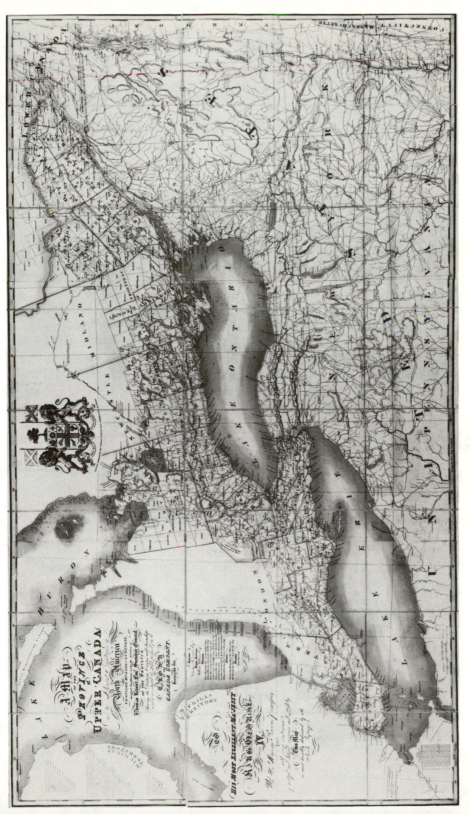

3 A Map of the Province of Upper Canada, compiled by James G. Chewett, c. 1830 (Public Archives of Ontario)

Conclusion

In November 1828 a report in the *Colonial Advocate* announced the arrival of Sir John Colborne, the new lieutenant governor of Upper Canada. A "New Era" in colonial development was at hand, editor William Lyon Mackenzie proclaimed. With the naturalization issue finally resolved and the departure of Lieutenant Governor Maitland, it was hoped that Upper Canadians could now embark on the road to prosperity, united in their allegiance to the king and in their commitment to the development of a progressive North American community.[1] A number of Upper Canadians, as they looked back over the past forty years of the colony's history, also considered this an auspicious time. "When the country was first settled," a report of the Northumberland County Agricultural Society stated in June, "the exertions of the Agriculturals were principally confined to the clearing of the land and preparing it for the reception of seed ... these days of hardship and unremitting toil are happily passed away." At last, "improvement is advancing slowly but surely" and settlers could look confidently forward to the time when "their adoptive country ... will ... appear in all the glorious array of beautiful cultivated fields," strong and prosperous, with a "numerous, enterprising and enlightened population."[2]

For both second- and third-generation Upper Canadians and for the growing number of new arrivals, the progress of the colony since the War of 1812 was heartening. Despite the postwar depression, her economy had expanded, keeping pace with the steady increase in population. At the end of 1828 the Welland Canal was within weeks of completion and construction was well under way on the new Rideau Canal project. Moreover, life in the towns and in the backwoods of the province had been significantly enhanced by the increasing number of social and economic organizations which had sprung up. In 1828 Upper Canada seemed at last very close to fulfilling Lieutenant Governor Simcoe's vision of a unified, prosperous community – a jewel of the empire and a prized British possession in North America.

Those Upper Canadians who expected Lieutenant Governor Colborne's arrival to herald a new era of "good feeling" were soon disillusioned, however. Certainly 1828 was a watershed in colonial development; but it really marked only the end of the beginning of serious political controversy in Upper Canada. Though the alien question had finally been resolved to the satisfaction of the vast majority in the province, new issues were already surfacing which threatened to divide the colony even more bitterly. In the colonial press, Rev. John Strachan was engaged in a vitriolic debate with the young Methodist preacher, Egerton Ryerson, over the establishment of the church, the disposition of the clergy reserves, and the educational needs of the colony.[3] In the spring of 1828 Mr Justice Willis had enraged the colonial administration by publicly questioning the competence of the Court of King's Bench. His subsequent suspension inflamed many reformers and revived memories of the past persecutions of Robert Thorpe and Robert Gourlay.[4] Most significant, however, had been the election that summer.

For the first time, Upper Canadian voters had elected more opponents than supporters of the government to the House of Assembly. To the chagrin of the executive, such "patriotic" agitators as William Lyon Mackenzie now joined the ranks of William Baldwin, John Rolph, and Marshall Bidwell. There was no question that, as Francis Collins of the *Canadian Freeman* commented with some glee, "the result of the late election has exasperated and alarmed the ministerial party beyond all reasonable grounds." Collins observed that the tories "think that the monster DISLOYALTY generated by the labours of the *radical* press has alone produced this great change in our political atmosphere." Collins and others attributed the results to other factors. Many believed that Upper Canadians had only shown their determination to elect men who were independent of the executive. For years, it was claimed, the colonists had seen "their laws trampled with impunity and outrage like an evil spirit, stalking abroad unmasked in open day." This "misrule and official corruption" had prompted many residents to vote against "the cringing sycophants who had betrayed their interests." In their stead, Upper Canadians had returned "a majority of independent and patriotic men" to the House of Assembly, men who, the reformers asserted, would "protect and support their rights and privileges."[5]

The election of 1828 marked the real beginning of increasingly organized and bitter political controversy in Upper Canada. From the time that Robert Gourlay had arrived to the final approval of the alien bill, Upper Canadians had evolved into an active and relatively knowledgeable electorate. As Lieutenant Governor Maitland and his supporters had found and as Lieutenant Governor Colborne would discover in 1828, the administration could no longer expect to pursue its programs without opposition. Over the past ten years, the executive had been increasingly forced to justify and defend its policies – not only before the elected Assembly, but also to the populace at large through the press and in public meetings. Moreover, dissent, though still associated by the tories with disloyalty, had gradually gained respectability. It was clear that the controversies of the previous ten years had been only a rehearsal for the vitriolic debates which would rock the colony in the 1830s.

It would be premature to conclude that, by the end of the 1820s, two political parties had emerged in Upper Canada. Most members of government, whether in the Assembly or on the executive, still adamantly and sincerely proclaimed their independence from any organized group. Rhetorically at least, Upper Canadians asserted that political parties and factions were destructive and, by their nature, inimical to good government. Nonetheless, the political debates throughout the decade had crystallized conflicting political ideologies. And though it was by no means united, the presence of a majority of antigovernment representatives in the House of Assembly, and the diffusion of viable opposition and government presses throughout the colony had legitimized and, to a certain degree, institutionalized dissent in the political process of Upper Canada.

The year 1828 was indeed the beginning of a new era in Upper Canadian life. It was, however, a new era which found itself confronted with many of the old issues which had been dividing Upper Canadians since 1791. Throughout the 1830s, the question of clergy reserves, of the duties of the House, of schools and a university, and of emigration continued to preoccupy the colonists. And, as had been the case for the past forty years, colonial leaders and, increasingly, a politically conscious electorate, considered these concerns and attempted to find answers for their many problems within their understanding of the two nations which still dominated their lives – Great Britain and the United States.

"The United States," the June 1828 report of the Northumberland Agricultural Society noted, "are increasing in population and power beyond all former calculations and experience." "One day or other," it was predicted, "the republic will grow to such a pitch of grandeur and might so as to rival, if not to eclipse, the present glory and splendour of Great Britain."[6] Many Upper Canadians in 1828 were confident that their colony would eventually also become "one of the finest countries ... in the world." This would only be possible, however, if it "continues under the fostering care and power and protection of their illustrious and kind parent."[7] Leading Upper Canadians at the end of the 1820s, like their predecessors of the 1790s, continued to be conscious of their unique and frequently precarious situation. The expanding republic to the south still posed a threat not only to the territorial integrity of Upper Canada but also to its hard-won institutions and British traditions. Though it appeared that the British government was finally beginning to appreciate the value of its North American colony, some residents remained apprehensive. The mother country might not be intending to abandon them but a growing number of Upper Canadians feared that if it condoned the ill-informed and misguided policies of the local administration, colonists might be forced into rebellion.

Moreover, in 1828, all influential Upper Canadians realized, to some degree at least, the impact that the two external powers still had on the colony's political development. Since 1791 the foundations had been carefully laid to create a distinct society in Upper Canada. Consciously, residents had tried to wed the Old World ideas of the British constitution, of the monarchy, and of the social and parliamentary traditions of Great Britain to the North American environment and New World beliefs and practices. As Hartwell Bowsfield has argued, Upper Canadians were determined to shape a community "able to move within its own orbit, separate from the United States, separate but not estranged from the imperial mother." Thus, at the same time that the colonists "proclaimed loyalty" to the British crown, they recognized Upper Canada's "place as a new and North American community in which conditions ... would necessarily influence and shape its attitudes."[8] Controversy between various elite groups in Upper Canada had arisen not so much over the acceptance of this premise, but rather over the relative degree to which either one or other factor – British or American ideas – should influence the institutional, social, and political life in the colony.

In the beginning, the divisions between the various regional leadership groups in Upper Canada had directly resulted from their differing backgrounds and their respective positions within Upper Canadian society. Physically and psychologically set apart from each other and primarily concerned about the immediate needs of their own community, residents in Kingston, Niagara, and York had often seen different things as they looked to Great Britain and the United States. This was inevitable. The American loyalists and merchants

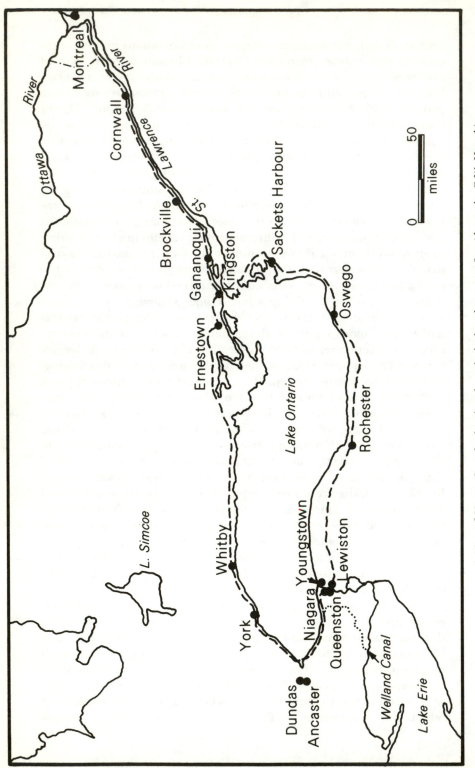

4 A Map of Upper Canada showing the principal settlements, 1825 (drawn by G.W. Hough)

and the British immigrants and government officials had had quite different perceptions of the needs and the future nature of the new land. For the first ten years, these divergent views had been reinforced by the isolation imposed by the frontier. Even after the threat and eventual calamity of war had drawn them together, varying regional viewpoints still persisted.

As the colony matured after 1815 and as a new generation of leaders began to confront new issues, differing perceptions of Great Britain and the United States continued to divide the Upper Canadian elite. At the same time, physical and political developments in the colony served to widen the debates, taking them out of their previously localized context and giving them a broader colonial interest and significance. The terms of the controversies remained basically the same, however – how to translate the principles and practices of the British constitution into a North American environment; how to maintain a distinctively British society while living in the shadow of an aggressive republican giant; how to use the example of economic prosperity presented by the United States without compromising the essential British nature of Upper Canadian society. In the postwar years, colonial leaders, like their predecessors, relied on their understanding of contemporary events in the United States and Great Britain to suggest answers to these questions. As views of the two nations and of the colony's relationship to each differed from one political group to another, so too did the solutions they presented.

The tory supporters of the government asserted that the overwhelming threat to the future of the colony emanated from south of the border. Only by maintaining strong and active ties with Great Britain and enforcing a conservative mould on colonial society could Upper Canada hope to survive. The reformers, on the other hand, considered that the danger to the province lay within Upper Canada herself. If the government began to respond to the needs of its people, it was asserted, and if Upper Canadians could share in the prosperity evident in the United States, then their allegiance to the crown would remain strong. This is not to say that in the 1820s the tories rejected all things American or that the reformers embraced the democratic ideals of the United States. Rather, these two evolving ideologies had their roots in and were sustained by a collective understanding of *both* the United States and Great Britain. And though the United States was the colony's closest neighbour, differing perceptions of the British constitution and parliamentary traditions were at the heart of the controversy. The questions of emigration and settlement, of citizenship rights, and of the duties of the House of

Assembly served to crystallize the differences. Yet underlying the political controversy of the 1820s and present, indeed, since Simcoe had first arrived in Upper Canada, was the colony's attempt to find a unique and special identity. The United States and Great Britain provided the colonists with constant points of reference in their search. On the basis of their understanding of these two nations, which continued to play such a large part in colonial life, Upper Canadians sought to discover who and what they were.

Notes

ABBREVIATIONS

CHA	Canadian Historical Association
CHR	*Canadian Historical Review*
DCB	*Dictionary of Canadian Biography*
House of Assembly	*Journals and Proceedings of the House of Assembly*
Legislative Council	*Journals and Proceedings of the Legislative Council*
OH	*Ontario History*
OHS	Ontario Historical Society
PAC	Public Archives of Canada
PAO	Public Archives of Ontario
QUA	Queen's University Archives
TPL	Toronto Public Library
UCS	Upper Canada Sundries

INTRODUCTION

1 [Richard Cartwright], *Letters of an American Loyalist*, nos. I, IX.
2 This is particularly true of the earliest histories of the province. See for example William Canniff, *The History of the Settlement of Ontario (Upper Canada)*; Egerton Ryerson, *The Loyalists and Their Times*. Even some of the most recent studies published to commemorate the bicentennial of Ontario promote this interpretation. These include Christopher Moore, *The Loyalists*; Robert S. Allen and Bernard Pothier, eds., *The Loyal Americans*; Patrick Brode, *The Bone and the Sinew: The Life of Sir John Beverley Robinson*.
3 S.F. Wise, "The Origins of Anti-Americanism in Canada," 301. Professor Wise has written a number of provocative and impressive articles to substantiate this interpretation. These include "God's Peculiar Peo-

ple"; "Sermon Literature and Canadian Intellectual History"; "Colonial Attitudes from the Era of the War of 1812 to the Rebellions of 1837," *Canada Views the United States*, ed. Wise and Robert Brown, 16–43; "Upper Canada and the Conservative Tradition."

4 A.G. Bailey, "Evidences of Culture Considered as Colonial," *Culture and Nationality*, 178–99, 180. Bailey was writing of Canadian culture in the post-Confederation period. He noted that "the volume and pressure of external influences on the population of the Dominion and its antecedent provinces have always exceeded that impinging upon it from its 'own' historic past," though "the past has helped to determine the way in which these influences have been received." This finding applies equally well to British North America in the pre-Confederation period and particularly to Upper Canada at the beginning of the nineteenth century.

5 There are a number of studies, particularly by British and American scholars, of the transference of ideas, beliefs, and practices within this North Atlantic triangle. In addition to Bailey, "Evidences of Culture," see Frank Thistlethwaite, *The Anglo-American Connection in the Early Nineteenth Century*; J.B. Brebner, *The North Atlantic Triangle*; Bernard Bailyn, *The Ideological Origins of the American Revolution*; Gordon Wood, *The Creation of the American Republic*; Robert Kelley, *The Transatlantic Persuasion*; R.R. Palmer, *The World of the French Revolution*; Richard Hofstadter, *The Idea of a Party System*; Richard Buel, *Securing the Revolution: Ideology in American Politics*; David Paul Crook, *American Democracy in English Politics*; Carl Bridenbaugh, *Mitre and Sceptre*. Unfortunately, little detailed attention has been given to British North America's and particularly Upper Canada's relationship to the British-American axis in the pre-Confederation period.

6 Rhys Isaacs, *The Transformation of Virginia*, 324.

7 It had been suggested that most Upper Canadians were politically passive, uncaring, and apathetic. Wise, "Colonial Attitudes," 16; S.D. Clark, "The Backwoods Society of Upper Canada," *Developing Canadian Community*, 63–80, 74. After only a cursory examination, it would seem that these generalizations do not fit Upper Canadian frontier society.

CHAPTER ONE

1 Simcoe to Sir Joseph Banks, 8 January 1791, *The Correspondence of Lieutenant Governor John Graves Simcoe*, ed. E.A. Cruikshank, 1:18. (Hereafter referred to as *Simcoe Papers*.)

2 The precise number of residents in Upper Canada in 1791 is unknown; even the actual number of loyalists who arrived immediately after the

revolution is not clear. Figures vary from 6,000 loyalists (Talman, "The United Empire Loyalists," 4,) to 10,000 (Canniff, *History of Ontario*, 62). It is known that the population did gradually increase in the early years. Nonetheless, the figure of 10,000 in 1791 is, at best, an estimate of the white population.

3 Talman, "The United Empire Loyalists," 4. Some historians have suggested that many of the loyalists were relatively wealthy, educated men. Canniff, *History of Ontario*, 51. However, as Kathryn M. Bindon found in "Kingston: A Social History," 39–40, loyalists' claims suggest that most had left little property in the United States. Marla Waltman, "From Soldier to Settler," confirms these findings.

4 Marcus Hansen and J.B. Brebner, *The Mingling of the Canadian and American Peoples*, 66. See also Fred Landon, *Western Ontario and the American Frontier*; Gerald Craig, *Upper Canada: The Formative Years, 1784–1841*, 51. By 1810, Michael Smith estimated, 60 per cent of the population was American nonloyalist. *A Geographical View of the Province of Upper Canada*, 82.

5 *Kingston Gazette*, 25 September 1810. For accounts of ethnic and cultural backgrounds of early Upper Canadians, see among others Waltman, "From Soldiers to Settlers," 58; E. Rae, *Alexander MacDonnell and the Politics of Upper Canada*; Helen I. Cowan, *British Emigration to British North America*; M. McLean, "Peopling Glengarry County"; D.H. Akenson, *The Irish in Ontario*.

6 A comprehensive examination of the colony in the early years is beyond the scope of this work. Moreover, considerable scholarly attention has already been given to various aspects of life in pre-War of 1812 Upper Canada. See for example Craig, *Upper Canada*; S.D. Clark, *The Developing Canadian Community* and *Movements of Political Protest in Upper Canada*; Goldwin French, *Parsons in Politics*; Lillian Gates, *Land Policies of Upper Canada*; G.P. de T. Glazebrook, *Life in Ontario*; E.C. Guillet, *Early Life in Upper Canada*; Akenson, *The Irish in Ontario*; Landon, *Western Ontario*; Hansen and Brebner, *Mingling of Peoples*; Stuart Ivison and F. Rosser, *The Baptists in Upper and Lower Canada before 1820*; J.K. Johnson, *Historical Essays in Upper Canada*; G.C. Patterson, *Land Settlement in Upper Canada*; Gerald Tulchinsky, ed., *To Preserve and Defend*. In addition, there is a host of articles, theses, and local studies which are too numerous to list.

7 J.J. Talman's collection of *Loyalist Narratives from Upper Canada* provides some of the best first-hand accounts of life in early Upper Canada. All these refer to the isolation and the problems of travel and loneliness that constantly confronted the pioneer farmers. For a very suggestive discussion of the oral culture and its interaction with a more formal

written one, see Rhys Isaac, *The Transformation of Virginia*, a study of life in colonial Virginia. Though by no means strictly similar to life in early Upper Canada, the situations are in many ways quite comparable.

8 Clark, "The Backwoods Society," 66.

9 Isaac Weld, *Travels through the States of North America and the Provinces of Upper and Lower Canada*, 2:89, 65.

10 Biographical information about all of these men can be found in *DCB*, vols. 3,4,5, and in Errington, "The Eagle, the Lion and Upper Canada." Unfortunately, there has been almost no other attention given to many of the individuals who made up the colonial elite. The one notable and most useful exception is Bruce Wilson's *The Enterprises of Robert Hamilton*.

11 Wilson, *Robert Hamilton*, argues that Hamilton's contacts with the Montreal merchants "and his good reputation with the army opened up wide avenues for dispensing patronage." Moreover, "trade, government and social regulation were inextricably interwined." Wilson's conclusions concerning Hamilton are equally applicable to Cartwright in Kingston. For a general discussion of the development of local elites and their political, social, and economic relationships, and the importance of, among other things, indebtedness in defining rank, see Isaacs, *Transformation of Virginia*.

12 Weld, *Travels*, 89. See also discussion in Robert Burns, "The First Elite of Toronto," 81.

13 See Craig, *Upper Canada*; Edith Firth, *The Town of York*, and particularly Bruce Walton, "The End of All Order: A Study of Upper Canadian Conservative Response to Opposition, 1805–1811."

14 T.H. Breen, *Puritans and Adventurers*, 3. This collection of articles examines the transference of culture from the Old World to the New. Breen notes that in Massachusetts, between 1630 and 1660, migrants attempted to preserve their local communities from external influence. And each village, he argues, maintained a different character and outlook. Breen contends that the character of the New World was partly determined by specific Old World antecedents. It is likely that each community in Upper Canada had its own unique character which evolved partly as a response to its residents' attempts to reestablish the life of their former homes in the United States.

15 Smith, *A Geographical View*, 61, cites that in 1810, Upper Canada had a population of 75,000. However, as before, this can only be considered the roughest of estimates. Regardless of this increase, Clark cogently argues in "The Backwoods Society of Upper Canada" that throughout the pre-1812 period, life in the towns of the colony had very little to do with that in the back country. However, a number of travellers noted the importance of the back country trade in the economic growth and prosperity of Kingston and Niagara. And certainly, on the evidence

of the advertisements that appeared in the local papers, the contact between Kingston, Niagara, and York and their respective hinterlands was gradually increasing before the War of 1812. See *Kingston Gazette* and *Upper Canada Gazette*, 1810–12; Smith, *A Geographical View*; Weld, *Travels*; Craig, *Upper Canada*.

CHAPTER TWO

1 *House of Assembly*, 18 September 1792, 1–2.
2 Ibid., 2.
3 Cartwright to Todd, 21 October 1792, Cartwright Papers, QUA. Unless otherwise noted, all Cartwright correspondence cited is in this collection.
4 The history of the early settlement of Upper Canada and particularly of British policies with regards to land and aid has been ably set out by Gates, *Land Policies of Upper Canada*, and Craig, *Upper Canada*. Policies fluctuated considerably over the early years. The continual problem of identifying legitimate loyalist claims was further complicated by inadequate registration and surveying techniques. Inevitably these problems generated considerable dissatisfaction and discontent, which after the turn of the century led to popular support for Justice Thorpe and his associates. See chap. 3.
5 There were frequent advertisements in the colonial press for both potash and pearl ash and the Assembly made specific provisions for subsidizing the growing of hemp. See for example *Upper Canada Gazette*, 22 June 1802; 22 February 1806; *House of Assembly*, 26 May 1801, 276; 16 March 1808. For a general discussion of the benefits Upper Canadians received see Craig, *Upper Canada*, 5–6.
6 Howard Temperley, "Frontierism, Capitalism and the American Loyalists in Canada." Temperley argues that the Turnean model of frontier development does not apply to Upper Canada, for the continuous financial support afforded to residents and the annual injection of capital significantly affected colonial development and accelerated the process of economic and social differentiation in the evolution of a hierarchical society.
7 [Cartwright], *Letters of an American Loyalist*, no. IX.
8 *Kingston Gazette*, 9 June 1812. Amelia Harris recalled that the militia "used to meet one day in the year for Company exercise" and there was also always a general muster on the king's birthday. "Reminiscences of Amelia Harris," in *Loyalist Narratives*, 109–48, 126. Reports of the celebrations which appeared annually in the local newspapers invariably included a list of the toasts given at the formal dinner and sometimes lists of some of the prominent residents in attendance.
9 Potter, *The Liberty We Seek*, 92. The historiography of the American

Revolution and of the loyalists' part in it is extensive. In addition to Potter see among others Bailyn, *Ideological Origins of the American Revolution*; Pauline Maier, *From Resistance to Revolution*; William Nelson, *The American Tory*; Richard Calhoon, *The Loyalists in Revolutionary America*; Richard Bushman, *From Puritan to Yankee*; Alan Heimert, *Religion and the American Mind*.

10 *House of Assembly*, 9 June 1800, 131; 8 July 1793, 41. The stylized rhetoric used in addressing the king or in referring to him publicly had almost a rote formula which the colonists seemed to consciously use. In time of perceived peril, or on special occasions, the standard rhetoric was somewhat embellished. The discussion here of colonial attitudes to the sovereign is an attempt to incorporate all the images and ideas frequently associated with the king. In most cases, though only one reference is given, the sentiments are repeated, in slightly different language and form, in the numerous addresses that were sent to England or in the proceedings of the legislature throughout the first twenty-five years of the colony's history.

11 *Upper Canada Gazette*, 9 March 1799; *House of Assembly*, 5 July 1796, 61. References to this perceived familial relationship between the king and his subjects were an integral part of the rhetoric of official addresses of the period.

12 *House of Assembly*, 5 July 1798, 61; 8 March 1810, 361.

13 *Legislative Council*, 3 June 1793, 32.

14 *Upper Canada Gazette*, 9 March 1799; See also *Legislative Council*, 9 July 1793, 32; *House of Assembly*, 8 July 1793, 41.

15 *Legislative Council*, 2 June 1794, 37; Rev. Alex. Sparks, *A Sermon Preached ... at Quebec, February* 1, 1804, 33–4; The theme of "remoteness" from Europe seemed to preoccupy many influential Upper Canadians. Almost all references to the Napoleonic Wars noted this fact, and often the colonists were almost apologetic. Yet at the same time, though clearly supportive of British efforts, the colonists were relieved and pleased that they could not be expected to take an active part in these endeavours.

16 *House of Assembly*, 3 June 1793, 24. The *Upper Canada Gazette* was particularly careful to keep its readers informed of British victories. This was not always the case with the two Niagara papers, the *Canada Constellation* and the *Niagara Herald*, though they did always include brief announcements of major British victories. This is not to say that influential Upper Canadians in Kingston and Niagara were not interested in and concerned about the European war. However, it is likely that all Upper Canadians received most of their news of the battles from American newspapers. The general colonial interest in European affairs and particularly in the war with France is also evident in private

correspondence where they received considerable attention. For example, at the turn of the century, Cartwright and Hamilton occasionally discussed international affairs and the implication of various European developments for their own businesses. See Cartwright Papers, QUA, particularly Cartwright to Hamilton, 16 October 1799; Cartwright to Strachan, 11 March 1804, and throughout May 1807; Cartwright to Todd and other business associates. Frequent references also appear in the Strachan papers, PAO.

17 *Upper Canada Gazette*, 18 May 1799, ironically, a report taken from the *Gazette of the United States*; *Legislative Council*, 30 March 1810, 82.

18 *Upper Canada Gazette*, 10 November 1798; 5 January 1799. The editor wrote in 1798 that "we have once more the satisfaction of announcing ... the pleasing intelligence of the defeat of the French fleet, an event which if true, we hope will have a tendency to humble that vile, detestable and tyrannical nation, the French republic."

19 Ibid., 9 March 1799; 30 December 1807; 18 May 1799.

20 Jacob Mountain, *Thanksgiving Sermon, January* 10, 1799, 18.

21 *House of Assembly*, 31 May 1802, 254.

22 Sparks, *A Sermon*, 12; *House of Assembly*, 9 February 1804, 419.

23 *Legislative Council*, 30 March 1810, 82.

24 *House of Assembly*, 3 June 1794, 38.

25 Ibid., 29 June 1799, 123; *Legislative Council*, 2 June 1794, 37; *House of Assembly*, 13 June 1799, 102; *Legislative Council*, 9 February 1804, 205.

26 *Legislative Council*, 9 July 1793, 82.

27 Ibid., 3 March 1810, 361. Some of the best examples of the highly stylized rhetoric used in addressing the king can be found in Strachan, *Discourse on the Character of King George the Third*; [Cartwright], *Letters of an American Loyalist*; *A Letter to the Right Honourable Lord Castlereagh*.

28 *House of Assembly*, 29 June 1799, 123.

29 [Cartwright], *Letters of an American Loyalist*, no. IX.

30 *A Letter to Lord Castlereagh*, 12–13.

31 *House of Assembly*, 7 June 1800, 131. The recognition of the importance of the constitution by the leaders of the colony was not restricted to the formal addresses by government or to a few sermons and pamphlets. Individual Upper Canadians also made frequent references to it in their private correspondence. Cartwright wrote to Sir John Johnson, 12 December 1797, that "the establishment of British Laws and Form of Government was most advantageous to the state," and as shall be seen its implementation was of constant concern to various leaders. See also his letters to Isaac Todd; Craig, *Upper Canada*, 20–65; Wilson, *Robert Hamilton*, 101.

32 *Upper Canada Gazette*, 30 August 1806; *House of Assembly*, 6 June 1800, 129.

33 The idea of society being a compact was explicitly set out by many of the leaders of the colony. In an address to the jury of the Home District, the chief justice, 2 November 1799, spoke of "the origin and object of good governments." According to the editor of the *Upper Canada Gazette,* he "showed the nature of the social compact and how necessary it is for the happiness of man." This concept was part of the ideology that many prominent Upper Canadians had brought with them to the colony. See Janice Potter, *The Liberty We Seek*; Wilson, *Robert Hamilton*; "Richard Cartwright," *DCB*, 4; Wise, "Colonial Attitudes."

34 *House of Assembly*, 8 March 1808, 255; *Upper Canada Gazette*, 11 July 1793.

35 *House of Assembly*, 3 June 1793, 24; 2 June 1794, 38; *Upper Canada Gazette*, 11 July 1793.

36 *Upper Canada Gazette*, 2 August 1800.

37 *House of Assembly*, 11 October 1792, 118; 5 March 1803, 410.

38 Ibid., 13 June 1794, 139.

39 Perhaps the best example of this is Sir Isaac Brock, who throughout his tenure in Upper Canada was continuously agitating for a more favourable posting. Matilda Edgar, *Ten Years of Upper Canada in Peace and War*. Brock was not alone in this, however. Sir Francis Gore spent much of his tenure as lieutenant governor on leave in England; Peter Russell, General Hunter, and Alexander Grant were all well past their prime and did not seem to welcome their appointments. Craig, *Upper Canada*, 42–3.

40 Cartwright to Todd, 1 October 1794. See also Cartwright to Hunter, 23 August 1799, in which Cartwright specifically commented that many Upper Canadians had originally chosen this area in preference to Nova Scotia. Cartwright was not the only one in this position. Thomas Markland, Robert Macaulay, John Kirby, Lawrence Herchmer, all of Kingston, Joel Stone of Brockville, and a host of others had for any number of reasons chosen Upper Canada over Quebec and in some cases North America over Britain or the West Indies. *DCB*, 6; Akenson, *The Irish in Ontario*; Wilson, *Robert Hamilton*.

41 Cartwright to Hunter, 23 August 1799.

42 Cartwright and Hamilton, Speech on the Judicature Act, 1794; Cartwright to Todd, 21 October 1792. Hamilton and a number of the early community leaders shared this viewpoint. Wilson, *Robert Hamilton*, 105–25; Craig, *Upper Canada*, 31–2.

43 Memorandum of Simcoe to Dundas, 30 June 1791, *Simcoe Papers*, 1: 27.

44 Simcoe to Dundas, 16 September 1793, *Simcoe Papers*, 2: 55. For further details of Simcoe's plans for the colony, see S.R. Mealing, "The En-

thusiasms of John Graves Simcoe," *Historic Essays on Upper Canada*, ed. J.K. Johnson, 302–16; Craig, *Upper Canada*, chap. 1.

45 Cartwright to Todd, 1 October 1794. Similar sentiments were expressed in Cartwright to Todd, 14 October 1793, and were shared by Robert Hamilton and others. Wilson, *Robert Hamilton*.

46 Cartwright to Todd, 14 October 1793.

47 Cartwright and Hamilton, Speech on the Judicature Act.

48 Cartwright to Todd, 1 October 1794. Local leaders were also opposed to Simcoe's commercial policies. Wilson, *Robert Hamilton*, 112–27; Craig, *Upper Canada*, 31–2.

49 Simcoe to Dundas, 16 September 1793, *Simcoe Papers*, 2: 53, 256.

50 Cartwright to Todd, 1 October 1794. As Wilson notes in *Robert Hamilton*, "Todd was the eyes and ears of the major Upper Canadian merchants in London," but Simcoe failed to recognize his influence or that of the local merchants on the political as well as economic development of the colony.

51 Cartwright to Todd, 1 October 1794.

52 Cartwright and Hamilton's relationship with both Hunter and Gore certainly developed beyond the point of a basic political association. Cartwright admired Hunter a great deal and on the latter's death he wrote to his son James in Quebec, 5 July 1805, "as Governor we shall never get one more able or more willing to promote the welfare of the Province." Cartwright corresponded regularly with Hunter, Gore, and Justice Alcock and frequently his letters included specific suggestions for new policies. By the time that Gore arrived in the colony in 1807, Cartwright and Hamilton's positions were well established, and they were two of the older and most respected members of Upper Canadian society. A common response to the Thorpe affair undoubtedly cemented their relationships. For further discussion of the political ideas of Cartwright and Hamilton, and their changing relations with the leaders in York, see Wilson, *Robert Hamilton*; Craig, *Upper Canada*; "Richard Cartwright," *DCB*, 4.

CHAPTER THREE

1 Richard Cartwright to James Cartwright, 23 October 1805, Cartwright Papers, Port Hope Collection, QUA.

2 Wise, "Colonial Attitudes," 22.

3 *Kingston Gazette*, 5 February 1811.

4 Weld, *Travels*, 2: 90; Hansen and Brebner, *Mingling of Peoples*, 66.

5 Michael Smith, *A Geographical View*, 82; Cartwright to Hunter, 23 August 1799.

6 To facilitate this contact, ferries joined both Kingston and Niagara to contiguous American communities. See references in *Upper Canada Gazette*, particularly 19 April 1797, and numerous travellers' accounts including John Lambert, *Travels through Canada and the United States*, 268–9; John Melish, *Travels through the United States of America*, 539; La Rochfoucault Liancourt, *Travels in Canada*, 77. See also Stephen Roberts, "Imperial Policy, Provincial Administration and Defences in Upper Canada," for a discussion of the impact of travel time on British policy.

7 Robert Gourlay, *Statistical Account of Upper Canada*, 115; Liancourt, *Travels*, 44. Rev. John Stuart kept up a regular correspondence with friends in the United States. Stuart to Rev. White, Misc. Ms., PAO. See also among others Joel Stone Papers, Solomon Jones Papers, QUA; Wilson, *Robert Hamilton*.

8 D'Arcy Boulton, *A Sketch of His Majesty's Province of Upper Canada*, 32.

9 The St Lawrence-Great Lakes system was of primary importance to residents on both sides of the border until well after the War of 1812. See Donald Creighton, *The Empire of the St. Lawrence*; Craig, *Upper Canada*; Wilson, *Robert Hamilton*. For customs records of the Kingston area, see RG 16, 133, Alex. Hagerman Collection, Collection of Customs, PAC; Stone Papers, Accounts 1803–9, QUA.

10 Cartwright to George Davison and Co., 11 November 1797, stressed that free trade was essential. Both Lambert, *Travels*, 239, and Melish, *Travels*, 539, noted that trade with New York flourished in these early years, and certainly the Cartwright correspondence, QUA; the Baldwin Papers, particularly the letters of Quetton St. George, TPL and PAO; Hamilton correspondence cited in Wilson, *Robert Hamilton*, 101–27; and advertisements in the local newspapers all attest to the importance of American trade. Even at the personal level, Upper Canadians depended on American peddlers for many of their goods. See Richardson Wright, *Hawkers and Walkers in Early America*; Brian Osborne, "Trading on the Frontier."

11 Richard A. Preston, *Kingston before the War of 1812*, xxiii.

12 In part this can be inferred from the sources available to indigenous editors after an Upper Canadian press emerged in 1793. In addition, the letters in the Cartwright Papers, QUA and the Strachan Papers, PAO, make numerous and specific references to articles appearing in American newspapers.

13 For a complete breakdown of news content and sources of the *Kingston Gazette* between 1810 and 1815, see Jane Errington, "Friend and Foe: Kingston Elite and the War of 1812."

14 *Upper Canada Gazette*, 4 July 1807. For a complete listing, discussion and analysis of federalist newspapers and their importance to colonial

editors, see Errington, "The Eagle, the Lion and Upper Canada," appendix and bibliographic note.

15 For a cogent discussion of the relationship between the press and the community on the frontier in an American colonial setting, see Robert Weir, "The Role of the Newspaper Press in the Southern Colonies"; Sidney Korbe, *The Development of the Colonial Newspaper*; Richard Merritt, *Symbols of American Community*.

16 George Rawlyk, "The Federalist-Loyalist Alliance in New Brunswick, 1784–1815." See also Jane Errington and George Rawlyk, "The Federalist-Loyalist Alliance of Upper Canada."

17 *Upper Canada Gazette*, 9 November 1796.

18 *Kingston Gazette*, 9 September 1810. For a full discussion of the importance of the land and the farming to Upper Canadians, see Robert Fraser, "Like Eden in Her Summer Dress," though this thesis is primarily concerned with the postwar years.

19 *Kingston Gazette*, 29 March 1811.

20 *Upper Canada Gazette*, 29 March 1797. This consciousness of the similarity of Upper Canada and the northeastern United States was acknowledged time and again in the newspapers and in the correspondence of Upper Canadians and Americans. See also Ralph Brown, ed., *Mirrors of the Americas*.

21 Cartwright to Hunter, 23 August 1799.

22 *Niagara Herald*, 14 November 1801. See also 28 March 1800.

23 Cartwright to Hunter, 23 August 1799.

24 In "Role of the Newspaper Press," 131, Weir writes that though the individual's "direct access to the newspapers was undoubtedly small," the group "who received their news from the members of the first group was probably much larger ... the newspapers were almost certainly available in many taverns" where they were read aloud. See also Robert Merritt, "Public Opinion in Colonial America."

25 See for example *Upper Canada Gazette*, 29 March 1797; *Niagara Herald*, 28 February 1801; *Kingston Gazette*, 6 November 1810; 4 December 1810, a letter from *Agricola*; 25 January 1811, from the *Connecticut Courant*; 12 March 1811, from the *American Mercury*; 2, 19 May 1811.

26 *Kingston Gazette*, 10 December 1810.

27 Ibid., 2 May 1811; *Upper Canada Gazette*, 29 March 1797.

28 *Upper Canada Gazette*, 22 March 1797; 26 May 1810, from the *New York Spectator*; *Niagara Herald*, 28 February 1801; *Kingston Gazette*, 6 November 1810; 16 May 1811; 22 February 1806.

29 The first specific reference appeared in the *Upper Canada Gazette*, 15 March 1797. See also 29 March 1797; 15 November, 15 February, 1806.

30 *Kingston Gazette*, 16 May 1811. See also *Niagara Herald*, 13 February l802; *Upper Canada Gazette*, 19 November 1808.

31 *Kingston Gazette*, 6 November 1810.

32 Ibid., 6 November 1810; 2 November 1811; *Canada Constellation*, 4 January 1800.

33 See for example *Upper Canada Gazette*, 25 January 1797; 9 June 1810; 29 January 1812.

34 American attempts to combat smallpox and other diseases appeared frequently. See for example *Upper Canada Gazette*, 1 February 1797; 20 June 1801; *Niagara Herald*, 14 February 1801. There was also growing attention to drunkenness and the need to form temperance societies, a concern which was not actually picked up in Upper Canada until well after the War of 1812. See for example *Kingston Gazette*, 18 December 1811, "Thoughts on a Public House from New York"; *Upper Canada Gazette*, 11 November, 16 December 1797.

35 See for example *Niagara Herald*, 4 April 1801; 16 January, 13 February, 1802.

36 *Upper Canada Gazette*, 22 March 1797; *Kingston Gazette*, 28 February 1811; *Niagara Herald*, 4 April 1801; 13 February 1802.

37 *Kingston Gazette*, 7 May 1811.

38 Ibid., 1, 15 January 1811. The debate started 4 December 1810 and continued until 23 January 1811.

39 *Upper Canada Gazette*, 9 November 1796.

40 *Kingston Gazette*, 29 January 1811.

41 *Upper Canada Gazette*, 1 November 1796; 14 September 1799.

42 Ibid., 14 September 1799. The *Upper Canada Gazette* provided only a broad outline of the political controversy. It was the *Canada Constellation* and the *Niagara Herald* that gave the colonists some specific analysis of the election. For example, the *Constellation* reported the growing opposition of the republicans to the attorney general's proposed Sedition Act (29 September 1799). A year later, the *Herald* told its readers of the quandary the federalists had found themselves in with respect to Aaron Burr (6 March 1801, from the *Mercantile Advertiser*). In addition, Upper Canadians in the Niagara region learned of the problems of the electoral system, which appeared to favour the republicans. See *Niagara Herald*, 21, 28 February, 3 March 1801; *Upper Canada Gazette*, 30 August 1800, from the *New York Herald* of 20 July 1800.

43 *Upper Canada Gazette*, 7 February 1801.

44 Strachan to James Brown, 31 March 1801, John Strachan Papers, PAO. All other citations from Strachan's letters are taken from this collection unless otherwise noted.

45 Strachan to Brown, 9 October 1808. See also a letter to Brown, 21 October 1809.

46 Strachan to Brown, 21 October 1809; 20 October 1807; 27 October 1803.

47 For a full discussion of how this became an integral part of the imperialists' ideological defence against the United States, see Carl Berger, *The Sense of Power*.

48 *Kingston Gazette*, 21 May 1811.

49 Ibid., 23 April 1811. See also Strachan's letter to the *Kingston Gazette*, writing as "Reckoner," 3 September 1811. Strachan had already discussed this issue with Brown in a letter, 21 October 1809. The effects produced by "licentious liberty," he wrote, were evident in the "frequency of their elections" which "keeps them at a continual boil." Generally, Strachan believed that British practices were far superior.

50 *Niagara Herald*, 21 February 1801, from an unspecified American paper.

51 *Upper Canada Gazette*, 11 January 1800; 3 August 1800, from the *New York Gazette*; 20 July 1800; *Niagara Herald*, 21 February 1801.

52 *Niagara Herald*, 28 February 1801.

53 Ibid., 13 June, 1801; 28 February 1801; Linda Kerber, *Federalists in Dissent*, 123. For a detailed discussion of federalist reaction to the 1800 election, see also David Hackett Fischer, *The Revolution in American Conservatism*.

54 *Kingston Gazette*, 31 October 1812.

55 Strachan to Brown, 20 October 1807. See also introductory comments in Strachan's *A Discourse on the Character of King George the Third*.

56 *Kingston Gazette*, 5 February, 29 January 1811.

57 The Upper Canadian press included many reports of political scandal and violent crime in the United States. Among other things colonists seemed to be intrigued by witchcraft (*Upper Canada Gazette*, 4 August 1804; *Canada Constellation*, 23 November 1799) and by slavery (*Canada Constellation*, 27 September 1799; 29 January 1802; *Upper Canada Gazette*, 9 November 1811). And like our press today, there were numerous accounts of "horrid murder" (*Canada Constellation*, 5 July 1799; *Upper Canada Gazette*, 14 July 1798).

58 La Rochfoucault Liancourt, *Travels*, 60; E.A. Cruikshank, "Immigration from the United States into Canada," 275; John Maude, *Trip to Canada*, 60. Just before the War of 1812, Michael Smith concluded in *A Geographical View*, 101, that "the opinion of many in Upper Canada now is that the province ought to be conquered for the good of the inhabitants on both sides."

59 Cartwright to Hunter, 23 August 1799.

60 Wilson, *Robert Hamilton*, 102.

61 *Niagara Herald*, 7 November 1801.

62 Ibid., 13 March 1801, from Addison's *Spectator*.

63 *To the Electors of the County of Essex*, broadside, 1800, PAO; *Upper Canada*

Gazette, 15 March 1800, "To the Free and Independent Electors of the County of York" from "Cato"; *Niagara Herald*, 20 June 1801, "To the Electors of the East Riding of York" from a "Lincoln Elector"; *Upper Canada Gazette*, 15 March, 16 August 1800.

64 *Upper Canada Gazette*, 17 March 1804.

65 For a complete discussion and analysis of the Thorpe affair, see Walton, "An End to All Order."

66 *Upper Canada Gazette*, 26 January 1805.

67 Thorpe to Edward Cooke, 24 January 1806, quoted in Walton, "An End to All Order," 55–6. These included providing redress for Methodists in the colony, changing the land granting system, and controlling the revenue. ibid., 62.

68 Ibid., 67.

69 Ibid., 80, 86, 87. The term "party" was used frequently by colonial officials to describe the Thorpe group.

70 "Sketch of the Conduct of Justice Thorpe," found in the Cartwright Papers, QUA, composed by Cartwright and apparently revised by Justice Alcock and Lieutenant Governor Gore. Walton, "An End to All Order," 91.

71 *Letter to Lord Castlereagh*, 2; Gore to Windam, 13 March 1809, CO 42/349,59 quoted in Walton, "An End To all Order," 87.

72 Richard Cartwright to James Cartwright, 22 January 1807, Cartwright Papers, Port Hope Collection, QUA.

73 *Letter to Lord Castlereagh*, 2.

74 Walton, "An End to All Order," 112–88.

75 *Letter to Lord Castlereagh*, 2.

76 Gore to Windam, 13 March 1807, CO 42/341, 59, quoted in Walton, "An End to All Order," 87.

77 *Letter to Lord Castlereagh*, 2.

78 *House of Assembly*, 19 March 1810, 375–6.

79 *Upper Canada Gazette*, 27 June 1807.

80 [Cartwright], *Letters of an American Loyalist*, no. 1.

81 For a general discussion of religion and particularly various attitudes towards the Methodists, see G.S. French, *Parsons and Politics*; Preston, *Kingston before the War of 1812*; E. Firth, *The Town of York*, and two groundbreaking studies on colonial religion, Donald Matthews, *Religion in the Old South* and George Rawlyk, *New Light Letters and Songs*.

82 Cartwright, "Memorandum Respecting the State of the Episcopal Church in Upper Canada," presented to General Brock, Cartwright Papers (undated), QUA. See also comments by Strachan in his papers.

83 Strachan to Brown, 13 July 1806. See also 27 October 1803; Strachan to Solomon Jones, 16 March 1812, Solomon Jones Papers, QUA, and a number of articles by Strachan in the *Kingston Gazette* signed "Reckoner."

84 Cartwright to Collins, 1789. See also Cartwright to Henry Motz, 31

May 1790. Cartwright wrote to Hunter, 15 May 1805, that students who went to the United States "must of necessity imbibe in some degree prejudices unfavourable" to Upper Canada. See also Hartwell Bowsfield, "Upper Canada in the 1820's: Development of a Political Consciousness," chap. 2; J.L.H. Henderson, *John Strachan, 1778–1867.*

85 Robert Gourlay, *Statistical Account*, 246. See also Smith, *A Geographical View*, 61; C.E. Phillips, *The Development of Education in Canada*; G.W. Spragge, "Elementary Education in Upper Canada."

86 *Kingston Gazette*, 25 September 1810.

87 Richard Cockerell, *Thoughts on Education.* Strachan was also aware of this problem and in an attempt to help alleviate it wrote *A Concise Introduction to Mathematics.* See also letter from Strachan to Reid, 11 February 1812; Cartwright to Hunter, 5 May 1805; *Kingston Gazette*, 13 November 1810; Gourlay, *Statistical Account*, 246; Smith, *A Geographical View*, 61.

88 *Kingston Gazette*, 16 April 1811. The first announcement was made 9 April 1811. Barnabas Bidwell had arrived in Upper Canada in the winter of 1811. Four years earlier he been appointed attorney general of Massachusetts under a republican government. However, it seems that he was forced to flee the United States under a cloud, for charges were laid that he had embezzled party funds. See a letter of Simon Larned to Barnabas Bidwell, 25 March 1810, Bidwell Papers, QUA.

89 *Kingston Gazette*, 16, 23 April 1811.

CHAPTER FOUR

1 A.R.M. Lower, *Colony to Nation*, 1.

2 *Kingston Gazette*, 25 September 1810.

3 Preston, *Kingston before the War of 1812*, lxxxiv. Preston notes that there was a constant problem with desertions. See Mackenzie to Green, 8 September 1808, 247; Capt. J. Carnie to Green, 13 September 1803, 205. La Rochfoucault Liancourt remarked in *Travels*, 80, that there were particular problems in the Niagara area. See also Burt, *The United States, Great Britain and British North America*, 379–90. For a particular discussion of the later period see Peter Burroughs, "Tackling Army Desertion."

4 *Niagara Herald*, 9 September, 3 October 1801.

5 Ibid., 3 October 1801. Similar problems did exist in the Kingston region. With the boundary as yet unmarked, there was considerable controversy over Carleton Island and other islands in the St Lawrence. See Preston, *Kingston before the War of 1812*; Rev. John Stuart's reference to his son James concerning his runaway slaves finding refuge on the American side, 6 March 1802, Stuart Papers, PAO.

6 First mention of the problem appeared in the *Upper Canada Gazette*, 28

July 1798, when a proclamation was issued offering rewards for the capture of counterfeiters. See also *Kingston Gazette*, 2 October 1810.

7 Matilda Edgar, *General Brock*, 109. Smuggling was a problem which plagued Upper Canadian authorities for the first forty years of the colony's history and it was continually commented on by residents, visitors, and officials on both sides of the border. See for example *Upper Canada Gazette*, 10 July 1794; 6 September 1799; *Kingston Gazette*, 12 December 1810; Cartwright to Gore, 5 November 1808; La Rochfoucault Liancourt, *Travels*, 62; Melish, *Travels*, 239; A.L. Burt, *The United States, Great Britain and British North America*.

8 Report of Hart Massey, 14 March 1809, quoted in William Flick, *The History of the State of New York*, 5:199.

9 *Kingston Gazette*, 25 September 1810. See also 6 November 1810; *Upper Canada Gazette*, 10 July 1794; 14 June 1797.

10 *Kingston Gazette*, 2 October, 6 November 1810.

11 Ibid., 6 November, 11 October 1810.

12 This problem of defining the international border plagued all of British North America from 1783 until well into the 1820s. The *Upper Canada Gazette* reported the first commissioners' meetings, 2, 9 November 1796. However, a report, 2 March 1806, noted that the members of the House of Assembly were still concerned about the question of jurisdiction. See also *Kingston Gazette*, 6 November 1810.

13 See among others *Upper Canada Gazette*, 10 July 1792; 14 June 1797; *Kingston Gazette*, 25 September, 6 November 1810.

14 *Upper Canada Gazette*, 31 May 1799; 27 January 1798. For further examples, see chapter 2.

15 For a complete discussion of these events, see Burt, *The United States*; James Hannay, *History of the War of 1812*; Craig, *Upper Canada*; Egan Clifford, "The Origins of the War of 1812."

16 *Upper Canada Gazette*, 10 July 1794.

17 Cartwright to Todd, 1 October 1794. Prominent Upper Canadians followed closely the events of 1793 and 1794. Both Cartwright and Hamilton (and undoubtedly other merchants of the colony) were aware that it was essential for the continuance of their economic well-being that amicable relations be sustained along the border. See among other things Cartwright to Major Lockbridge, 10 October 1794, in which Cartwright commented that "some weeks ago [we] expected to have been ere now at war with our neighbours the States." The *Upper Canada Gazette* also provided its readers with accounts of the various official attempts to resolve the points at issue. Starting in April 1793, Roy included reports of American negotiations with the Indians on the frontier and diplomatic relations between the American and British governments.

18 Cartwright to Todd, 1 October 1794.

19 Richard Hofstadter, *The Idea of a Party System*, 90; Kerber, *Federalists in Dissent*, 33. See also Richard Buel, *Securing the Revolution*; James Banner, *To The Hartford Convention*; Lance Banning, *The Jeffersonian Persuasion* for detailed accounts of the American response to the French Revolution and its effects on the political life of the nation.

20 *Upper Canada Gazette*, 18 June 1801.

21 Ibid., 18 May 1799, from the *Gazette of the United States*.

22 Ibid., 28 December 1796; 1 February 1797; See also 15 March, 3 May, 28 June 1797.

23 Ibid., 4 October, 9 December 1797. See also 28 June 1797, from an unnamed American paper; 5 July 1797, from a report from Boston; 25 August 1798, in which a report from Washington urged American merchants to arm themselves against French privateers.

24 Ibid., 4 August 1798.

25 Ibid., 22 December 1798, from a speech of J. Trumbull to the legislature of Connecticut, calling for the need to prepare the militia to fight against France; 14 September 1799, from a report of a meeting at Lancaster, Pa.

26 Ibid., 14 September 1799; 5 July 1797, from the *Gazette of the United States*.

27 Ibid., 14 September 1799.

28 *Niagara Herald*, 4 April, 3 October 1801; *Upper Canada Gazette*, 7 February 1801.

29 *House of Assembly*, 31 May 1802, 254; *Upper Canada Gazette*, 29 November 1806, from the *Mercantile Observer*.

30 *Upper Canada Gazette*, 1 August 1807. On 8 August 1807 the editor noted that this account taken from the *Boston Repository* "speaks in a language of reason, of patriotism and of truth."

31 Ibid., 15 August, 5 September, from the *Boston Palladium*, 10 October 1807.

32 Ibid., 10 October 1807, predicted that there would be no war, though on 8 August 1807 the paper had noted that the Americans were already beginning to make preparations. On 2 March 1808 a report from Washington claimed that the danger was past and suggested that the next step was war with France. A month later, Strachan wrote to Solomon Jones that "The alarm of war becomes louder and louder, but I am still at ease." 12 April 1808, Jones Papers, QUA. Strachan noted "the war-like preparations" in Kingston in a letter to John Macaulay (3 January 1808, Macaulay Papers, PAO) and that "the militia is in readiness in case Jonathan should attempt an invasion." In addition, William Jones wrote to his uncle, Solomon Jones, from Detroit, "war is almost a sure thing ... the *Whig* and the *Tory* parties of 76 and 77

were never more violent than are the Democrats and Federal Factions here now." 27 July 1809, Jones Papers, QUA.

33 Cartwright to Gore, 2 April 1807. It was believed that even in the Kingston area, in what had traditionally been the heartland of British support, some were supporting Thorpe. This fear was explicitly acknowledged in the address of the *House of Assembly*, 10 March 1810.

34 Cartwright, 15 December 1807, Speech to the Militia of the County of Frontenac, Cartwright Papers.

35 [Cartwright], *Letters from an American Loyalist*, no. 1. Other replies to the Jackson pamphlet included the anonymous *Letter to the Right Honourable Lord Castlereagh* (1810) (though internal evidence suggests that this may have been written at least in part by Cartwright) and Strachan's *A Discourse on the Character of King George the Third*. In addition, the colonial press frequently printed articles on the importance of the British connection to Upper Canadians.

36 Cartwright, Speech to the Militia, 1807.

37 *Upper Canada Gazette*, 12 February 1808.

38 Ibid., 12, 20 February 1808, taken from the *Boston Palladium*. This fear that France was gradually gaining control of the national administration in the United States increased as relations between the United States and Great Britain deteriorated. See for example ibid., 20 January, 2 March 1808.

39 Ibid., 20 January 1808, from the *New York Evening Post*. See also 12 February 1808. The *Upper Canada Gazette* from 5 August 1807 relied almost completely on federalist reports for its news of the deepening crisis in British-American relations. And in all instances, these reports called on the American government to use reason and not provoke a war. The federalist reports pointed out to Upper Canadians that the administration of the United States was hostile to Great Britain and partial to the French (1 January 1808, from the *New York Evening Post*) and that if America went to war, they could not hope to win (20 February, 15 August 1807). Even John Strachan, in a letter to Brown, 20 October 1807, wrote that "the administration of the United States is now evidently in the French interest. The Jeffersonian party or republicans, as they call themselves have always shown themselves hostile to Britain." See also Strachan to Brown, 9 October 1808.

40 *Upper Canada Gazette*, 2 March 1808.

41 Ibid., 20 January 1808, report from the *New York Evening Post*, on a report from Washington; 23 December 1807.

42 Ibid., 12 February 1808.

43 Ibid., 22 February 1809.

44 Ibid., 27 August 1809, from the *Baltimore Federal Republican*. See also a letter from J. McDonell to Quetton St. George, 23 January 1808,

Baldwin Papers, PAO; reports from the *Albany Gazette*, 23 December 1807, that told of petitions against the war presented by the townspeople of New England.

45 *Upper Canada Gazette*, 5 April 1808, letter to the governor of Massachusetts from James Sullivan; 8 February 1809.

46 On 22 February 1809 the *Upper Canada Gazette* included reports from Rhode Island that the custom houses there were closed and that the militia refused to enforce the embargo. *A Memorial from the State of Massachusetts to the Senate and House of Representatives* was published in full, 22, 29 March 1809. On 1 January 1809 it was reported that the governor of Delaware had refused to call out the militia. On 30 April 1808 it was predicted that there would be open resistance to the embargo and as late as 27 August 1808 it was reported that at Oswego there was considerable conflict over its enforcement. It was not only through the newspapers, however, that Upper Canadians followed federalist opposition to the policies of the republican administration. A number of federalist pamphlets were also available north of the border as evidenced in advertisements in the colonial press. These included *The New Crisis* by an "Old Whig"; *A Letter from the Honourable John Quincy Adams to the Honourable Harrison Otis*; John Lovell, *Thoughts upon the Conduct of Our Administration in Relation to both Great Britain and France*; Lovell, *Mr Madison's War*; Lovell, *Peace Without Dishonour, War Without Hope*; *Honourable Timothy Pickering's Speech in the Senate*, 13 November 1808. In these pamphlets and in a host of others available in the colony, the federalists vehemently attacked the policies of their government.

47 *Kingston Gazette*, 29 January 1811.

48 *Upper Canada Gazette*, 30 April 1808. The editor wrote, "we must feelingly deprecate a rupture with the American government," but he predicted that the United States would be the only loser. Yet a petition from the inhabitants of Prince Edward County (*House of Assembly*, 15 March 1808, 270–2) noted the hardships that Upper Canadian farmers and merchants were experiencing. Quetton St.George noted that he considered smuggling his goods across the lake (St.George to Andrew McGill, 18 January 1808, Baldwin Papers, TPL), for he found it almost impossible to get supplies by the regular routes; see also 21 January 1808, Charles Fortum to St. George. A Mr Walton in Schenectady, 23 January 1808, noted that he expected to use sleighs to get his goods across the lake. Baldwin Papers, PAO.

49 *Upper Canada Gazette*, 30 April 1808.

50 Ibid., 12 February 1808, from an unnamed American paper.

51 Ibid., 2 March 1808, reported from Washington; 30 July 1808.

52 Ibid., 12 February 1808. As Strachan wrote to Brown (21 October

1809), Upper Canadians were "in a state of suspense" for "their neigh-bours have so little honour." He noted that the "ruling class was still hostile to Britain" though the northern states were against war. Despite this uncertainty, regular contact on a personal level continued through out the period. On 1 July 1809 Solomon Jones attended the launching of a new ship at Ogdensburg and Strachan wrote to him, 21 May 1809, that "I congratulate you on the prospect of peace with our neighbours; we are too near the frontier to make war agreeable." For further ref-erences to this need to maintain harmony, see *Kingston Gazette*, October 1810, for an ongoing discussion between "A Loyalist" believed to be Strachan, and "A Friend of Peace," Barnabas Bidwell.

53 *Kingston Gazette*, 28 January 1812.

54 *House of Assembly*, 3 February 1812, 4–5.

55 *Kingston Gazette*, 5 March 1811, from the *Salem Gazette*, on a report from Washington. In the *Kingston Gazette*, detailed proceedings of the congressional debates started in 23 April 1811 and continued through-out the next thirteen months, appearing in almost every issue. The *Upper Canada Gazette* also provided its readers with extensive coverage of the debates.

56 *Kingston Gazette*, 19 November 1811. On 12 December 1811 Miles noted that the *Chesapeake* affair had been resolved and he hoped that relations between the two principals would improve. Yet in this same issue it was observed that though the British were anxious for a reconciliation, the American government did not seem to be. *Kingston Gazette*, 4 June – 11 November 1811. It was regarded as an "unfortunate action" (4 June 1811) when the *President* and the *Little Belt* exchanged fire. The Americans thought that the British captain had been impressing Amer-ican nationals and the British officer believed that he was under attack. The first mention of the affair in the *York Gazette* was on 13 June 1811, when the editor commented briefly on "this unpleasant occurrence."

57 See Craig, *Upper Canada*, 72.

58 Melish, *Travels through the United States*, 485. Travellers and residents both commented on this. By 1810 the leaders of the colony believed that *they* (the American settlers) were not sufficiently attached to *our* cause. This "them-us" point of view prevailed until well after the War of 1812. In 1810 John Macaulay wrote to his friend John Bethune that "evil principles are beginning rapidly to find their way into this country and to corrupt the loyalty of some of the best of our subjects." 21 December 1810, Macaulay Papers, PAO.

59 *Kingston Gazette*, 12 May 1812, in a letter to the editor from "John Bull."

60 Ibid., reprinted in the *York Gazette*; 4 February 1812. The propaganda campaign initiated by the leaders of Upper Canada is ably discussed

in R. Bowler, "Propaganda in Upper Canada during the War of 1812." Bowler argues that the British propaganda "was more often than not the result of organized effort ... its techniques, within the limitations of the period, were of some sophistication"(27). Some residents realized the potential of a newspaper campaign. Cartwright, writing as "Falkland," contributed a number of articles to the *Kingston Gazette* obviously intended to arouse the general populace. John Strachan, in a letter to the governor general of British North America, 1 October 1812, was explicit about the matter: "It appears to me that the press might be rendered exceedingly useful at this crisis if properly conducted, not only in confirming the allegiance of the people, but in giving additional force to such measures as the Government might think it necessary to take for the defence of the Canadas and the annoyance of the enemy."

61 *Kingston Gazette*, 28 January 1812.

62 Ibid., 18 February 1812, from the *York Gazette*; 2 February 1812, "Address to the Inhabitants of Upper Canada" from "Loyalist." It has never been determined who "Loyalist" was, but it may well have been Strachan, for a letter under that pen-name had appeared a year earlier in the *Kingston Gazette*, in defence of Strachan's *Discourse*, and the Macaulay correspondence suggests that this had been written by Strachan. See Macaulay's discussions with John Bethune and John Beverley Robinson, 16 November, 21, 25 December 1810; 15 February 1811, PAO.

63 David Osgood, *A Solemn Protest against the Late Declaration of War*, 16. Osgood continued, "the law of our rulers calls us to rob and slaughter our fellow-men, our brethren, with whom we have ties of blood, of interest, of manners, of speech or opinion and of religion." This assumption that the American federalists were the most civilized group in the United States was a constant refrain in the colonial press for the next three years.

64 *Kingston Gazette*, 26 May 1812. The belief that any war would seriously harm their businesses emerged again and again in the American reports that the Upper Canadian editors picked up during this period. To the leaders of the colony, such reasoning must have been quite persuasive, for many of them could appreciate and sympathize with it.

65 Ibid., 26 May 1812, letter to Independent Electors from "John Bull"; 18 February 1812; *York Gazette*, 4 March 1812, from the *Boston Repository*; Osgood, *A Solemn Protest*, 16. Upper Canadians read federalist pamphlets which claimed that "it is in effect a French War and not an American one." *Mr Madison's War*, 7. The editor of the *York Gazette*, 4 March 1812, noted that "Federalists were every where warned to take care how they opened their mouths."

66 *Kingston Gazette*, 18 February 1812. Indeed, it was predicted by Osgood

in *A Solemn Protest*, 16, that all must now expect civil war for this was Mr Madison's war. See also letter of "John Bull," *Kingston Gazette*, 12 May 1812.

67 *Kingston Gazette*, 28 January, 18 February, 12 May 1812, from "John Bull."

68 Ibid., 28 January 1812.

69 Ibid., 26 May 1812, letter to Independent Electors from "John Bull."

70 Ibid., 11 February, 30 June, 18 February 1812. A number of articles by "Falkland" also appeared in the *York Gazette*. For the most part, these were shortened versions of his *Letters of an American Loyalist* of 1810.

71 *Kingston Gazette*, 11 February, 12 May 1812, letters to the editor from "Falkland." Both letters stressed that "the advantages are preponderate on our side when we throw into the scale the assured co-operation and support of the best disciplined troops in the world, eager for an opportunity to emulate the brilliant exploits of their fellow soldiers in Spain and Portugal." See also a letter from "Falkland," 3 March 1812.

72 Ibid., 3 March, 18 February 1812.

73 *House of Assembly*, 25 February 1812, 4.

74 *York Gazette*, 4 February 1812 and on. See also *Kingston Gazette*, 18, 25 February 1812. Reports in both the *Kingston Gazette* and the *York Gazette* were reminiscent of the coverage given to the *Chesapeake* affair in 1807–9. Rarely did a week go by from the autumn of 1811 to the end of 1812 without federalist reports of the worsening situation, complete with their condemnation of the policies of the American government. See for example *Kingston Gazette*, 5 May 1812, from a report in the *National Intelligencer*; 26 May 1812; *York Gazette*, 4 March, 22 April, 4 July 1812. In this last report the editor wrote that the French were "the polluting touch which has sealed the willing eyes of America's great rulers from seeing the deformity of the rash step she had taken." See also Bowler, "Propaganda."

75 From the *Boston Gazette*. The announcement in the *York Gazette*, 28 July 1812, also from Boston, concluded that it was "totally unnecessary, inexpedient and impolitic."

76 *Kingston Gazette*, 30 June 1812, from the *Albany Gazette*.

77 Ibid., 14 July 1812. See also *York Gazette*, 11 July 1812. The garrison at Niagara apparently received the news at the end of June.

78 Certainly Stephen Miles continued to rely on American sources. See Errington, "Friends and Foes."

79 *York Gazette*, 28 July 1812.

80 See Stephen Mecredy, "Some Military Aspects of Kingston's Development during the War of 1812." In addition to the Mecredy thesis, there are a number of general texts which have provided much of the

background for this discussion. See Burt, *The United States*; Hannay, *History of the War of 1812*; Pierre Berton, *The Invasion of Canada* and *Flames Across the Border*; Morris Zaslow, ed., *The Defended Border*. Both Craig, *Upper Canada* and George F.G. Stanley, *The War of 1812*, also provide an extensive bibliography for the period.

81 *Kingston Gazette*, 14 July 1812. Not all agreed with these sentiments, however. Strachan advocated that the Upper Canadian forces should be aggressive. He wrote to John Richardson, "A successful attack instead of irritating the Federalists will produce the contrary effect by furnishing them with additional proofs of the incapacity of their present rulers ... A successful attack will dispirit the Democrats and ruin their whole plan of operations." And without an attack, Strachan believed that the Canadians would be disheartened. 30 September 1812.

82 Indeed, in the eastern district of the colony at least, individuals continued to move back and forth across the border with impunity. Solomon Jones seems to have crossed regularly and become "perfectly acquainted with the sentiments of various characters, military and civilian." 7 July 1812, Report to the Commanding Officer of Dundas, Jones Papers, QUA. Two months later Strachan charged that "there has been too much communication in your quarter." Strachan to Jones, 6 October 1812, Jones Papers, QUA.

83 *Kingston Gazette*, 14, 28 July 1812. See also *York Gazette*, 28 July 1812, for the same report and *Kingston Gazette*, 19 September 1812, extracts from the proclamation.

84 *Kingston Gazette*, 14 July 1812. In a speech to his constituents, *Kingston Gazette*, 28 July 1812, from the *Spirit of 76*, John Randolph declared that "it is war against the liberty and happiness of mankind." See also *Kingston Gazette*, 20 January, 9 March 1813, 27 July 1813, speeches of Mr Josiah Quincy; 22 March 1814, speeches of John Randolph; report in *York Gazette*, 29 August 1812, from New Hampshire which concluded that if they "could perceive the present war was JUST; if we could perceive that OUR RIGHTS and LIBERTIES required it," they would cooperate. Other state opposition was reported in *Kingston Gazette*, 28 July, 11 August 1812; *York Gazette*, 11 July 1812. Upper Canada also continued to receive a number of federalist pamphlets which vehemently condemned the actions of the American administration. These included, *Address to the Free and Independent People of Massachusetts*; Jacob Bigelow, *The War of the Gulls*; W. Phillips, *An Appeal to the Good Sense of the Democrats and the Public Spirit of the Federalists*. For a clear and much more comprehensive discussion of New York's response to the war, see Harvey Strum, "New York and the War of 1812."

85 *Kingston Gazette*, 14 July 1812, from the *Connecticut Courant*.

86 Ibid., 26 September 1812.

87 Ibid., 27 July 1813, part of Quincy's speech to the Senate of Massachusetts; 1 June 1813. See also *York Gazette* report from Boston (28 July 1812) which concluded, "we consider our country as now basely and ignominiously sold to the Tyrant and full destroyer of the World."

88 *Kingston Gazette*, 14 July 1812; Osgood, *A Solemn Protest*, 14–15. This assumption that the republicans were morally degenerate pervaded all of Upper Canadian and indeed federalist thinking during this period. Partly, it was believed that this resulted from their acceptance of the institution of slavery. One Upper Canadian wrote that "the heads" of the republican party "are the avowed patrons of slavery and dealers in human blood." *Kingston Gazette*, 28 January 1812. See also Strachan to Brown, 21 October 1809.

89 *Kingston Gazette*, 27 July 1813.

90 Ibid., 14 July 1812; *York Gazette*, 29 August 1812. This report concluded ironically that this had happened "in a land alleged to be the only one where true liberty exists, whose citizens boast that they are the 'freeest and most enlightened in the world'."

91 *Kingston Gazette*, 18 August 1812. The report referred to the beginning of an American "reign of terror." On 29 August 1812 it was reported that the Baltimore mob had profaned the Sabbath. Riots the following year in Buffalo only confirmed for many North American conservatives the evil effects of French influence. See also 23 January 1813.

92 Ibid., 18 August 1812.

93 *York Gazette*, 5, 12 December 1812.

94 *Kingston Gazette*, 26 September 1812, from the *Connecticut Courant*.

95 Ibid., 29 June 1813, from a report from Oswego.

96 Ibid., 28 July 1812, from the *Connecticut Herald*.

97 Ibid., 25 January 1814, from the *Albany Register*; 8 June 1813. See also 21 January 1815; Phillips, *An Appeal*, 14, who noted that "the Federalists from the beginning set themselves against the wayward and wicked measures of our government."

98 *Kingston Gazette*, 1 March 1814, from "a letter to a Gentleman in New York" from his "friend in Plattsburgh." These federalist attacks against specific members of the executive increased significantly as the war progressed. In addition to their attacks on Madison, they also began to censure the secretary of war. See for example 7 July, 3 August 1813, accusing the administration of graft and corruption; 5, 24 January, 15 February, 1 March 1814.

99 Ibid., 1 March, 5 June 1814. This report concluded that the Montreal disaster "overshadows all with gloom and wrings the heart of every American with the bitterness of anguish."

100 Ibid., 5 January 1814; 14 August 1813. See also 10 August 1813; 15

February 1814 for reports of American lack of confidence in their army.

101 Ibid., 15 February, 25 January 1814.

102 Ibid., 15 February, 22 July 1814, from a report from Georgetown, which concluded, "what is granted to defend our country, the sacred soil of our birth ... NOTHING."

103 Ibid., 24 October 1812, from a report from York. This was the very beginning of the creation of the myth of General Brock. On 29 August 1812 the *Kingston Gazette* gave a full account of Brock's capture of Detroit and reported "the man Brock" was "terrible to their imaginations." The rapidity of his movements, his unexpected appearance, his skilful and determined attack "appall'd and struck terror into their hearts." The *York Gazette*, 17, 24 October 1812, reported both the initial victory at Queenston Heights and Brock's funeral, complete with poetry, the eulogy, and a full description of the funeral procession. These were also included in the *Kingston Gazette*, 24, 31 October 1812, together with full coverage of his arrival at Kingston and York, 5, 12 September 1812. For a sensitive discussion of General Brock the hero, see Keith Walden, "Isaac Brock: Man and Myth."

104 *Kingston Gazette*, 18 August 1812, a report from General Proctor.

105 Ibid., 28 July 1812, Brock's speech from the throne to the legislature.

106 *York Gazette*, 10 November 1812, an Extra, concerning the landing at Fort Erie; *Kingston Gazette*, 20 November 1813. See also 6 April, 25 May, 1 June, 27 July, 13 November 1813.

107 *Kingston Gazette*, 27 November 1813.

108 Ibid., 20 April 1813. The society was founded by a group of influential residents of York and Kingston in March 1813. In the proceedings which officially launched the affair, it was stated that "the country is never more secure than when defended by its faithful and loyal and industrious inhabitants."

109 Ibid., 6 April 1813, a speech of Alan McLean, speaker of the House of Assembly, addressed to the president of Upper Canada.

110 Ibid., 14 July 1812, from the *Connecticut Courant*.

111 Ibid., 25 May 1813, from the *Quebec Gazette* from an open letter addressed to Madison. This identification of the Upper Canadian situation with that in Great Britain was made by both the colonists and the Americans. See Osgood, *A Solemn Protest*; Spark, *A Thanksgiving Sermon ... 1814*; Strachan, *A Sermon at York ... 1814*. This awareness of European events was also demonstrated by the considerable space that the York and Kingston editors gave to them during the war. For example, in the spring of 1813 long detailed reports appeared of activities on the Russian front. See *Kingston Gazette*, January-May 1813.

112 *Kingston Gazette*, 10 August 1813; 13 September 1814.

113 Ibid., 9 October 1813. "Falkland" introduced the report on the formation of this London society which he asserted must "surely inspire us with fresh motives for perseverance and all our energies in defense of our country."

114 Ibid., 14 July 1812, a letter to the editor from "Camillus"; 6 April 1813, a speech of the speaker of the House of Assembly. This belief was one of the central arguments that such men as Strachan put forward. In his *Sermon to the Legislature ...* 1812, 24–5, Strachan appealed to Upper Canadians to be "Christian soldiers." "Go forth then to battle, my Brethren, clothed in the Christian armour, our cause in just." He asserted that "our Heavenly Father will enable us to endure all the hardships." See also Strachan, *Sermon at York ...* 1814.

115 *Kingston Gazette*, 13 July 1813, from *Boston Gazette*. This comparison of the European and North American theatres of war is interesting for it extends the traditional French-Republican against British-Federalist-Upper Canadian analogy to include Russia.

116 Sparks, *A Thanksgiving Sermon ...* 1814, 8. Sparks continued, "Providence is on our side against a Horn of the Beast."

117 *Kingston Gazette*, 20 July 1813, from the *Boston Gazette*. This article concluded that "the fact that Upper Canadians have been able to repulse us is an indication of Divine Providence"; *Kingston Gazette*, 10 August 1813, from the *Utica Gazette*, which believed that God was on the side of Russia.

118 Ibid., 27 April 1813, reported from New York.

119 Ibid., 18 May 1814, from *Relph's Philadelphia Federal Gazette*; 15 February, 14 December 1814. This was a constant refrain of federalist protest in the United States. A report from Boston, 3 November 1814, charged that the government "will be able to squeeze out enough by hook or by crook to pay their own salaries; the public consideration is another affair."

120 *York Gazette*, 21 January 1815, taken from a speech of Cyrus King of Massachusetts. See also *Kingston Gazette*, 3 November, 14 December 1814.

121 The end of the war in Europe was heralded as a major triumph for Upper Canadians. The colonial government proclaimed a Day of Thanksgiving, *Kingston Gazette*, 11 May 1814, and a number of sermons were given and celebrations were held in honour of the occasion.

122 *York Gazette*, 25 February 1815; *Kingston Gazette*, 1, 8 April 1815.

123 *Kingston Gazette*, 5 June 1815.

124 Upper Canadians were clearly aware of the continuing discontent of the federalists. In the *York Gazette*, 8 February 1815, a report from the *New Hampshire Gazette*, 14 December 1814, told of the convening of the

Hartford Convention and wondered if the federalists would really secede. For a complete discussion of the demise of the federalists see Fischer, *Revolution in American Conservatism*, and Banner, *To the Hartford Convention*.

CHAPTER FIVE

1 John Howison, *Sketches of Upper Canada*, 77.
2 A.R.M. Lower, *Colony to Nation*, 197.
3 Howison, *Sketches*, 24, 40–1.
4 The development of roads and transportation services in Upper Canada after the war is graphically chronicled in the various advertisements that appeared in the colonial press. On 7 June 1817 the *Kingston Gazette* contained a notice that a steamship service was available from Quebec to Niagara, with stops at Ernest Town, New Castle, and York. On 31 March 1818 the Bay River Steam Boat Company announced the commencement of a service from Prescott to the Carrying Place and on 12 February 1819 it was stated that the steamboat *Frontenac* now travelled from Queenston to Montreal. In addition, advertisements in the *Kingston Gazette* between 1816 and 1818 told of the development of stage travel in the colony. See 6 July, 19 October, 30 November 1816; 18, 25 January, 9 December 1817. See also E.C. Guillet, *Pioneer Travel in Upper Canada*, 144; Craig, *Upper Canada*.
5 For example, *Kingston Gazette*, 13 June 1815, included a notice from James Chapman that he would provide regular service, three times a week, to Sacket's Harbour. On 7 June 1817 another advertisement appeared for a service by sail to the American port.
6 Alan Wilson, "The 1820's," *Colonists and Canadians*, ed. J.M.S. Careless, 144, notes that the population of Upper Canada was 90,000 in 1820; William Bell, *Hints to Emigrants*, 245, cites 200,000, a figure with which John Strachan in a report on emigration concurred. Strachan Papers, 1827, PAO. Charles Fothergill, *Reflections on the Value of British North America*, 34, suggested a population of 160,000 in 1825.
7 Scholars have given little attention to social life in the colony in the period. The local press chronicles, however, the rapid development of various types of schools, both public and private, the popularity of local theatre, dances, public lectures, and circuses, and a host of community of affairs. For a general discussion of this, see among others Glazebrook, *Life in Ontario*; Phillips, *Development of Education in Canada*; Guillet, *Early Life in Upper Canada*.
8 Clark, "The Backwoods Society of Upper Canada," *The Developing Canadian Community*, 69. For a brief discussion of the rise of reform in Upper Canada in the early years, see Richard Splane, *Social Welfare in*

Ontario; Patricia Malcolmson, "The Poor in Kingston, 1815–1850," *To Preserve and Defend*, ed. G. Tulchinsky, 281–97; Bindon, "Kingston: A Social History"; Susan Houston, "The Impetus to Reform."

9 Strachan to Bishop, 6 July 1816, noted that York had a population of 710 in 1815. In 1819 James Strachan, *A Visit to ... Upper Canada*, stated that it had increased to 1,058. Bell, *Hints to Emigrants*, 175, estimated that Kingston had 2,000 and York about 1,500 residents in 1824. Michael Cross, "The 1820's," *Colonists and Canadians*, ed. J.M.S. Careless, 133, cites 2,800 for York in 1830. John Goldie, *A Diary of a Journey through Upper Canada*, 18, found in 1819 that York was "superior" in society and culture. See also T.W. Acheson, "The Nature and Structure of York Commerce in the 1820's," *Historical Essays on Upper Canada*, ed. J.K. Johnson, 171–93.

10 Graeme Patterson writes in "Studies in Elections and Public Opinion," 504, that "there was no locus of power in Upper Canada." Instead, there were local compacts whose influence persisted into the 1830s. Patterson fails to consider, however, that decisions made in York did have an increasing impact on colonial affairs.

11 *DCB*, 6.

12 As in the early period, biographical information about prominent Upper Canadians in the postwar period is sadly sparse. There is a recent biography of John Beverley Robinson by Patrick Brode, *The Bone and the Sinew*. For other biographical material see Robert J. Burns, "The First Elite of Toronto"; Bowsfield, "Upper Canada in the 1820's"; *DCB*, 5, 6.

13 The correspondence between Strachan and his students and among the boys is extensive. See in particular Strachan Papers; John Beverley Robinson Papers; Macaulay Papers, PAO. See also David Mills, "The Concept of Loyalty"; Fraser, "Like Eden in her Summer Dress"; Bowsfield, "Upper Canada in the 1820s"; Brode, *The Bone and the Sinew*.

14 There is considerable dispute over what exactly the Family Compact was. Wise, "Origins of Anti-Americanism," 301, asserts that in both personnel and in beliefs, the Family Compact can be traced back to 1791 and the arrival of John Graves Simcoe. He equates the group with the ruling conservative elite which dominated colonial politics. After the war, Wise contends, "it was, in part, a coalition between a central bureaucracy and local conservative elites." "John Macaulay, A Tory for All Seasons," 186. The network, he continues, was based on a combination of political patronage and family and personal connections. The role of Strachan was very important to political life in the colony. However, the suggestion that the connection can be traced back to 1791 is not convincing. The Family Compact was virtually unknown even in the 1820s. Graeme H. Patterson, "The Myths of Responsible

Government and the Family Compact," 346. For further discussion of the problem, see Mills, "Concept of Loyalty"; R. Saunders, "What Was the Family Compact?" *Historical Essays on Upper Canada*, 122–39; Bowsfield, "Upper Canada in the 1820's"; Phillip Buckner, *The Transition to Responsible Government*, 72–8.

15 The growth of reform sentiment in Upper Canada is sometimes traced back to the activities of Justice Thorpe in 1808 and 1809. Dent, *The Story of the Upper Canadian Rebellions*. For the most part, however, historians link the reformers of the 1820s and 1830s with the activities of Robert Gourlay and with the elections of 1824 and 1828. See Aileen Dunham, *Political Unrest in Upper Canada*; Eric Jackson, "The Organization of the Upper Canadian Reformers," *Historical Essays*, 196–222; Bowsfield, "Upper Canada in the 1820's"; Paul Romney, "A Conservative Reformer in Upper Canada."

16 For a discussion of the usage of "country" and "court" in politics, see J.G.A. Popock, *The Machiavellian Moment*, 402–22. Popock notes that the "court" party was traditionally associated with patronage, dependence, and corruption. "Country" party was a term used by gentry and freeholders who saw themselves as free, independent, and virtuous. In the American context, the country/court division was often equated with the many against the few or by some with the republicans against the federalists. See Banning, "Jeffersonian Ideology Revisited"; Murrin, "The Great Inversion or Court versus Country."

17 *House of Assembly*, 7 February 1816, 171-2, the reply of the House to the Speech from the Throne.

CHAPTER SIX

1 Strachan, *A Sermon Preached at York on the* 3rd Day of June, Being the Day Appointed for General Thanksgiving, 1814, 22–3, 38, 34.

2 Strachan, "Reasons against Removing the Seat of Government," enclosed in a letter from John Beverley Robinson to Lord Bathurst, 20 February 1816, John Beverley Robinson Papers, PAO; *Observer*, 9 December 1825.

3 *House of Assembly*, 7 February 1817, 316; 20 March 1818, 562.

4 Ibid., 2 February 1821, 268.

5 *Kingston Chronicle*, 9 June 1820.

6 Ibid., 24 March 1820.

7 *House of Assembly*, 6 February 1816, 169; 4 February 1817, 312.

8 Ibid., 2 February 1816, 171.

9 *Kingston Chronicle*, 9 June 1820.

10 *House of Assembly*, 2 February 1821, 268; Strachan, "Reasons against Removing the Seat of Government," 35.

11 Charles Fothergill, *A Sketch of the State of Upper Canada*, 17.

12 *United Empire Loyalist*, 6 January 1827. This sense of overwhelming gratitude was particularly apparent in the colonial press in 1815 and 1816 and in the addresses to the king and the prince regent from the House of Assembly. See also *Report of the Loyal and Patriotic Society*; *A Form of Prayer and Thanksgiving ... 1815*; *General Union of All the British Provinces of North America*; Rev. Alex. Sparks, *A Sermon Preached in the Scotch Church ... Quebec*, 1814; Rev. J. Burns, *True Patriotism: A Sermon Preached in ... Stanford, Upper Canada*; Rev. J. Bethune, *A Sermon Preached at Brockville ... being a General Day of Thanksgiving*.

13 Strachan, *Sermon at York ... 1814*, 32. See also *United Empire Loyalist*, 5 January 1828, New Year's Address; *House of Assembly*, 2 February 1821, 268.

14 *Niagara Spectator*, 11 June 1818, from (ironically) the *American Monthly Review*.

15 Ibid.

16 Rev. T. Philips, *A Loyal Sermon preached on St. George's Day*, 1826, 7; *Observations on the Importance of the North American Colonies*, 17. This identification with Great Britain and with Englishmen in particular had been evident since before the War of 1812 and it clearly persisted well into the 1820s.

17 Fothergill, *Sketches*, 51.

18 *House of Assembly*, 6 February 1816, 169.

19 Strachan, *Sermon at York ... 1814*, 34–5. In an address to the prince regent, the House of Assembly also paid tribute to "the blood of their youth" which "had flowed freely." The colonists had guarded their lives and their property, to make good "the solemn pledge of faith and loyalty to the Parent Country." *House of Assembly*, 20 March 1818, 562.

20 The mythology about Canadian participation in the War of 1812 started soon after its conclusion and the writings of John Strachan were particularly instrumental in helping to create and propagate the myth. See among others *Sermon at York ... 1814* and *The Report of the Loyal and Patriotic Society*, of which John Strachan was the secretary. The idea of a colony united in support of its British institutions was soon picked up by the tories in the 1820s and used by them throughout the 1830s. See Mills, "Concept of Loyalty"; Walden, "Isaac Brock: Man and Myth." By the late 1860s, historians of the period had immortalized the myth. See Canniff, *History of Ontario*. For the imperialists of the 1880s, it formed the underpinning of their belief in the unity of the empire. See Berger, *The Sense of Power*; Lower, *Colony to Nation*.

21 T.S. Ashton, *The Industrial Revolution 1761–1830*, 106; For general accounts of the unrest in Great Britain, see R.J. White, *Waterloo to*

Peterloo; F.O. Darvall, *Popular Disturbances and Public Order in Regency England*; E.P. Thompson, *The Making of the English Working Class*.

22 *House of Assembly*, 4 February 1817, 312. See also 7 February 1816, 170.

23 Ibid., 4 February 1817, 313; 7 February 1817, 316; *Kingston Chronicle*, 5 April 1820. See also *Kingston Gazette*, 14 November 1814; *Upper Canada Gazette*, 17 September 1818.

24 *Kingston Chronicle*, 25 June 1819.

25 Ibid., 1 January 1819.

26 Ibid., 25 June 1819.

27 Ibid., 24 September, 10 December 1819. See also *Upper Canada Gazette*, 11 October 1819. Reports of meetings in the industrial towns of England received considerable space in the colonial press throughout 1819 and 1820. See for example the *Upper Canada Gazette* and the *Kingston Chronicle*, September 1819 to March 1820.

28 *Kingston Chronicle*, 3 December 1819, from the *Quebec Gazette*.

29 Ibid., 7 January 1820. See also *Kingston Chronicle*, 1 October 1819; *Upper Canada Gazette*, 28 October 1819.

30 *Kingston Chronicle*, 3 December 1819.

31 Ibid., 10 December 1819; 7 January 1820. A report of 24 September 1819 referred to "the turbulent and seditious spirit" in England, which was threatening law and order. See also 1, 15 October, 19 November 1819. A report in the *Upper Canada Gazette*, 21 October 1819, told of the "deep seated spirit of unrest."

32 *Kingston Chronicle*, 12 November 1819.

33 Ibid. See also 3 December 1819.

34 Ibid., 22 August 1819; 14 January 1820. See also 19 November 1819; *Upper Canada Gazette*, 21 October 1819. The remarkable similarity in rhetoric is evident when we consider Potter, *The Liberty We Seek*, chap. 2.

35 *Kingston Chronicle*, 14 April, 25 February, 7 January 1820. See also 22 October 1819.

36 Ibid., 14 April 1820. See also *Upper Canada Gazette*, 3 August 1820, which included a report of Lord Grenville's speech concerning the revolutionary activities against the government.

37 *Kingston Chronicle*, 10 December 1819. The concern of the government in England and of the authorities in Upper Canada about the radical reformers was compounded by the support the reformers were to receive from the case of the attempted divorce of Queen Caroline. Both the *Kingston Chronicle* and the *Upper Canada Gazette* provided considerable coverage of Lord Grenville's arrival in London and the queen's subsequent trial by the House of Lords. As the editor of the *Upper Canada Gazette* commented, 2 November 1820, though the House

could be expected to be impartial, they nonetheless could not help but disapprove of the queen's apparent alliance with "the demagogues."

38 *Kingston Chronicle*, 25 February, 14 January 1820. See also 2 November 1820.

39 Ibid., 25 February, 1 January 1820. See also a report, 19 November 1819, which noted that most Britons did not follow the cause of radical reform.

40 Ibid., 14 April 1820; 12 October 1819; 25 February 1820; 1 October 1819.

41 *Weekly Register*, 25 April 1822, concerning debates in the House of Commons on parliamentary reform.

42 *Kingston Gazette*, 18 November 1817. See also reports in the *Niagara Spectator* and the *Upper Canada Gazette*.

43 Gourlay, "Address Written from Jail," in *Statistical Account*, cccclxvi (also published in the *Niagara Spectator*, 27 June 1819); Gourlay, "Second Address," *Statistical Account*, 2: 472 (also printed in *Kingston Gazette*, 27 February 1818).

44 *Kingston Gazette*, 7 April 1818. Miles, in Kingston, noted that the Gourlay affair had increased his circulation (1 September 1818) and scarcely a week went by without some reference to and lengthy comment on the matter. Only the *Upper Canada Gazette* attempted to remain aloof. Yet those in York were informed of and concerned about Gourlay's activities. See the private correspondence in the Strachan Papers, Robinson Papers, and Macaulay Papers, PAO.

45 *Kingston Gazette*, 25 November 1817. See also 14 July 1818, a letter to the editor from "Hope." The notices and eventual proceedings of various meetings of "respectable yeomen farmers" appeared in both the *Kingston Gazette* and the *Niagara Gleaner*. See issues in January, February, and March 1818. For a general account of the Gourlay affair, see Craig, *Upper Canada*; Gerald Bloch, "The Visions of Robert Gourlay"; L.D. Milani, *Robert Gourlay, Gadfly*.

46 *Niagara Spectator*, 16 June 1818, letter to the editor from Richard Leonard; William Baldwin to Harvey, 22 June 1818, Baldwin Papers, TPL; *Niagara Spectator*, 29 July 1819; *Kingston Gazette*, 12 May 1818. See also *Kingston Chronicle*, 11 June 1819; letters to the editor from Richard Beasley, *Kingston Gazette*, 24 November 1818; from a "Resident Landowner," 24 March 1818; from Charles Stuart, *Kingston Chronicle*, 9 July 1819.

47 John Simpson, *An Essay on Modern Reformers*, 13. See also *Kingston Gazette*, 4 August 1818, letter to the editor from "Oxygen"; 12 May 1818; 26 May 1818, in which "Spectator" wrote that the "most turbulent and seditious subjects in Upper Canada were generally native of Great Britain"; *Niagara Spectator*, 6 August 1818.

48 *Kingston Gazette,* 21 July 1818. See also *Niagara Spectator,* 4 August 1818, letter to the editor from "Traveller," who had first supported Gourlay's ideas but had come to suspect his motives.

49 *House of Assembly,* 20 May 1818, 562–3. In 1818 "Bystander" published *Resolutions and Addresses ... of the Commons House of Assembly of Upper Canada,* in which he included a commentary and his minutes of the proceedings of the House.

50 *Kingston Gazette,* 18 August 1818. See also 15 September 1818 which included a letter to the editor from "Bob Short" supporting the verdict. He wrote, "if the verdict of the Jury ever expressed the public sentiment, it was in that case." In the same September issue, "Junius" demanded, however, that "the partial, arbitrary and illegal conduct of some of the Justices of the Peace" be rectified.

51 For an account of the proceedings, see Milani, *Robert Gourlay;* Craig, *Upper Canada,* "A Briton Banished"; Bowsfield, "Upper Canada in the 1820's." Contemporary newspaper accounts did include a draft of the petition to be sent to the prince regent. See *Niagara Spectator,* 14 May 1818; *Kingston Gazette,* 2 June 1818, and some of the resolutions of the delegates, *Kingston Gazette,* 22 September 1818.

52 Strachan to Macaulay, 8 December 1818, Macaulay Papers, PAO. Strachan had been one of the first to regard Gourlay with suspicion. His correspondence with Macaulay during this time is filled with his concern for the continued peace and harmony of the colony. He had clearly been appalled by the partiality of the *Kingston Gazette* and congratulated Macaulay on his handling of the matter in the *Kingston Chronicle.* 30 July 1819, Macaulay Papers, PAO. In addition, there seems to be no question that the last chapter of James Strachan's *A Visit to Upper Canada,* which roundly condemned Gourlay, was written by John Strachan who was not alone in his apprehensions. For example, William Baldwin also expressed concern in a letter to Lt. Col. Harvey, 22 June 1818, Baldwin Papers, TPL.

53 *House of Assembly,* 17 October 1818, 8; 22 October 1818, 16.

54 Ibid., 22 February 1820, 207. The government lifted the "gagging" bill in 1819 and by 1820 many Upper Canadians were remarking on the tranquillity of the province.

55 Charles Fothergill, "Port Hope Meeting," 1818, 7, in Gourlay, *Narrative of a Journey; Kingston Chronicle,* 5 March 1819.

56 Craig, *Upper Canada,* 99. See also Bowsfield, "Upper Canada in the 1820's," 148–50; Mills, "Concept of Loyalty," 46.

57 *United Empire Loyalist,* 20 October 1827; *Kingston Chronicle,* 10 November 1825; *Niagara Gleaner,* 26 November 1823. See also *Niagara Gleaner,* 25 June 1825; *Kingston Chronicle,* 11 March 1825.

58 *United Empire Loyalist,* 9 March 1920. See also 16, 23 March 1820. These

sentiments also appeared in Peter Robinson's Appeal to the Free and Independent Electors of York, *York Gazette*, 8 May 1816; Henry Boulton's appeal, *Upper Canada Gazette*, 23 March 1820; Halton's appeal, *Upper Canada Gazette*, 6 February 1817, to list only a few.

59 *York Gazette*, 8 May 1816, to the Electors of York; *United Empire Loyalist*, 23 March 1820. This latter issue includes the appeals of Henry Boulton, Peter Robinson, John Beverley Robinson, and William Baldwin.

60 *Kingston Chronicle*, 26 October 1821, in a letter to the editor from "John Barleycorn," the pen-name used by W.W. Baldwin.

61 *Upper Canada Gazette*, 23 March 1820.

62 "A Freeman," *To the Electors of the Town of York*, broadside, TPL. See also a comment in the *Upper Canada Gazette*, 24 June 1824, that "the PEOPLE of this PROVINCE" must "DO THEIR DUTY" and "return men for their Representatives as may be a credit to themselves ... and the bulwark of their country." In 1820 both Benjamin Hawk and John Playter called on their respective electors to choose an independent representative. Playter called for one who "takes pride in being a farmer, and being free from employment of the government." See Election Broadsides, TPL.

63 *Upper Canada Herald*, 10 May 1825. See also 14 June, 12 November 1825.

64 Ibid., 17 May 1825; 7 June 1819; *Kingston Chronicle*, 29 April 1825. Many members of the House of Assembly saw themselves as independent men, not members of any party. See for example references in *Colonial Advocate*, 2 September 1824; 2 February 1828; York *Weekly Register*, 9 September 1827; *Upper Canada Herald*, 8 November 1825; 18 October 1825; Bowsfield, "Upper Canada in the 1820's," chap. 7.

65 *Upper Canada Gazette*, 23 March 1820. See also Henry Boulton's appeal, *To the Free and Independent Electors of York and Simcoe*, 1824, broadside, TPL, in which he specifically refuted charges that his position as a member of the executive had compromised his ability to represent his constituents. "I will," he wrote, "to the utmost of my power, support the interests of the Farmers of this Happy Colony without fear, favour, or affection."

66 *Kingston Chronicle*, 4 January 1822. See also the *Observer*, 19 December 1825, in which the editor noted "the present struggle for popularity and power."

67 See for example *Upper Canada Herald*, 26 April 1825; *Kingston Chronicle*, 28 March 1823.

68 *Upper Canada Herald*, 8 November, 18 October 1825. In a letter to the editor of the *Weekly Register*, 15 July 1824, Robinson was criticized as being a "crown lawyer." See also criticisms reprinted in the *United Empire Loyalist*, 10 November 1827.

69 *Upper Canada Herald*, 8 November, 17 May 1825. "One of the People" noted that though controversy was "unfortunate," it did concern "a most important constitutional issue." It was the "doctrine that the People's Representatives" are "the appointed guardians of the public purse." *Upper Canada Herald*, 16 April 1825.

70 *Upper Canada Gazette*, 13 February 1825.

71 *Kingston Chronicle*, 29 April 1825. See also 13 February 1825, in which the editor remarked, "such as the Cobbetts of England, so are the observers of Canada."

72 *Upper Canada Gazette*, 13 February 1823; *Upper Canada Herald*, 18 October 1825, quoting from the *Kingston Chronicle*. This criticism was not restricted just to the public press. For example, Robert Stanton, now editor of the *United Empire Loyalist*, formerly the *Upper Canada Gazette*, wrote extensively to John Macaulay in 1826 of the antics and almost traitorous activities of the "Patriots" in the House. And by 1828 he had begun to equate them with the radical reformers in England. Macaulay Papers, PAO.

73 In 1819 H.C. Thomson started the *Upper Canada Herald* in Kingston. That same year, Macaulay and Pringle, having purchased the presses of the *Kingston Gazette*, commenced publication of the *Kingston Chronicle*. By 1825 the *Niagara Gleaner*, the *Brockville Recorder*, and the *Observer* and the *Colonial Advocate* in York were all thriving. Within five years, the colony was also supporting the *Canadian Freeman*, the *Farmers Journal*, and the *Gore Gazette*.

74 *Upper Canada Herald*, 8 November 1825; *Kingston Chronicle*, 21 June 1822; *Upper Canada Herald*, 12 April 1825, advertisement for the *Canadian Freeman*. The question of the freedom and independence of the press seemed to preoccupy Upper Canadians increasingly after the War of 1812. In 1823, for example, the *Upper Canada Gazette* ran a series of articles by "Eusebius" on the need for a free but responsible press. In addition, all the other newspapers frequently included articles on the role of the press in society. See among others *Kingston Chronicle*, 15 August 1823; *Farmers Journal*, 1 March 1826; *Niagara Gleaner*, 22 July 1826; *Upper Canada Gazette*, 20 November 1823. In part, this was undoubtedly a response to the growing political role that the press was playing.

75 *Gore Gazette*, 3 March 1827. See also among others *Kingston Chronicle*, 3 January 1823; *Weekly Register*, 10 February 1823.

76 *Niagara Gleaner*, 13 November 1824; *Gore Gazette*, 3 March 1827.

77 *Kingston Chronicle*, 3 December 1824. See also debates in the *Kingston Chronicle*, 2 February 1823; *Weekly Register*, 25 September 1823.

78 *Kingston Chronicle*, 3 December 1824.

79 *Gore Gazette*, 7 December 1828; 2 February 1824; *Kingston Chronicle*, 3

December 1824. See also *Weekly Register*, 10 February 1823; 21 July 1825; *Kingston Chronicle*, 27 December 1828.

80 *Farmers Journal*, 14 June 1826; *Niagara Gleaner*, 6 November 1824. See also *Gore Gazette*, 7 December 1827; *Niagara Gleaner*, 22 September 1828.

81 *Weekly Register*, 28 October 1824.

82 *Kingston Chronicle*, 3 December 1824. See also Stanton's letters to Macaulay throughout 1826, Macaulay Papers, PAO; *Kingston Chronicle*, 21 June 1822; *Weekly Register*, 28 October 1824.

83 *United Empire Loyalist*, 10 May 1828. See also 7 July 1825.

84 *Gore Gazette*, 8 March 1828. See also *Kingston Chronicle*, 3 December 1824.

85 *Upper Canada Herald*, 12 April 1825, from the proposal for the *Canadian Freeman*; *Colonial Advocate*, 10 June 1824.

86 Francis Collins, *To the Loyal, Patriotic and Independent Anglo-Americans of Upper Canada*, 12; *Upper Canada Herald*, 7 June, 17, 10 May 1825.

CHAPTER SEVEN

1 *Upper Canada Herald*, 22 November 1825, from the *New York Commercial Advertiser*.

2 Strachan, "A Letter to Thomas Jefferson," *Quebec Gazette*, 4 April 1815.

3 Landon, *Western Ontario*, 40.

4 Wise, "Colonial Attitudes," 41.

5 *Gore Gazette*, 16 June 1827. See also Robert Baldwin's extensive correspondence with J. Samson in New York, March 1821–May 1828, and Quetton St George's letters to William Bryon of New York and Myles, Ellice and Co., Baldwin Papers, TPL. Even Strachan kept in touch with the bishop of New York. Strachan Papers, 1818–19, PAO.

6 *Kingston Gazette*, 8 July 1817; 28 July 1818.

7 *Niagara Spectator*, 8 June 1816. See also *Kingston Gazette*, 21 September 1816, concerning a steamship service that now linked New York to Albany; *Upper Canada Gazette*, 25 September 1817, 10 February 1820, reports of travel on the St Lawrence and the building of a new road through Maine to the Canadas; 23 June 1825, concerning a proposed canal from Montreal to Boston. In the *Niagara Gleaner*, 28 May 1825, the editor noted that as a result of the new stage service from Young's Town to Rochester, he could receive New York papers in five days, "faster than any other paper in Upper Canada." See also A. Flick, ed., *History of the State of New York*.

8 *United Empire Loyalist*, 31 March 1827. See also *Kingston Gazette*, 6 January 1818, concerning manufacturing in New York, from the *New York Ontario Messenger*; *Kingston Chronicle*, 15, 22 January 1819, reports of

a New York society for the relief of the poor; 2 July 1819, on the growing problem with banks in the United States; 10 November 1826, on the industrial development of Philadelphia; *Upper Canada Gazette*, 8 January 1818, a report of the Colonization Society of New York; 5 July 1818, concerning financing of new projects in the United States; 30 November 1820, about schools in New York; *Niagara Gleaner*, 9 July 1825, on the New York school system.

9 *Upper Canada Gazette*, 30 November 1820; *Kingston Gazette*, 3 February 1818, from the *Raleigh Register*. See also the *Kingston Gazette*, 17 August 1816, on crops in New Hampshire, Vermont, and Maine; *Niagara Gleaner*, 17 September 1825.

10 *Upper Canada Gazette*, 30 November 1820.

11 *Kingston Gazette*, 17 November 1818. See also 2 September 1818, from the *Daily Advertiser*; 10 August 1816, reports from the *New Hampshire Sentinel* and Philadelphia; 12 August 1817, reports from Vermont, New Jersey, and Sacket's Harbour; 15 July 1817, concerning the growing of potatoes; 3 February, 17 November 1818, both from New York; *Upper Canada Gazette*, 30 January 1817, from the *Connecticut Courant*; 6 August 1818, from Salem; 26 November 1818, from Jefferson County.

12 *Kingston Gazette*, 22 March 1817.

13 Ibid., 22 December 1822; 1 April 1823; 23 January 1822; 21 October 1823. See also *Kingston Gazette*, 6 October 1818; *Upper Canada Gazette*, 30 June 1825. Reports of canal building in the United States received increasing attention. In 1817 the *Upper Canada Gazette* printed numerous reports of the progress being made on the Erie. See for example 16, 23 January, 6 March 1817. This interest was also reflected in the Kingston and Niagara journals. After 1825 the newspapers also began to print accounts of various Upper Canadian endeavours to improve inland water communications. The *Farmers Journal* and the *Niagara Gleaner* in particular show their readers' special interest in these developments. In addition, the House of Assembly commissioned a report on the progress and the techniques being used by the Americans. See *Kingston Chronicle*, 1 April 1823; *Farmers Journal*, 19 July 1826; Craig, *Upper Canada*, 151; Fraser, "Like Eden in Her Summer Dress."

14 *Niagara Gleaner*, 25 July 1823. See also *Upper Canada Gazette*, 31 March 1827.

15 *Niagara Gleaner*, 4 December 1824; *Farmers Journal*, 26 April 1825; *Kingston Chronicle*, 27 December 1824. The building of canals was central to the tories' policy for the economic development of Upper Canada after the War of 1812. Certainly Strachan considered it important, for he submitted a number of articles on canal building to Macaulay for publication in the *Kingston Chronicle* (Strachan to Macaulay, 11 March 1819) and was concerned about development of the St Lawrence River.

Strachan to Macaulay, 4 October 1821, Macaulay Papers, PAO. The *Kingston Chronicle*, throughout October 1826, also printed in full the report to the House of Assembly on the development of the New York canals. Fraser, "Like Eden in Her Summer Dress," provides an extensive discussion of John Beverley Robinson's belief that without economic development, and especially the creation of canals linking all parts of the colony, the political development and, indeed, survival of the colony were in jeopardy. See also Craig, *Upper Canada*, 150–5.

16 *Farmers Journal*, 1 February 1826. See also *Upper Canada Gazette*, 25 June 1825.

17 *Farmers Journal*, 26 April 1826; *Niagara Gleaner*, 25 July 1823. See also *Farmers Journal*, 1 February 1826; 29 March 1826; *Upper Canada Gazette*, 30 June 1825; 31 March 1827.

18 *Niagara Gleaner*, 24 July 1824. The Welland Canal was not the only canal which Upper Canadians started to build in the 1820s. After 1825 organization had already been started for the Rideau Canal, which was expected "to greatly increase the prosperity" of the colony. Ibid., 28 June 1826.

19 *Kingston Chronicle*, 23 June, 7 January, 15 April 1820.

20 Ibid., 17 November 1826.

21 *Upper Canada Gazette*, 27 August 1819; *Kingston Chronicle*, 8 June 1821; 23 June 1820. Upper Canadians particularly admired the "enterprising" nature of Americans and the adjective was frequently used to describe the Yankees themselves and their accomplishments.

22 See Flick, *History of New York*; A. Kass, *Politics in New York State, 1800–1830*; Lee Benson, *The Concept of Jacksonian Democracy*.

23 *Kingston Chronicle*, 29 January 1819. See also 24 November 1820.

24 Ibid., 22 January 1825; 24 November 1820. See also 28 January 1820; 20 December 1822; 21 January 1825; *Upper Canada Gazette*, 16 January 1817; 27 January 1825; *Kingston Gazette*, 4 November 1817; *Upper Canada Herald*, 5 April 1825.

25 *Farmers Journal*, 27 February 1828, from a New York paper. References to the New York and Erie canals that appeared in the colonial newspapers almost always included a reference to the contribution that Clinton had made to their development. For references to "Clinton's achievements," among others see *Upper Canada Gazette*, 16 January 1817; 5 March 1818; *Niagara Gleaner*, 4 December 1824; 19 November 1825; *Kingston Chronicle*, 18 January, 27 December 1822; *Colonial Advocate*, 27 September 1824.

26 *Farmers Journal*, 27 February 1828. See also *Gore Gazette*, 23 February 1828.

27 *Kingston Chronicle*, 7 January, 23 June 1820.

28 Ibid., 15 April 1825.

29 See for example *Kingston Chronicle*, 10 February 1816, from the *Delaware Gazette*; 10 August 1821; *Upper Canada Gazette*, 1 January 1818. Strachan seemed to be particularly concerned about this. In a series of letters to Col. Harvey in Quebec at the end of 1815 and the beginning of 1816, he proposed to write an "accurate" history of the War of 1812, so as to correct the many "gross misrepresentations made by many Americans."

30 *Upper Canada Gazette*, 5 September 1822.

31 *Kingston Chronicle*, 23 June 1820.

32 *Upper Canada Gazette*, 18 December 1823. See also *United Empire Loyalist*, 29 September 1826; 31 March 1827.

33 *Kingston Chronicle*, 23 August 1828; *United Empire Loyalist*, 3 March 1827. See also *Kingston Chronicle*, 22 December 1822; 25 July 1823; *Niagara Gleaner*, 4 December 1824; *Farmers Journal*, 19 July 1826; *United Empire Loyalist*, 23 September 1826.

34 *Kingston Chronicle*, 28 January, 4, 11 February 1825.

35 Gourlay, "Address from Jail," *Niagara Spectator*, 18 May 1819. Gourlay's use of comparisons with New York increased throughout 1818 and early 1819. See among others *Kingston Gazette*, 26 May 1818; *Niagara Spectator*, 8 July 1819, containing his vitriolic reply to Charles Stuart.

36 *Kingston Chronicle*, 4 June 1819.

37 Ibid., 9 July 1819. See also 11 June 1819.

38 Ibid., 4 June 1819. See also 11 June 1819, a letter to the editor from "Loyalist"; 9 July 1819, letter to the editor from Charles Stuart.

39 *Colonial Advocate*, 18 May 1824. See also 20 January 1825.

40 *Weekly Register*, 27 May, 3 June 1824. See also 27 September 1824; 9, 27 September 1826.

41 *Colonial Advocate*, 21 December 1826. Mackenzie also suggested, 7 December 1826, that Upper Canadians should look to examples in Nova Scotia and and New Brunswick. See Bowsfield, "Upper Canada: The 1820s," 351, for a discussion of Mackenzie's use of British constitutional examples. Nonetheless, Mackenzie did use the United States as a constant point of reference. For example, he often spoke of the differences in educational facilities, newspaper reporting, and the freedom of the press. See for example 4 December 1824; 7 December 1826; 19 April, 17 May, 21 June, 22 November 1827.

42 *Farmers Journal*, 19 July 1826.

43 *Upper Canada Gazette*, 1 April 1822.

44 *Farmers Journal*, 15 November 1826.

45 See among others *Kingston Gazette*, 23 December 1815; 21 December 1816; 5 April 1817; 19 May 1818; *Kingston Chronicle*, 26 February 1819; 28 December 1821; 24 December 1823; 13 December 1828; *York Gazette*, 13 March 1816; 16 January 1817; 9 December 1819; 1 January

1824; 6 January 1825; *Niagara Spectator*, 27 June 1817; *Niagara Gleaner*, 24 December 1827; *Colonial Advocate*, 30 December 1824; 7 May 1825.

46 See for example *Upper Canada Gazette*, 26 February, 5 March 1818; 6 January 1825; *Niagara Gleaner*, 13 May, 27 November 1824; 15 January, 19 November 1825; *Kingston Chronicle*, 29 January, 20 November 1819; 20 April 1821; *Gore Gazette*, 8 January 1825; 12 May 1827.

47 *Kingston Chronicle*, 17 November 1826.

48 Ibid., 23 June 1820.

49 *Niagara Gleaner*, 7 February 1817. See also John Bethune, *A Loyal Sermon Preached at Brockville*, 1816, 17, in which he spoke of the "ruling faction in the United States" and the principles of "hatred, rage and party spirit" which governed it.

50 *Kingston Gazette*, 4 January 1817.

51 *Upper Canada Gazette*, 16 December 1826, from the *Auburn Free Press*. Comment was made concerning the ill-fated attempts of Adams to bring harmony to the Congress. Frequently derogatory references were made in the tory press to the "idle vapourings of American politicians." *Kingston Chronicle*, 22 November 1819. On 26 February 1819 the editors of the *Chronicle* commented on "the tinsel glare" of American politics. Even William Lyon Mackenzie condemned the "party quarrels" in the United States. *Colonial Advocate*, 26 April 1827.

52 *Niagara Gleaner*, 26 November 1827. See also *Farmers Journal*, 7 May 1828. Upper Canadians also remarked privately on the political controversies in the United States and the ill-effects of political parties. For example, in a letter to Macaulay, 10 July 1816, Strachan commented on the discontent in Congress. Macaulay Papers, PAO.

53 *Niagara Spectator*, 11 November 1817.

54 *Kingston Gazette*, 6 January 1818. Two years earlier, Macaulay had received a letter from his cousin in Newbury, 10 July 1816, which noted that "the severe party spirit has lost something of its violence owing in some measure to the quiet accession of votes to what is called the Democratic party." Macaulay Papers, PAO.

55 *Upper Canada Gazette*, 9 December 1819.

56 *Kingston Gazette*, 4 November 1817. See also 11 November 1817. The continuing awareness of political developments and of the party system in the United States is perhaps best illustrated in a letter, written by Strachan to the *Kingston Chronicle*, 11 February 1820, in which he explicitly detailed the number of seats each party had in Congress.

57 *Kingston Chronicle*, 14 July 1826.

58 *Niagara Gleaner*, 22 July 1826; *Farmers Journal*, 19 July 1826, from the *New York Spectator*; *Colonial Advocate*, 7 April 1825. See also *Kingston Chronicle*, 6 December 1825.

59 See for example *Niagara Gleaner*, 9 July 1825; 12 December 1827;

Farmers Journal, 17 May, 20 September 1826; *Kingston Gazette*, 1 July 1819; *Upper Canada Gazette*, 7 July 1825; *Kingston Chronicle*, 14 April, 2 June 1820; 28 February, 15 August 1823; *Upper Canada Herald*, 19 July 1825.

60 William Morgan had been an aspiring author in New York who had proposed to write a history and commentary on Masonry in the United States. In 1827 he was abducted, and it was rumoured that the secret Masonic order had been responsible for this and perhaps for his death. Throughout 1827 the kidnapping was a newspaper sensation. All the Upper Canadian newspapers provided extensive coverage of the "latest developments," and particular interest was shown by the *Colonial Advocate* and those papers in the western districts of the colony. See specifically the *Kingston Chronicle*, 6 April 1827, containing Clinton's offer of a reward of $1,000 if Morgan was recovered alive and $2,000 if he was dead and his murderers were apprehended; *Farmers Journal*, 14 March 1827.

61 Alexander Arbuthnot and Robert Ambister had apparently chosen to stand with their Indian associates and take up arms against the American army. After their execution, the question arose whether, indeed, the two merchants were still British subjects. See George Dangerfield, *The Era of Good Feeling*, 121–36.

62 *Kingston Chronicle*, 21 May 1819, from the *Connecticut Mirror*.

63 *Upper Canada Gazette*, 2 January 1818; *Kingston Chronicle*, 1 January 1819.

64 *Upper Canada Gazette*, 7 January 1818; 7 January 1819, from the *Baltimore Telegraph*. See also *Kingston Gazette*, 27 October 1818.

65 *Upper Canada Gazette*, 7 January 1819, from the *American Daily Advertiser*; *Kingston Chronicle*, 1 January 1819.

66 *Upper Canada Gazette*, 7 January 1819, from the *American Daily Advertiser*.

67 *Kingston Chronicle*, 29 January, 21 May 1819.

68 Ibid., 22 January 1819, editorial comment. See also *Upper Canada Gazette*, 15 October 1818, from the *New York Spectator*; 11 March 1819, an article from the *Petersburgh Intelligencer* noting the controversy that was rocking Congress.

69 *Farmers Journal*, 7 May 1828.

70 *Upper Canada Gazette*, 27 May 1824; *Farmers Journal*, 7 May 1828. See also *Niagara Gleaner*, 27 May 1824.

71 *Kingston Gazette*, 29 July 1817.

72 *House of Assembly*, 1817, 316.

73 The issue first appeared in the *Kingston Gazette*, 23 September 1817, concerning the question of Mississippi. Then on 28 April 1818 the question of Missouri, Illinois, and Michigan was raised. See also reports in *Kingston Gazette*, 29 December 1818; *Upper Canada Gazette*, 4 Novem-

ber 1819; 24 February 1820; *Kingston Chronicle*, 25 February, 24, 31 March 1820.

74 *Upper Canada Gazette*, 23 March 1820, from the *American Repertory*; *Kingston Chronicle*, 31 March 1820, from the *New York Daily Advertiser*. See also *Farmers Journal*, 21 October 1826, from the *New York Spectator*; *Upper Canada Gazette*, 2 September 1826, from the *Commercial Advertiser*.

75 *Kingston Chronicle*, 31 March 1820. Reports in the same issue from the *Connecticut Courant* noted that all the states below the 36th parallel were now slave states.

76 *Kingston Chronicle*, 22 December 1820. See also 29 December 1820.

77 Ibid., 25 February 1820, from the *Utica Patriot*.

78 Ibid., 31 March 1820, from the *New York Daily Advertiser*. See also ibid., 21 February 1820, letter to the editor from "Scrutator."

79 Ibid., 22 December, 25 February 1820. See also *Upper Canada Gazette*, 14, 21, 28 December 1820.

80 *Kingston Chronicle*, 30 November 1821.

81 *Upper Canada Gazette*, 12 September 1822. *Farmers Journal*, 25 December 1826. See also *Upper Canada Gazette*, 2, 9 July 1825; 2 September 1826; *Niagara Gleaner*, 30 July 1825, report from Virginia; 9 February 1826; *Farmers Journal*, 21 March 1827, containing a report concerning Georgia and the problems of "peace" in the Union.

82 *Colonial Advocate*, 23 March 1826, from the *National Intelligencer*.

CHAPTER EIGHT

1 Craig, *Upper Canada*, 85. For a view of British policies with respect to the British American colonies in general, and particularly with regard to the granting of responsible government, see Buckner, *Transition to Responsible Government*.

2 *Kingston Chronicle*, 7 December 1821.

3 Ibid. First the *Kingston Gazette* and then the *Chronicle* provided extensive coverage of the negotiations. See *Kingston Gazette*, 19 October 1816, concerning the various islands in the St Lawrence; 14 December 1816, concerning the boundary line; 4 January, 1 July 1817; 2 December 1817, regarding the St Lawrence survey; 26 May, 15 September 1818; *Kingston Chronicle*, 17 December 1819; 4 January 1821.

4 *Kingston Chronicle*, 19 July 1822. The overall issue was still being considered well into the 1830s. For example, see *Niagara Gleaner*, 20 November 1824; 3 December 1827; 16 June 1828, from the *Boston Centinel*; the *Farmers Journal*, 26 July 1826; *Upper Canada Herald*, 27 November 1827; *Kingston Chronicle*, 19 July 1822; 15 December 1826, from the *New York Times*; *Upper Canada Gazette*, 5 August 1826.

5 See for example *Kingston Gazette*, 30 December 1815; 6 January 1816;

13 January 1816, which included reports of an incident at Detroit involving the murder of an Indian and the contentious question of which government had the authority to investigate and prosecute the offender; 10 February 1818, concerning a kidnapping in the Kingston area.

6 See for example *Kingston Gazette*, 12 October, 2, 9 November 1816; 26 April 1817; *Kingston Chronicle*, 6 August 1819; 2 June 1820; 28 February, 15 August 1823; *Upper Canada Herald*, 26 April, 19 July 1825; *Niagara Gleaner*, 3 September 1825.

7 *Kingston Gazette*, 30 December 1815.

8 Ibid., 2 November 1816. See also 13 January, 21 October, 9 November 1816; *Niagara Gleaner*, 16 June 1828. Strachan in a letter to Macaulay, 19 February 1821, also mentioned the importance of maintaining good relations with the United States. Macaulay Papers, PAO.

9 *Upper Canada Gazette*, 20 October 1817.

10 *Kingston Gazette*, 2 June 1818. See also 9 June 1818; *Upper Canada Gazette*, 19 October 1816; Bethune, *A Sermon Preached at Brockville*, 1816, 19.

11 *A Form of Prayer and Thanksgiving ...* 1815.

12 *Kingston Gazette*, 26 September 1815; 2 March 1816. Numerous reports began to appear in the *Upper Canada Gazette* and the *Kingston Gazette*. Also *Niagara Spectator*, 8 November 1816; *Kingston Gazette*, 9 November 1816.

13 *Upper Canada Gazette*, 14 May 1818; *Kingston Chronicle*, 1 January 1819. See also *Upper Canada Gazette*, 26 February 1818, from the *Montreal Herald*. This concern persisted throughout the next decade. For example, Strachan, in a letter to Horton, 25 May 1824, wrote of the "growing power of the United States," and in an address at Woolwich, 28 April 1824, voiced the same concern.

14 *Kingston Gazette*, 24 February 1818.

15 *Kingston Chronicle*, 24 December 1819; *Kingston Gazette*, 15 December 1818. These sentiments had been asserted, perhaps with more hope than conviction since the end of the War of 1812. See also *Upper Canada Gazette*, 30 January 1817; 19 March, 2 July 1818; *Kingston Chronicle*, 24 December 1819.

16 *Upper Canada Gazette*, 8 April 1819. This article advocated that the government should keep the militia in order, for all were willing to fight; *Niagara Gleaner*, 8 July 1819.

17 *Kingston Chronicle*, 8 December 1820; See also 1, 29 January, 24 December 1819; *Kingston Gazette*, 6 December 1816; *Farmers Journal*, 24 May 1826.

18 *Kingston Chronicle*, 7 October 1827; *Niagara Gleaner*, 8 July 1819. A report in *Upper Canada Gazette*, 20 February 1823, asserted that "the Americans are fully determined on settling their settlements quite across

the continent." See also *Upper Canada Gazette*, 23 February 1817; 13 March 1823; 22 January, 3 March 1825; *Niagara Gleaner*, 8 July 1819; 22 January 1825. Moreover, after the War of 1812, Great Britain reimposed her Navigation Act, to the detriment of the American carrying trade. Reports of the effects of this on the American economy, and subsequent American reaction, received a great deal of attention in the colonial press. Upper Canadians realized that the resulting tensions between the two powers would inevitably affect their own position. See for example *Kingston Chronicle*, 19 February, 7 September 1819; 12 May, 2 June 1820; *Upper Canada Gazette*, 2 July 1818; *Niagara Gleaner*, 17 May 1822; 22 January 1825.

19 *Kingston Chronicle*, 10 December 1819. See also 22 June 1821.

20 Ibid., 22 June 1821. See also 1 June 1820.

21 Strachan to John Macaulay, 13 June 1820, Macaulay Papers, PAO. He found Walsh's paper "too flat" and believed "it will not succeed."

22 *Kingston Chronicle*, 1 January 1820.

23 Ibid., 18 February 1820, Letter 4. "Scrutator" was definitely Rev. John Strachan, for in his personal correspondence with Macaulay, then editor of the *Kingston Chronicle*, Strachan made frequent allusion to the letters he had sent for publication in response to Walsh. See 10, 17 April, 18 June, 15 July 1820, Macaulay Papers, PAO.

24 *Kingston Chronicle*, 17 March 1820, Letter 7.

25 Ibid., 21 July 1820, Letter 14.

26 Ibid., 11 February 1820, Letter 3; 4 February 1820, Letter 2.

27 Ibid., 4 February 1820; 25 August 1822.

28 Ibid., 22 June 1822.

29 Ibid., 11, 18 February, 14 July 1820.

30 Ibid., 4 February 1820; Strachan to Macaulay, 8 November 1822, Macaulay Papers, PAO. This is based on information that he had received from "A Gentleman in Philadelphia."

31 *Upper Canada Gazette*, 18 May 1824.

32 *Colonial Advocate*, 11 April 1824. As early as 17 August 1820, the editors of *Upper Canada Gazette* had begun to notice a change in sentiment. See also 24 December 1823.

33 John Stuart, *A Plan for Legislative Union*, 33; Strachan, *Sermon Preached at Woolwich*, 28 April 1824. See also Fothergill, "Port Hope Meeting," in Gourlay, *Narrative of a Journey*. Fothergill claimed in 1818 that Americans considered union of the continent essential, "*in order* to complete, as they term them, their territorial arrangements."

34 *United Empire Loyalist*, 9 December 1826. At the same time, however, the newspapers continued to report on American rearmament. In addition to previous references, see *Kingston Chronicle*, 12 July 1822, con-

cerning forts on the Great Lakes; *Farmers Journal,* 12 December 1826, a report of the new troops arriving at American forts.

35 *Kingston Gazette,* 24 February 1818.

36 Strachan to Lieutenant Murray, 29 March 1815.

37 Strachan, "Reasons Against Removing the Seat of Government," private memorandum, enclosed in a letter of John Beverley Robinson, 20 February 1816, Robinson Papers, PAO.

38 Strachan to Murray, 29 March 1815.

39 Residents of Kingston undoubtedly believed that, as the largest and the most promising of all Upper Canadian centres, their city should house the seat of government. Strachan himself recognized that some Kingstonians were in agreement with the government's proposals; however, he suggested that these were only a few land speculators. Yet, as Stephen Miles remarked in the *Kingston Gazette,* 29 June 1816, many were disappointed.

40 *Niagara Gleaner,* 13 August 1825, from the *Upper Canada Herald.*

41 *Kingston Chronicle,* 17 June 1820.

42 *Farmers Journal,* 6 December 1826, from the *New York Times; Upper Canada Gazette,* 19 March 1818; *Niagara Gleaner,* 8 May 1825.

43 *Upper Canada Gazette,* 1 February 1821.

44 Ibid. See also Strachan, "Reasons Against Removing the Seat of Government"; *Colonial Advocate,* 3 January 1828; *Kingston Chronicle,* 19 August 1822, which included a report that the "prosperity of one affected the other."

45 *Upper Canada Gazette,* 1 February 1821; 1 February 1826.

46 Ibid., 17 June 1826.

47 *Niagara Gleaner,* 16 June 1828.

48 *United Empire Loyalist,* 17 June 1826; *Upper Canada Gazette,* 2 February 1821.

49 *Kingston Gazette,* 18 November 1815.

50 Ibid., 1 February 1817. See also 30 December 1815, a letter to the editor from "Resident" stating that trade from the United States would make Kingston prosperous.

51 Ibid., 30 December 1815.

52 *House of Assembly,* 13 March 1816, 240–1. Throughout 1816 and 1817 there was considerable controversy voiced in the *Kingston Gazette* over who should have the right to run steamboats on the St Lawrence River. From 17 February 1816 the debate revolved for about two months around the question of monopolies and whether Americans should have the right to service Upper Canadian communities.

53 *Kingston Gazette,* 6 April 1816. See also 3 June 1816, letter to the editor from "Honestus"; 23 March 1816.

54 Ibid., 24 February 1816. See also 23 March 1816, expressing a concern that the province "will become a nursery for American seamen." These sentiments were echoed in an address from the Legislature of Nova Scotia on the question of trade, *Kingston Chronicle*, 7 September 1819.

55 *Kingston Gazette*, 23 March, 24 February 1816.

56 Ibid., 3, 17 February 1816.

57 Ibid., 6 January 1816, letter to the editor from "Yankee"; 10 February 1816.

58 Ibid., 23 March 1816, letter to the editor from "True Briton"; 17 November 1817.

59 Ibid., 6 April 1816. See also 13 April 1816 for further discussion of the steamship issue; 10 February 1816.

60 Ibid., 24 April 1816. However, on 17 June 1817 a new controversy arose over the introduction of Waterloo and York coppers into the colony. The next week, 24 June 1817, "Green Grocer" complained that Upper Canadians were being duped by American speculators; on 15 July 1817 it was reported that two tons of coppers had been brought into the colony from Sacket's Harbour.

61 Ibid., 3 May 1817, letter to the editor from "Camden." See also *Kingston Chronicle*, 4, 5 May 1819; on 30 July 1819 the editors applauded the decrease in duties which they claimed was resulting in a decrease in smuggling; 17 September 1819; on 4 August 1820 Thomas Dalton placed a notice concerning the need for protection from American grains and spirits. For a general discussion of economic relations between the Canadas and the empire and within the colonies see D. Creighton, *Empire of the St. Lawrence*; C. Goodwin, *Canadian Economic Thought: The Political Economy of a Developing Nation*.

62 See *Kingston Chronicle*, 25 June 1819, which noted that "the effects of the great change which has taken place in the political condition in Europe had adversely affected American trade"; 7 January 1820, a report noting that "the United States are only beginning to feel the effect of commercial duties"; 13 August 1819.

63 *Kingston Gazette*, 2 July 1817.

64 *Kingston Chronicle*, 17 March, 8 September 1820.

65 Ibid., 17 March 1820. See also 18 May 1821.

66 Ibid., 31 August 1821. See also 18 May 1821, which noted that the new bill "only had the effect of adding to our difficulties."

67 Ibid., 17, 24 March 1820. The concern about trading relations with the United States was much in the news throughout 1820 and 1821. And even Strachan apparently opposed the new trading regulations. In a letter to Macaulay, 10 May 1821, he cryptically noted that it would be better to term them "non-intercourse" regulations. See also letter to Macaulay, 27 March 1821, Macaulay Papers, PAO.

68 *Kingston Chronicle*, 10 September 1819; *Upper Canada Gazette*, 2 February 1821, reported from the *Quebec Review*. See also *Kingston Gazette*, 24 February 1818, reported from the *Colonial Journal*; 8 September 1818; *Upper Canada Gazette*, 24 February 1818; *United Empire Loyalist*, 17 June 1826.

69 *Kingston Chronicle*, 22 September 1820. See also 17 August, 2 November 1821. The colonial press included quite lengthy reports on the proceedings of the House of Commons and the House of Lords on the matter.

70 Ibid., 22 September 1822; 10 March 1820.

71 Ibid., 22 September 1922.

72 Ibid., 20 March 1820.

73 *Upper Canada Herald*, 3 August 1825. See also 8 March 1825.

74 *Upper Canada Gazette*, 27 November 1822; 6 May 1823.

75 *Upper Canada Herald*, 23 August 1825.

76 Ibid., 8 March 1825. Of surviving "opposition" papers, it was the *Upper Canada Herald* which provided the most comprehensive coverage of this commercial concern and the constitutional debates in the House of Assembly.

77 *Colonial Advocate*, 28 February 1825. See also *Upper Canada Herald*, 8 March 1825, which noted the disadvantages of Upper Canada's internal geographical position.

78 *Upper Canada Herald*, 2 August 1825, letter to the editor from "A Matter of Fact." See also *Colonial Advocate*, 27 May 1824. Echoing arguments presented just after the War of 1812 and in Kingston in 1816, the reformers noted that the present situation encouraged smuggling. See *Upper Canada Herald*, 25 April, 14 June, 2, 25 August 1825.

79 *Niagara Gleaner*, 6 August 1825.

80 *Kingston Chronicle*, 18 March 1825; *Niagara Gleaner*, 19 March 1825. See also *Niagara Gleaner*, 6 August 1823; *Kingston Chronicle*, 1 April 1825.

81 *Kingston Chronicle*, 11 March 1825; *Niagara Gleaner*, 6 August 1825; 13 August 1825. See also *Kingston Chronicle*, 18 March 1825, where the editors referred to the "grumblers." A week earlier the editor of the *Chronicle* had noted that "the only thing wanted by us ... is a further relaxation of the British corn laws in our favour."

82 *Gore Gazette*, 15 September 1827. In the *Kingston Chronicle*, 11 October 1826, the editor wrote, "it is the anxious desire of the parent state to retain, cherish and promote the welfare of the colony ... the country itself is sufficiently sensible to the value of the protection of England and in no respect wishes to be separated from her." See also 1 January 1819; 28 January 1820; *Gore Gazette*, 1 May, 19 June 1827; 16 August 1828; *United Empire Loyalist*, 17 June, 9 December 1826; *Farmers Journal*,

6 December 1826. Concern over British-American trading relations did persist for the rest of the decade. See for example *Colonial Advocate*, 5 April 1827; *Canadian Freeman*, 18 January 1827; *Kingston Chronicle*, 6 October 1826; *United Empire Loyalist*, 23 June 1827; 22 March 1828.

83 *Kingston Gazette*, 20 November 1810.

84 Robert Baldwin to an unknown correspondent, 22 June 1818, Baldwin Papers, TPL.

85 *Kingston Gazette*, 11 May 1816.

86 Robert Baldwin to an unknown correspondent, 22 June 1818, Baldwin Papers, TPL.

87 *Kingston Gazette*, 11 May 1816.

88 The instructions were issued by the colonial executive on 14 October 1815. A second directive was sent out, instructing all magistrates to take note and inform the executive of all aliens in the colony, and of their character, and reminding them not to issue the oath of allegiance. Circular to Solomon Jones, 14 October 1815, Upper Canada Sundries, RG5 AI, PAC. See Craig, *Upper Canada*, 89; Landon, *Western Ontario*, chap. 4.

89 Strachan, *A Letter to the Right Honourable the Lord Selkirk*.

90 Baldwin to unknown correspondent, 22 June 1818, Baldwin Papers, TPL. See Landon, *Western Ontario*, chap. 4; Craig, *Upper Canada*, 90–2, for a detailed discussion of the concern expressed by residents in the western districts of Upper Canada over the exclusion of American immigrants. Robert Dickson and Col. Nichol, both landowners, were very upset and made numerous representations to the executive to have the order rescinded. In 1817 Nichol raised the matter in the Assembly.

91 *Kingston Gazette*, 18 November 1817. For specific discussion of Gourlay's proposals, see Bowsfield, "Upper Canada in the 1820's," chap. 3; Craig, *Upper Canada*, "A Briton Banished"; Milani, *Robert Gourlay*.

92 For example see *Kingston Gazette*, 7 September 1816, in which it was noted that between 12,000 and 15,000 emigrants had arrived in the United States that year; *Upper Canada Gazette*, 3 April, 10, 17 July 1817; 3 July 1818; 1 July 1826; *Kingston Chronicle*, 3 July 1817; 3 April 1818; 28 January 1820.

93 *Kingston Gazette*, 17 February 1818.

94 Ibid., 17 February, 24 March 1818; 17 March 1818. See also 7 April 1818; *Kingston Chronicle*, 4 June, 9 July 1819.

95 Fothergill, "Port Hope Meeting," in Gourlay, *Narrative of a Journey*. See also Baldwin to unknown correspondent, 22 June 1818, Baldwin Papers, TPL.

96 *Upper Canada Gazette*, 1 February 1821, from the *Quebec Review*.

97 *Kingston Chronicle*, 28 January 1820. See also 2 April 1819; *Upper Canada Gazette*, 2 May, 13 June 1822.

98 *Upper Canada Gazette*, 1 February 1821, from the *Quebec Review*.

99 *Kingston Chronicle*, 2 April 1819. See also 1 January 1819; 2 April 1819, from the British press; 11 June 1819; 17 December 1819, on the great expense for labour and settlement in Upper Canada; 28 January 1820; *Upper Canada Gazette*, 7 July 1817, on the barren soil in Upper Canada; Craig, *Upper Canada*, 128; Cowan, *Emigration*, both noting government's reluctance in this period to subsidize large numbers of emigrants.

100 *Kingston Chronicle*, 6 August 1819; 28 January 1820. See also 25 August 1820.

101 *Niagara Spectator*, 5 September 1819; *Kingston Chronicle*, 6 August 1819. See also 2 November 1821; *Upper Canada Gazette*, 1 February 1821. As early as 11 November 1817, an article in the *Kingston Gazette* remarked on the need for emigrant societies in Upper Canada.

102 *Kingston Chronicle*, 6 August 1819. See also 9 September 1819; 2 November 1821. A number of Upper Canadians supported James Buchanan's attempts to encourage British settlers who had originally arrived in New York to move north to Upper Canada. See *Kingston Gazette*, 3 April 1817; 3 January 1817. For other problems relating to emigration, see *Kingston Chronicle*, 25 June 1819; 13 October 1826; *Niagara Spectator*, 5 August 1819; *Gore Gazette*, 7 July 1827; *Upper Canada Gazette*, 3, 17 July 1817; *Farmers Journal*, 16 August 1826.

103 *Upper Canada Gazette*, 1 February 1821. Charles Stuart had arrived in the colony shortly after the War of 1812 and had settled near Lake Simcoe.

104 *Kingston Chronicle*, 17 December 1819.

105 Ibid., 28 January 1820. A notice of John Howison's *Sketches of Upper Canada* first appeared in the *Upper Canada Gazette*, 30 May 1822. It is likely that Howison was "Traveller" writing in the colonial press at the time of the Gourlay affair. James Strachan's *A Visit to the Province of Upper Canada* was another attempt both to inform and encourage emigration. See also John Strachan, *Remarks on Emigration from the United Kingdom, addressed to William Horton* (1827), mentioned in the *Kingston Chronicle*, 6 April 1827. For a general study of travel literature during this period, see G.M. Craig, ed., *Early Travellers in the Canadas, 1791 to 1867*; Daniel Keon, "The New World Idea in British North America."

106 *Niagara Gleaner*, 6 November 1824. See also *Gore Gazette*, 24 April 1827. For a general account of British immigration policies during this period, see Cowan, *Emigration*.

107 *Kingston Chronicle*, 25 March 1825; *Niagara Gleaner*, 12 March 1825. The controversy over the Canada Land Company revolved around a

pamphlet entitled *A Warning to the Canada Land Company*, published in Upper Canada in 1825. The anonymous author attempted to illustrate that the proposals of the new company would be detrimental both to the colony and to its shareholders. See Craig, *Upper Canada*, 135-8, and selected issues of the colonial press in the spring of 1825, particularly the *Upper Canada Herald*.

108 *Kingston Chronicle*, 2 November 1821; 28 July 1820.

109 Reprinted in *Kingston Chronicle*, 27 May 1827.

110 *Kingston Chronicle*, 6 August 1819; 21 February 1821, House of Assembly debates.

111 Ibid., 13 August 1823.

CHAPTER NINE

1 W.D. Powell to Gore, 23 January 1817, in a report to the Executive Council, UCS, RG 1 E3, PAC.

2 *Kingston Gazette*, 14 April 1818. Among others see also Samuel Smith to Powell, 14 April 1818, UCS, RG 1 E3, PAC; Baldwin to an unknown correspondent, 22 June 1818, Baldwin Papers, TPL; Ernest Cruikshank, "A Study in Disaffection"; Landon, *Western Ontario*.

3 Strachan, *A Letter to the Right Honourable Lord Selkirk*. See also Baldwin to unknown correspondent, 22 June 1818, Baldwin Papers, TPL; Thomas Smythe to William Halton, 20 January 1816, UCS, RG 5 A1, PAC.

4 Gourlay, *Statistical Account*, 2: 416, 478. Also printed as "Address to the Resident Landowners of Upper Canada," *Niagara Spectator*, 11 February 1818; *Kingston Gazette*, 18 February 1818. See also *Kingston Gazette*, 7, 14 April, 14 May 1818; 14 July 1818, letter to the editor from "Hope."

5 *Kingston Gazette*, 17 March 1818, letter to the editor from Richard Leonard. See also *Kingston Chronicle*, 4 June, 9 July 1819.

6 *Kingston Chronicle*, 22 February 1822, from coverage of the House of Assembly debates, 1822. The *Chronicle* noted that if Bidwell was admitted, "it appears to us that the sons of Monroe, or Adams, or all American citizens have equal claims to the rights, privileges and immunities of British subjects." See also 15 February 1822, remarks of Mr Van Koughnett. Throughout the 1820s the *Kingston Chronicle* and the *Upper Canada Gazette* provided detailed coverage of the House of Assembly debates.

7 *Kingston Chronicle*, 22, 29 February, 22 March 1822. See also 2 May 1823, for the arguments put forward by Christopher Hagerman.

8 Ibid., 25 April, 9 May 1823. See also 9 April 1823. The debates, first concerning Barnabas and then Marshall Bidwell, were obviously of considerable interest to a number of Upper Canadians, for they re-

ceived extensive coverage in the press. Strachan was also clearly upset by the issue. In a letter to Macaulay, 18 November 1821, he considered that it was "a disgrace to the Province." See also Robinson to Macaulay, 13 December 1821, Macaulay Papers, PAO; Bowsfield "Upper Canada in the 1820's," 251–5; Mills, "The Concept of Loyalty," 56.

9 *Kingston Chronicle*, 15 February 1822.

10 Ibid., 22 February 1822. See also 2 May 1823, remarks by Mr Hagerman.

11 Ibid., 22 February 1822.

12 Ibid., 11 January, 15 March 1822. The concern of the *Chronicle* over the present House of Assembly was also reflected in the private papers of many leading tories. Strachan wrote that "in truth, the present House exhibits a very curious assemblage of foreign importation ... including Mr Randall ... Mr Pelly, a refugee of no good thing and Mr Bidwell." Strachan to Macaulay, 25 November 1821. See also Robinson to Macaulay, 18 November 1821, Macaulay Papers, PAO.

13 *Kingston Chronicle*, 8 February 1822. See also 1, 22 February 1822.

14 Ibid., 1 February 1822. See also 8 February 1822, 2 May 1823, remarks of Mr Nichol; February 22, 1822, remarks of Mr Hamilton; Buckner, *Transition to Responsible Government*.

15 Ibid., 22 February 1822. See also 28 February 1822; 9 May 1823.

16 Ibid., 5 September 1823, from the *Upper Canada Herald*.

17 Ibid., 8 February 1822. See also 22 February 1822; 14 February 1823.

18 Ibid., 5 September 1823.

19 *Upper Canada Herald*, 12 March 1822, cited in John Garner, *The Franchise and Politics in British North America* 1755–1867, 169. Bowsfield suggests that in 1822 and 1823 most Upper Canadians had little real appreciation of the legal and political implications of the Bidwell affair. This, he argues, developed only with the alien question in 1825. "Upper Canada in the 1820's," 25. There seems to be little question, however, that politically active Upper Canadians in the government and throughout the colony were well aware of the problems that the Bidwell issue posed. The coverage of the Assembly debates in the colonial press throughout 1822, 1823, and 1824 undoubtedly brought the issue before the people and reflected their growing interest in the matter. It seems that the longer the issue was left unresolved, the more attention it received from various contributors to the press.

20 *Kingston Chronicle*, 29 March 1823, from the *Upper Canada Herald*. See also 22 March 1822, letter to the editor from "Thwack"; *Weekly Register*, 13 March 1823, a comment from the *Montreal Herald*.

21 *Kingston Chronicle*, 9 May 1823. Hagerman, in a letter to Macaulay, considered that this decision was "abominable." 17 February 1823, Macaulay Papers, PAO.

22 Mills, "The Concept of Loyalty," 79. The British case involved the rights

of an American citizen, born after the peace treaty, to inherit land in England. It was decided that as the parents had obviously renounced their allegiance to the king, the child was an alien and had no right to hold property. See Garner, *Franchise and Politics*, 169–70. The administration was very concerned that if the present titles to land were suspect and perhaps competely invalid, this would harmfully affect colonial development. See F.G. Quealey, "The Administration of Peregrine Maitland," 528; Mills, "The Concept of Loyalty," 72.

23 *Upper Canada Herald*, 22 November 1825, supplement. See also the *Colonial Advocate*, 8 December 1825. Indeed, all the colonial newspapers printed Maitland's address, though for the most part without comment.

24 *Kingston Chronicle*, 20 April 1827. For a detailed discussion of the various bills presented and the problems of the colonial executive, see Garner, *Franchise and Politics*, 164–9. The executive found itself caught between an increasingly intransigent Assembly and a Colonial Office reluctant to become involved in what proved to be a very unpopular issue.

25 *Canadian Freeman*, 1 December 1825. See also *Gore Gazette*, 3 March 1827, which noted that "an extraordinary degree of excitement continued to exist in the public's mind." The alien question dominated the Upper Canadian press throughout 1827 and early 1828, in addition to the extensive coverage afforded through the legislative debates. Starting in 1825, it also evoked the publication of a number of pamphlets on the issue. See for example *Proceedings Concerning the Conferring of Civil Rights on Certain Inhabitants of Upper Canada*; Collins, *To the Loyal Anglo-Americans*.

26 *Gore Gazette*, 10 March 1827. This theme was expressed again and again by the supporters of the original bill. See also *Kingston Chronicle*, 16 February 1827; 23 February 1827, remarks of Mr McLean; 25 March 1827; *Farmers Journal*, 24 March 1827; *Gore Gazette*, 17 March 1827, concerning meetings at Hamilton and Ancaster.

27 *Kingston Chronicle*, 20 April 1827.

28 *Farmers Journal*, 21 March 1827. See also *United Empire Loyalist*, 21 April 1827, concerning a charge to the Grand Jury. This seems to have been the first occasion when both the tories and the reformers attempted to organize their support across the colony. See Bowsfield, "Upper Canada in the 1820's," 260; Mills, "The Concept of Loyalty."

29 *Kingston Chronicle*, 20 April 1827. Watkins Miller noted, in the *Gore Gazette*, 7 March 1827, that "none are in the least danger of being considered aliens who have not, at some period or other, been citizens of the United States, or subjects of some other foreign power, either by birth or naturalization." See also *United Empire Loyalist*, 31 March 1827; *Kingston Chronicle*, 16 March 1827.

30 *Colonial Advocate*, 5 January 1826, letter to the editor from "Catharus"; *Kingston Chronicle*, 11 May 1827. See also *United Empire Loyalist*, 17 March 1827.

31 *Kingston Chronicle*, 20 April 1827. *Colonial Advocate*, 5 January 1826. The loyalist heritage was fundamental to the tories' proposals for naturalization. See for example *Gore Gazette*, 10 March 1827; *Kingston Chronicle*, 26 February, 20 April 1827. For a general discussion of this aspect, see Mills, "The Concept of Loyalty," 76; Bowsfield, "Upper Canada in the 1820's."

32 *Farmers Journal*, 25 April 1827. See among others *Gore Gazette*, 24 March 1827; *Kingston Chronicle*, 22 December 1826, letter to the editor from "Stepsure"; *Farmers Journal*, 7 March 1827, letter to the editor from Watkins Miller.

33 *Kingston Chronicle*, 22 December 1826; *United Empire Loyalist*, 17 March 1827.

34 *Colonial Advocate*, 15 December 1825, remarks by Mr Fothergill and Mr Clarke. The presence of Charles Fothergill among the ranks of the reformers was short-lived. As Paul Romney persuasively argues in "A Conservative Reformer in Upper Canada," Fothergill was really an "English Whig." Moreover, the advocates of reform were never really unified in this early period. See also *Gore Gazette*, 17, 24 March 1827; *United Empire Loyalist*, 28 April 1827; 27 January 1828. The *Colonial Advocate* provided what were apparently complete reports of the legislative debates for 1825 and 1826.

35 *Kingston Chronicle*, 9 February 1827. See also 23 February 1827, remarks by Mr Hamilton.

36 *Colonial Advocate*, 15 December 1825; *Kingston Chronicle*, 16 February 1827. See also *Niagara Gleaner*, 25 February 1828, remarks of Mr Bidwell; *Colonial Advocate*, 12 December 1826, editorial comment.

37 *Colonial Advocate*, 19 January 1826; 26 January 1826, Rolph resolution.

38 Ibid., 15 December 1825. See also *United Empire Loyalist*, 27 January 1827, remarks of Mr Randall.

39 *Colonial Advocate*, 19 January 1826.

40 *Kingston Chronicle*, 9 February 1827. See also *United Empire Loyalist*, 27 January 1827. John Lefferty of Lincoln County remarked that he "would rather suffer his arm to rot from his shoulder than consent to call himself an alien."

41 Collins, *To the Loyal Anglo-Americans*, 16.

42 *Colonial Advocate*, 15 December 1825, remarks of Mr Fothergill.

43 Collins, *To the Loyal Anglo-Americans*, 16; *Kingston Chronicle*, 9 February 1827. See also 23 February 1827, remarks of Mr Fothergill; *United Empire Loyalist*, 27 January 1827.

44 Collins, *To the Loyal Anglo-Americans*, 13. See also *Canadian Freeman*, 14

May 1828, in which Collins charged that, in fact, the instructions received concerning the alien bill had been drawn up by Strachan, not by officials in London; *United Empire Loyalist*, 27 January 1827. Bowsfield, "Upper Canada in the 1820's," 265–7, provides a lengthy discussion of the growing agitation against Strachan over this issue.

45 *Colonial Advocate*, 2 February 1826, remarks of Mr Bidwell; 29 March 1826.

46 *Canadian Freeman*, 9 April 1827; Collins, *To the Loyal Anglo-Americans*, 16. See also *Kingston Chronicle*, 15 December 1826.

47 *Canadian Freeman*, 14 April 1827; *Colonial Advocate*, 15 March 1826. Before any bill was presented in the House, Mackenzie had been confident that nothing would be done in "direct opposition to the spirit and measures of the British constitution." However, it soon became clear to him and many of the reformers that the executive was indeed determined to use the constitutional principle for its own political ends. See also *Colonial Advocate*, 9 August 1824; *United Empire Loyalist*, 23 December 1826; 27 January, 16 February 1827.

48 *Colonial Advocate*, 2 February 1826.

49 *Kingston Chronicle*, 23 February 1827. Petitions were circulated extensively throughout Upper Canada in 1827 and particularly in York, where a concerned group distributed one petition which was roundly condemned by the tories. See for example *Gore Gazette*, 10 March 1827; *Kingston Chronicle*, 13 March, 29 July 1827; *United Empire Loyalist*, 31 March 1827. Nonetheless, the petition received considerable support and was taken to England for presentation by Robert Randall. See Garner, *Franchise and Politics*, 165.

50 *Farmers Journal*, 7 March 1827, letter from Watkins Miller. As Mills argues in "Concept of Loyalty," 15, the tories equated any form of dissent with disloyalty.

51 *United Empire Loyalist*, 17 March 1827; *Kingston Chronicle*, 16 March 1827; *Farmers Journal*, 7 March 1827. See also *United Empire Loyalist*, 25 April 1827; 27 January 1828; *Kingston Chronicle*, 23 March 1827, remarks of Mr Hamilton.

52 *Kingston Chronicle*, 11 May 1827.

53 *United Empire Loyalist*, 21 April 1827, report of the meeting at Kingston. See also 27 January 1827, editorial comment.

54 *Kingston Chronicle*, 16 February, 10 March 1827. See also *Gore Gazette*, 10 March 1827, editorial comment.

55 *Colonial Advocate*, 19 January 1826, remarks of Mr Morris.

56 Ibid., 5 January 1826. See also *Gore Gazette*, 24 March 1827, letter to the editor from Sylvester Tiffany. The *Kingston Chronicle*, throughout April 1827, ran a series of articles on the "Naturalization Bill and

Observations" which provided a point by point analysis of the tory position. See 13, 20, 27 April 1827.

57 *United Empire Loyalist*, 17 March, 21 February 1827.

58 *Colonial Advocate*, 5 January 1826; *Kingston Chronicle*, 5 May 1827. See also *Farmers Journal*, 21 February 1827; 16 July 1828, letter to the editor from Watkins Miller. An anonymous *Stepsure* advocated that the real friends of the aliens would not obstruct measures to rectify the problem, but would cooperate with the executive. *Kingston Chronicle*, 22 December 1826; 23 March 1827, letter from "John Bull" who condemned the present opposition which he considered tantamount to treason; *United Empire Loyalist*, 7 July 1828, attacking the editor of the *Colonial Advocate*, and asking, "are these the *real* friends of the people?" No, they were "demagogues."

59 *Colonial Advocate*, 29 January 1826. See also 7 April 1827; *Gore Gazette*, 24 November 1827.

60 *Farmers Journal*, 14 March 1827.

61 *Kingston Chronicle*, 16 March 1827, meeting at Johnstown; *United Empire Loyalist*, 27 January 1827.

62 *Farmers Journal*, 21 February 1827; *United Empire Loyalist*, 21 April 1827. Bowsfield notes, "Upper Canada in the 1820's," 272–4, that the tories saw the alien bill as an opportunity to "purify" the colony of all seditious elements, whether from the United States or from Great Britain.

63 *Kingston Chronicle*, 4 May 1827.

64 *United Empire Loyalist*, 21 April 1827.

65 *Colonial Advocate*, 5 January, 15 March 1826; *Kingston Chronicle*, 20 April 1827.

66 *Kingston Chronicle*, 15 December 1826.

67 Ibid., 2 February 1826.

68 Ibid., 18 May 1826, House of Assembly debates; 2 February 1826. See also 19 January 1826.

69 Mills, "The Concept of Loyalty," 1, 5.

CONCLUSION

1 *Colonial Advocate*, 27 November 1828.

2 *Report of the Northumberland County Agricultural Society*, 16 June 1828, in Bowsfield, "Upper Canada in the 1820's," 354.

3 This started in 1827, with Strachan's Ecclesiastical Chart, which was forwarded to Horton. Many in the colony charged that Strachan had consciously falsified his figures concerning the number of Church of England clergy in the colony. In reply to the Chart and to Strachan's proposals for a university in Upper Canada, Egerton Ryerson and a

number of other Upper Canadians began to submit numerous letters to editors, particularly of the opposition press. See *Upper Canada Herald* throughout 1827 and 1828; Craig, *Upper Canada*.

4 See for example *Upper Canada Herald*, 28 January; 4 February 1829; Craig, *Upper Canada*; Bowsfield, "Upper Canada in the 1820's," 347–8.

5 *Canadian Freeman*, 4 August 1828.

6 *Report of the Northumberland County Agricultural Society*, 17 June 1828.

7 Ibid.

8 Bowsfield, "Upper Canada in the 1820's," 206.

Bibliography

PRIMARY SOURCES

Manuscripts

Baldwin Papers. PAO and TPL
Barnabas Bidwell Papers. QUA
H.J. Boulton Papers. PAO
The Honourable Richard Cartwright Papers. QUA
Cartwright Papers, Port Hope Collection. QUA
William Case Journal, 1808–9. PAO
Election Broadside Collection, 1800–28. TPL
Elmsley-Macaulay Papers, 1792–1857. PAO
Solomon Jones Papers, 1787–1843. PAO
Jones Family Papers. QUA
Macaulay Papers. PAO
Archibald McLean Papers. PAO
Sir John Beverley Robinson Papers. PAO
Rogers Papers. PAO
Joel Stone Papers. QUA
John Strachan Papers, unpublished sermons, 1803–28; Letter Books. PAO
Stuart Family Papers. PAO
Washburn Papers. PAO
Upper Canada Sundries, v-viii. PAC

Newspapers

Canada Constellation 1799–1800
Canadian Freeman 1824–8
Colonial Advocate 1824–8

Farmers Journal and Welland Canal Intelligencer 1826–8
Gore Gazette 1827–8
Kingston Chronicle 1819–28
Kingston Gazette 1810–18
Niagara Gleaner 1817–28
Niagara Herald 1801–2
Niagara Spectator 1818–20
Observer 1820–8 (only a few issues survive)
St. David's Spectator 1816–19 (only a few issues survive)
Upper Canada Gazette 1793–1828
   1807, renamed *York Gazette*; 1817, *Upper Canada Gazette*; 1821, *York Weekly and Upper Canada Gazette*; 1822, *Weekly Register and Upper Canada Gazette*; 1826, *United Empire Loyalist and Upper Canada Gazette*
Upper Canada Guardian or Freeman's Journal 1807–10 (only a few issues survive)
Upper Canada Herald 1819–28

Government Documents and Publications

"Journals and Proceedings of the House of Assembly of the Province of Upper Canada." 1792–1804. *Sixth Report of the Bureau of Archives of the Province of Ontario*, ed. Alex Fraser. Toronto 1909.
– 1805–1811. *Eighth Report*. 1911.
– 1812–1818. *Ninth Report*. 1912.
– 1819–1821. *Tenth Report*. 1913.
– 1822–1824. *Eleventh Report*. 1914.
– 1825–1828. *Twelfth Report*. 1915.
"Journals of the Legislative Council of the Province of Upper Canada." 1792–1819. *Seventh Report of the Bureau of Archives of the Province of Ontario*. 1910.
– 1820–1824. *Twelfth Report*. 1915.
Draft Petition for the Re-Union of the Province of Upper and Lower Canada. Glengarry, Upper Canada: np 1822.
First Report of the Select Committee Appointed to Take into consideration the Internal Resources of the Province of Upper Canada ... . York: By Order of the House of Assembly, Upper Canada Gazette Office 1821.
First Report of the Upper Canada Central School on the British National System of Education. York: Charles Fothergill 1822.
A Form of Prayer and Thanksgiving ... for the Repeated Successes Obtained by the Allied Army in Portugal Spain ... . Quebec: John Neilson 1812.
A Form of Prayer and Thanksgiving ... for putting an end to the Late Bloody ... War upon the Continent of Europe. Quebec: John Neilson 1814.
A Form of Prayer and Thanksgiving ... to be Used on Thursday, the Sixth Day of April, 1815. Quebec: John Neilson 1815.

Proceedings at a Meeting of the Inhabitants of the Townships of Hope and Hamilton. York: R.C. Horne 1818.

Proceedings Concerning the Conferring of Civil Rights on Certain Inhabitants of Upper Canada. York: John Carey 1825.

Resolutions, Addresses etc. of the Commons House of Assembly and the Legislative Council as taken from the York Gazette by a Bystander. York: np 1818.

Resolutions on the Alien Question. York: House of Assembly 1825.

Contemporary Printed Sources

Anonymous
- *Address to the Free and Independent People of Massachusetts.* Boston: np 1812.
- *An Address to the People of the Canadas by a Friend to Natural and Equal Rights.* New York: np 180?
- *The American Traveller and Emigrant's Guide.* Shrewsbury: C. Hulbert 1817.
- *The British Spy or Letters to a Member of the British Parliament.* Newbury: np 1804.
- *The Canadian Inspector ... Containing a Collection of Facts Concerning the Government of Sir George Prevost.* Montreal: Nahum Mower 1815.
- *Canadian Letters – A Description of a Tour through the Province of Lower and Upper Canada in the Course of the Years 1792 and '93.* Reprint. *Canadian Antiquarian Journal,* 9, nos. 3,4 (1912).
- *Explanations of the Proceedings of the Loyal and Patriotic Society.* York: R. Stanton 1841.
- *To the Electors of York and Simcoe,* by "Fair Play." York: np 1824.
- *To the Electors of the Town of York,* by "Freeman." York: np 1820.
- *An Exposition of the Causes and Character of the Late War with Great Britain.* Washington: Published by the authority of the American Government 1815.
- *A Few Plain Directions for Persons Intending to Proceed as Settlers to His Majesty's Province of Upper Canada,* by "English Farmer." London: Baldwin, Cradock and Joly 1820.
- *To the Free and Independent Electors of the County of Essex.* np 1800.
- *Letter to the Right Honourable Lord Castlereagh etc..* Quebec: np 1809.
- *A Letter from a Gentleman to His Friend in England Descriptive of the Different Settlements in the Province of Upper Canada.* Philadelphia: W.W. Woodward 1795.
- *The New Crisis,* by "An Old Whig." New York: np 1810.
- *Observations upon the Outline of a Plan of Emigration to Upper Canada.* York: np 1822.
- *Origin and Progress of the Present Difficulties between the United States and Great Britain and France Considered,* by "A Citizen of Otsego County." Utica: np 1809.

– *Outline of a Plan of Emigration to Upper Canada*. London: np 1822.
– *Political State of Upper Canada in 1806–7 and 1815 and 1816*. Reprint. Ottawa: S.E. Dawson 1893.
– *Reflections upon the Value of the British West Indian Colonies and the British North American Colonies, 1825*. London: np 1826.
– *The Resources of the Canadas or Sketches of the Physical and Moral Means which Great Britain and her Colonial Authorities Will Successfully Employ ... against the Government of the United States*. Quebec: np 1813.
– *A Series of Reflections on the Management of Civil Rule in the Town of Kingston*, by "An Inhabitant." Kingston: H.C. Thomson 1827.
– *A View of the State of Parties in the United States of America*. Edinburgh: John Ballantyne and Co. 1812.
– *A Warning to the Canada Land Company, in a Letter Addressed to that Body by an Englishman Resident in Upper Canada*. Kingston: Herald Office 1824.
Adams, John Quincy. *A Letter From the Honourable John Quincy Adams to Honourable Harrison Gray Otis on the Present State of Our National Affairs*. Sag Harbour: Alden Spooner 1808.
Anderson, David. *Canada: or a View of the Importance of the British American Colonies*. London: J.M. Richardson 1814.
Ansley, Amos. *A Collection of Loyalist and Other Petitions, Letters ... Referring to the Land Boundary ... on the Bay of Quinte*. Kingston: np 1810.
Atcheson, N. *A Compressed View of the Points to be Considered in Treating with the United States of America*. London: np 1815.
Baldwin, Robert. *To the Free and Independent Electors of the County of York*. York: Francis Collins 1828.
– *The Reply of Robert Baldwin ... on Being Asked What Would Induce Him ... .* York: np 1828.
Baldwin, William Warren. *To the Free and Independent Electors of the Counties of York and Simcoe*. York: np 1820.
Bell, William. *Hints to Emigrants in a Series of Letters from Upper Canada*. Edinburgh: Waugh and Innis 1824.
Bethune, Rev. John. *A Sermon Preached at Brockville ... June, 1816 Being a Day of General Thanksgiving*. Montreal: William Gray 1816.
Bidwell, Barnabas. *The Prompter: A Series of Essays on Civil and Social Duties*. Kingston: H.C. Thomson 1821.
Bigelow, Jacob. *The War of the Gulls*. New York: The Dramatic Repository 1812.
Blane, William. *An Excursion through the United States and Canada during the Years 1822–1823*. London: 1824. Reprint. New York: Negro University Press 1969.
Boulton, D'Arcy. *Sketch of His Majesty's Province of Upper Canada*. London: C. Rickaby 1805.
– *To the Free and Independent Electors of York and Simcoe*. York: np 1824.

Brown, Ralph W., ed. *Mirrors of the Americas.* 1810. Reprint. New York: American Geographical Society 1943.

Burns, John. *True Patriotism. A Sermon Preached ... in Stanford, Upper Canada, 1814.* Montreal: Nahum Mower 1814.

Campbell, Patrick. *Travels in the Interior Inhabited Parts of North America in the Years 1791 and 1792.* Edinburgh: 1793. Reprint. Toronto: The Champlain Society 1937.

[Cartwright, Richard]. *Letters of an American Loyalist in Upper Canada, on a Pamphlet Published by John Mills Jackson.* Quebec: np 1810.

Cockrell, Richard. *Thoughts on the Education of Youth.* Newark: G. Tiffany 1795.

Collins, Francis. *To the Loyal, Patriotic and Independent Anglo-Americans of Upper Canada.* York: privately 1827.

Duncan, J.M. *Travels through Parts of the United States and Canada.* London: np 1823.

Fothergill, Charles. *Prospectus ... of ... the Canadian Annual Register, Being a View of the History, Politics, Literature and Growth of the Canadas.* York: Charles Fothergill 1822.

– *Reflections on the Value of British North America.* York: np 1825.

– *A Sketch of the Present State of Canada.* York: np 1822.

Goldie, John. *Diary of a Journey through Upper Canada and some of the New England States.* 1819. Reprint. Toronto: Wm. Tyrrell and Co. 1897.

Gourlay, Robert. *Address to the Jury at Kingston Assizes, in the case of the King v. Robert Gourlay, for Libel, With a Report of the Trial.* Kingston: Stephen Miles 1818.

– *Narrative of a Journey through the Midland, Johnston Eastern and Ottawa Districts ... .* Niagara: Niagara Spectator Office 1818.

– *Statistical Account of Upper Canada.* 2 vols. London: 1822. Reprint. Toronto: S.R. Publishers 1966.

Gray, Hugh. *Letters from Canada Written during a Residence there in the Years 1806, 1807 and 1808.* London: 1809. Reprint. Toronto: Coles Canadian Collection 1971.

Grece, Charles. *Facts and Observations Respecting Canada and the United States of America.* London: J. Harding 1819.

[Haliburton, Brenton.] *Observations upon the Importance of the North American Colonies to Great Britain,* by "An Old Inhabitant." Halifax: np 1825.

Hawk, Benjamin. *To the Free and Independent Electors of York and Simcoe.* Hawkes Mills: privately 1824.

Heriot, George. *Travels through the Canadas.* 2 vols. London: Richard Phillips 1807.

Howison, John. *Sketches of Upper Canada.* London: 1821. Reprint. Toronto: S.R. Publishers 1965.

Hudson, Rev. J. *A Sermon on the Death of His Late Royal Highness the Duke of York*. York: R. Stanton 1827.

Jackson, John Mills. *A View of the Political State in the Province of Upper Canada in North America*. London: np 1809.

Jarvis, William. *To the Free and Independent Electors of the Counties of Durham, Simcoe and the East Riding of the County of York*. York: privately 1800.

Lambert, John. *Travels through Canada and the United States in the Years 1806, 1807, 1808*. 2 vols. London: C. Cradock and W. Joy 1814.

La Rochfoucault Liancourt. *Travels in Canada*. 1795. Reprint. Toronto: William Renwick Riddell 1917.

[Lowell, John.] *Peace Without Dishonour, War Without Hope. Being a Calm and Dispassionate Enquiry into the Question of the Chesapeake and the Necessity and Expediency of War*, by "Yankee Farmer." Boston: np 1807.

— *Mr. Madison's War: A Dispassionate Inquiry into the Reasons Alleged by Mr. Madison for Declaring an Offensive and Ruinous War against Great Britain*, by "A New England Farmer." Boston: Russell and Cutler 1812.

— *Thoughts upon the Conduct of Our Administration in Relation to Both Great Britain and France*, by "A Friend of Peace." Boston: Repertory Office 1808.

Maude, John. *Visit to the Falls of Niagara in 1800*. London: Longman, Rees and Green 1826.

Melish, John. *Travels through the United States of America ... and travels through various parts of ... Canada*. Belfast: J. Smyth 1818.

A Memorial from the State of Massachusetts to the Senate and House of Representatives. Boston: np 1812.

Morgan, J.C. *The Emigrants Notebook and Guide with Recollections of Upper and Lower Canada during the Late War*. London: Longman, Rees and Green 1824.

Mountain, Lord Bishop Jacob. *A Sermon Preached at Quebec on ... January 10 1799, Being the Day Appointed for a General Thanksgiving*. Quebec: John Neilson 1799.

Ogden, J. *A Tour through Upper and Lower Canada by a Citizen of the United States*. Litchfield: np 1795.

Osgood, David. *A Solemn Protest against the Late Declaration of War, in a Discourse delivered on the Next Lord's Day after the Tidings of it were Received*. Cambridge: Hilliard and Metcalf 1812.

Phillips, Rev. T. *The Canadian Remembrancer. A Loyal Sermon Preached on St. George's Day, April 23, 1826*. York: Robert Stanton 1826.

[Phillips, W.] *An Appeal to the Good Sense of the Democratic and the Public Spirit of the Federalists*, by "A Citizen of Massachusetts." Boston: np 1814.

Pickering, Timothy. *Mr. Pickering's Speech in the Senate on the United States on the Resolution Offered by Mr. Hilliard to Repeal the Several Acts Laying an Embargo*. Boston: np 1808.

— *A Letter from the Honourable Timothy Pickering ... to His Excellency James Sullivan.* Boston: Greenough and Stebbins 1808.

Playter, Ely. *To the Free and Independent Electors of the Counties of York and Simcoe.* York: privately 1820.

Robinson, John Beverley. *To the Freeholders of the Town of York.* York: privately 1820.

— *To the Free and Independent Electors of the Town of York.* York: privately 1824.

— *To the Free and Independent Electors of the Counties of York and Simcoe.*, Newmarket: privately 1820.

— *A Letter on Canada in 1806 and 1817, during the Administration of Governor Gore.* York: Private circulation 1853.

— *Speech in Committee on the Bill Conferring Civil Rights on Certain Inhabitants of This Province.* York: np 1825.

Ryerson, Egerton. *Letters from the Reverend Egerton Ryerson to the Honourable and Reverend Dr. Strachan.* Kingston: Hugh Thomson 1828.

Sewell, John; Robinson, J.B.; Stuart, Charles; and Strachan, John. *General Union of All the British Provinces of North America.* London: W. Clowes 1824.

Simpson, John. *An Essay on Modern Reformers Addressed to the People of Upper Canada to which is added a Letter to Mr. Robert Gourlay.* Kingston: Stephen Miles 1818.

Smith, Michael. *A Geographical View of the Province of Upper Canada.* Philadelphia: Thomas and Robert Desliver 1813.

Smyth, David. *A Short Topographical Description of His Majesty's Province.* London: William Blumer and Co. 1799.

Sparks, Rev. Alex. *A Sermon Preached in the Scotch Presbyterian Church at Quebec ... on ... February 1, 1804, being the Day Appointed by Proclamation for a General Fast.* Quebec: John Neilson 1804.

— *A Sermon Preached in the Scotch Church ... on the 21st day of April, 1814, being a Day of General Thanksgiving.* Quebec: John Neilson 1814.

Strachan, James. *A Visit to the Province of Upper Canada in 1819.* Dundee: 1820. Reprint. Toronto: S.R. Publishers 1968.

Strachan, John. *An Appeal to the Friends of Religion and Literature in Behalf of the University of Upper Canada.* London: R. Gilbert 1827.

— *Arithmetic for Schools – A Precise Introduction to Practical Arithmetic for the Use in Schools.* Montreal: Nahum Mower 1809.

— *The Christian Religion, Recommended in a Letter by the Reverend John Strachan to His Pupils, Andrew Stuart and James Cartwright.* np 1807.

— *Copy of a Letter Addressed to R.J. Horton Esq. by the Reverend John Strachan ... Respecting the State of the Church of that Province.* London: np 1827.

— *A Discourse on the Character of King George the Third.* Montreal: Nahum Mower 1810.

— *Observations on the Provisions Made for the Maintenance of a Protestant Clergy in the Provinces of Upper and Lower Canada.* London: R. Gilbert 1827.

- *Remarks on Emigration from the United Kingdom addressed to Robert Wilmot Horton.* London: John Murray 1827.
- *A Report of the Loyal and Patriotic Society of Upper Canada.* Montreal: William Gray 1817.
- *A Sermon Preached on the Death of the Honourable Richard Cartwright, Preached at Kingston.* Montreal: William Gray 1816.
- *A Sermon Preached at York, Upper Canada ... on the Death of the Late Lord Bishop of Quebec.* Kingston: James McFarlane 1826.
- *Sermon Preached on the Death of the Reverend John Stuart, Preached at Kingston.* Kingston: Charles Kendall 1811.
- *A Sermon Preached at York before the Legislative Council and the House of Assembly.* York: John Cameron 1812.
- *A Sermon Preached at York, Upper Canada on the Third of June, Being the Day Appointed for a General Thanksgiving.* Montreal: William Gray 1814.
- *A Sermon Preached at Woolwich,* 1824. Strachan Papers, PAO.
- *To Thomas Jefferson of Monticello, Ex-President of the United States.* Extract from the *Quebec Gazette,* 15 April 1815. Military Extracts, PAO.
- Stuart, Charles. *Emigrants Guide to Upper Canada.* London: np 1822.
- Sutcliffe, Robert. *Travels in Some Parts of North America in the Years 1804, 1805 and 1806.* London: W. Alexander 1815.
- Walsh, Robert. *An Appeal from the Judgements of Great Britain Respecting the United States of America, Part First, Containing an Historical Outline.* Philadelphia: Mitchell, Armes and White 1819.
- Weld, Isaac. *Travels through North America and the Provinces of Canada.* 1807. Reprint. New York: Augusta Kelley 1970.
- Wenham, Rev. John. *A Sermon Preached before the Bishop of Quebec ... August, 1826.* Brockville: William Buel 1826.
- *Upper Canada Almanac,* 1804. York: John Bennet 1804.
- *Upper Canada Almanac,* 1827, 1828. York: Robert Stanton 1827, 1828.
- *The York Almanac and Provincial Calender,* 1821, 1822, 1823. York: 1821, 1822, 1823.
- *The York Almanac and Royal Calender of Upper Canada.* 1824, 1825, 1826. York: Charles Fothergill 1824, 1825, 1826.

Printed Collections

- Cruikshank, E.A., ed. *The Correspondence of Lieutenant Governor John Graves Simcoe and Allied Documents Relating to his Administration of the Government of Upper Canada.* 5 vols. Toronto: The Champlain Society 1923–31.
- *The Documentary History of the Campaign of the Niagara Frontier.* Welland: Lundy's Lane Historical Society 1908.
- *Documents Relating to the Invasion of Canada and the Surrender of Detroit, 1812.* Ottawa: King's Printer 1912.

Doughty, A.G., and McArthur, D.A., eds. *Documents Relating to the Constitutional History of Canada, 1791-1818*. Ottawa: King's Printer 1914.

Firth, Edith, ed. *The Town of York, 1793–1815*. Toronto: The Champlain Society 1962.

– *The Town of York, 1815–1834*. Toronto: The Champlain Society 1966.

Preston, Richard A., ed. *Kingston before the War of 1812*. Toronto: The Champlain Society 1959.

Robertson, John Ross, ed. *The Diary of Mrs. John Graves Simcoe*. Toronto: William Briggs 1911.

Shortt, Adam. *Early Records of Ontario, being Extracts from the Records of the Court of Quarter Sessions in the District of Mecklenburgh*. Kingston: np 1900.

Talman, James J., ed. *Loyalist Narratives from Upper Canada*. Toronto: The Champlain Society 1946.

Young, A.H., ed. *The Parish Register of Kingston, Upper Canada, 1785–1811*. Kingston: 1921.

SECONDARY SOURCES

Adams, James T. *New England in the Republic 1776–1850*. Gloucester, Mass.: Peter Smith 1960.

Akenson, D.H. *The Irish in Ontario: A Study in Rural History*. Kingston: McGill-Queen's University Press 1984.

Allen, H.C. *Great Britain and the United States*. London: Odhams Press 1954.

Ashton, T.S. *The Industrial Revolution*. London: Oxford University Press 1971.

Aspinall, A. *Politics and the Press*. London: Home and Van Thal 1949.

Bailey, A.G. *Culture and Nationality*. Toronto: McClelland and Stewart 1972.

Bailyn, Bernard. *The Ideological Origins of the American Revolution*. Cambridge, Mass.: Harvard University Press 1967.

Banner, James M. *To the Hartford Convention: The Federalists and the Origins of Party Politics in Massachusetts, 1789–1815*. New York: Alfred A. Knopf 1970.

Banning, Lance. *The Jeffersonian Persuasion: Evolution of a Party Ideology*. Ithaca: Cornell University Press 1978.

– "Jeffersonian Ideology Revisited." *William and Mary Quarterly* 43 (1986): 3–34.

Bell, David. *Early Loyalists: Saint John. The Origin of New Brunswick Politics*. Fredericton: New Ireland Press 1983.

– "The Loyalist Tradition in Canada." In *Canadian History before Confederation: Essays and Interpretations*, edited by J.M. Bumsted. Georgetown: Irwin-Dorsey 1972.

Benson, Lee. *The Concept of Jacksonian Democracy*. Princeton: Princeton University Press 1961.

Benton, William Allen. *Whig Loyalism: An Aspect of Political Ideology in the American Revolutionary Era.* Rutherford: Fairleigh Dickinson Press 1969.

Berger, Carl. *The Sense of Power: Studies in the Ideas of Canadian Imperialism, 1867–1914.* Toronto: University of Toronto Press 1970.

Berton, Pierre. *The Invasion of Canada.* Toronto: McClelland and Stewart 1981.

– *Flames Across the Border.* Toronto: McClelland and Stewart 1982.

Bethune, A.N. *Memoirs of the Right Reverend John Strachan.* Toronto: Henry Rowsell 1870.

Betts, George. "Municipal Government and Politics, 1800–1850." In *To Preserve and Defend: Essays on Kingston in the Nineteenth Century,* edited by Gerald Tulchinsky. Montreal: McGill-Queen's University Press 1976.

Bindon, Kathryn M. "Kingston: A Social History, 1785–1830." PH D thesis, Queen's University 1979.

Bloch, G. Robert. "Gourlay's Vision of Agrarian Reform." *Canadian Papers in Rural History,* vol. 3, edited by D.H. Akenson. Gananoque: Langdale Press 1982.

Boulton, James, T. *The Language of Politics in the Age of Wilkes and Burke.* Toronto: University of Toronto Press 1963.

Bowler, Reginald Arthur. "Propaganda in Upper Canada: A Study of Propaganda Directed at the People of Upper Canada during the War of 1812." MA thesis, Queen's University 1964.

Bowsfield, Hartwell. "Upper Canada in the 1820's: The Development of a Political Consciousness." PH D thesis, University of Toronto 1976.

Brebner, J.B. *The North Atlantic Triangle: The Interplay of Canada, the United States and Great Britain.* New Haven: Yale University Press 1962.

Breen, T.H. *Puritans and Adventurers: Change and Persistence in Early America.* New York: Oxford University Press 1980.

Bridenbaugh, Carl. *Mitre and Sceptre.* New York: Oxford University Press 1962.

Brode, Patrick. *The Bone and the Sinew: The Life of John Beverley Robinson.* Toronto: University of Toronto Press 1985.

Buckner, Phillip. *The Transition to Responsible Government.* Westport, Conn.: Greenwood Press 1985.

Buel, Richard. *Securing the Revolution: Ideology in American Politics 1789–1815.* Ithaca: Cornell University Press 1972.

Burns, Robert J. "God's Chosen People: The Origin of Toronto Society, 1793–1818." CHA *Historical Papers* 1973: 213–29.

– "The First Elite of Toronto: An Examination of the Genesis, Consolidation and Duration of Power in an Emerging Colonial Society." PH D thesis, University of Western Ontario 1975.

Burroughs, P. "Tackling Army Desertion in British North America," *CHR* 61 (March 1980): 28–68.

Burt, A.L. *The United States, Great Britain and British North America From the Revolution to the Establishment of Peace after the War of 1812.* 1940. Reprint. New York: Russell and Russell 1961.

Calhoon, Robert. *The Loyalists in Revolutionary America, 1760–1781.* New York: Harcourt Brace 1973.

Canniff, William. *History of the Province of Ontario (Upper Canada) ... .* Toronto: H.H. Hovey 1872.

Careless, J.M.S., ed. *Colonists and Canadians, 1763–1867.* Toronto: Macmillan Co. of Canada 1971.

Carroll, John. *Case and His Contemporaries.* Toronto: Wesleyan Conference Office 1871.

Carruthers, James Robertson. "The Little Gentleman, The Reverend Dr. John Stuart and the Inconvenience of Revolution." MA thesis, Queen's University 1975.

Childs, Harwood L. *Public Opinion: Nature, Formation and Role.* Princeton: D. Van Nostrand Co. 1965.

Clark, S.D. *The Developing Canadian Community.* 2nd ed. Toronto: University of Toronto Press 1971.

– *Movements of Political Protest in Canada, 1640–1840.* Toronto: University of Toronto Press 1959.

Clifford, Egan. "The Origins of the War of 1812." *Military Affairs* 38 (1974).

Colgate, William. *Nahum Mower, An Early Printer of Montreal.* Toronto: np 1964.

Colquhoun, A.H.U. "The Career of Joseph Willcocks." *CHR* 7 (1926): 287–93.

Cone, Carl B. *Burke and the Nature of Politics in the Age of the French Revolution.* Vol. 2. Lexington: University of Kentucky Press 1964.

Cook, Terry. "John Beverley Robinson and the Conservative Blueprint for the Upper Canadian Community." *Ontario History* 64 (1972): 79–94.

Cowan, Helen I. *British Emigration to British North America: The First Hundred Years.* Toronto: University of Toronto Press 1961.

Craig, Gerald. *Upper Canada: The Formative Years, 1784–1841.* Toronto: McClelland and Stewart 1963.

– ed. *Early Travellers in Upper Canada, 1791-1867.* Toronto: University of Toronto Press 1955.

– "The American Impact on the Upper Canadian Reform Movement before 1837." *CHR* 29 (1948): 333–52.

Creighton, Donald. *The Empire of the St. Lawrence.* 1937. Reprint. Toronto: Macmillan Co. of Canada 1956.

Crook, David Paul. *American Democracy in English Politics, 1815–1850.* Oxford: Clarendon Press 1965.

Cruikshank, E.A. "A County Merchant in Upper Canada 1800–1812." *Ontario Historical Society Papers and Records* 25 (1929): 145–90.

- "Immigration from the United States into Upper Canada, 1784–1812 – Its Character and Results." *Proceedings of the 39th Convention of the Ontario Educational Association* (1900): 263–83.
- "A Study of Disaffection in Upper Canada." *Transactions of the Royal Society of Canada* 6 (1912): 11–65.

Dangerfield, George. *The Era of Good Feeling*. New York: Harcourt, Brace and Co. 1952.
- *The Awakening of American Nationalism, 1815–1828*. New York: Harper and Row 1965.

Darvall, F.O. *Popular Disturbances and Public Order in Regency England*. New York: Augusta M. Kelly 1969.

Davis, David Briton, ed. *The Fear of Conspiracy*. Ithaca: Cornell University Press 1971.

Day, C.M. *Pioneers of the Eastern Townships*. Montreal: John Lovell 1863.

Dent, John Charles. *The Story of the Upper Canadian Rebellion*. Toronto: C. Blackett Robinson 1885.

Deutsch, Karl, et al., eds. *Political Community and the North Atlantic Area*. Princeton: Princeton University Press 1957.

Doobs, Leonard. *Propaganda: Its Psychology and Technique*. New York: Henry Holt and Co. 1948.

Dunham, Aileen. *Political Protest in Upper Canada, 1815–1836*. 1937. Reprint. Toronto: McClelland and Stewart 1963.

Earl, D.W.L. "British Views of Colonial Upper Canada, 1791-1841." *Ontario History* 53 (1961): 117–36.

Edgar, Matilda. *Ten Years in Upper Canada in Peace and War, 1805–1815*. Toronto: William Briggs Co. 1890.
- *General Brock*. The Makers of Canada Series. Toronto: Oxford University Press 1926.

Ellis, David Maldwyn. *Landlords and Farmers in the Hudson Mohawk Region, 1790–1850*. New York: Octagon Books 1967.

Emery, Edwin. *The Press and America*. 3rd ed. Englewood Cliffs, NJ: Prentice-Hall 1972

Engal, Mark, and Ernst, Joseph. "An Economic Interpretation of the American Revolution." *William and Mary Quarterly* 29 (1972): 3–32.

Errington, Jane. "The Eagle, the Lion and Upper Canada: A Developing Colonial Ideology. The Colonial Elites' Views of the United States and Great Britain, 1784–1828." PH D thesis, Queen's University, 1984.
- "Friend and Foe: Kingston Elite and the War of 1812." *Journal of Canadian Studies* 20 (1985): 53–79.

Errington, Jane, and Rawlyk, George. "The Loyalist-Federalist Alliance of Upper Canada." *The American Review of Canadian Studies* 14 (1984): 157–76.

Ewart, Alison, and Jarvis, Julia. "The Personnel of the Family Compact, 1791-1841." *CHR* 7 (1926): 209–21.

Feiling, K.G. *The Second Tory Party, 1714–1832*. London: Macmillan and Co. 1951.

Firth, Edith. *Early Toronto Newspapers, 1793–1867*. Toronto: McClelland and Stewart 1961.

Fischer, David Hackett. *The Revolution of American Conservatism*. New York: Harper and Row 1965.

Flick, Alexander, ed. *History of the State of New York*. New York: Columbia University Press 1934.

Flint, David. *John Strachan, Pastor and Politician*. Toronto: Oxford University Press 1971.

Fraser, Robert. "Like Eden in Her Summer Dress: Gentry, Economy and Society, Upper Canada, 1812–1840." PH D thesis, University of Toronto 1979.

French, Goldwin. *Parsons in Politics*. Toronto: The Ryerson Press 1962.

Garner, John. *The Franchise and Politics in British North America, 1755–1867*. Toronto: University of Toronto Press 1969.

Gates, Lillian F. *Land Policies of Upper Canada*. Toronto: University of Toronto Press 1968.

Glazebrook, G.P. de T. *Life in Ontario – A Social History*. Toronto: University of Toronto Press 1968.

Gribbin, William. *The Church Militants*. New Haven: Yale University Press 1973.

Guest, Harry H. "Upper Canada's First Political Party." *Ontario History* 54 (1962): 275–96.

Guillet, Edwin C. *Early Life in Upper Canada*. Toronto: Ontario Publishing Co., 1933.

– *Pioneer Inns and Taverns*. Toronto: Ontario Publishing Co. 1954.

– *The Pioneer Farmer and Backwoodsman*. Toronto: University of Toronto Press 1963.

– *Pioneer Travel in Upper Canada*. Toronto: Ontario Publishing Co. 1963.

Gundy, H. Pearson. *Early Printers and Printing in the Canadas*. Toronto: Bibliographic Society of Canada 1957.

– *The Spread of Printing in Canada*. New York: Abner Schram 1972.

– "Hugh C. Thomson: Editor, Publisher and Politician, 1791–1834." In *To Preserve and Defend: Essays on Kingston in the Nineteenth Century*, edited by Gerald Tulchinsky. Montreal: McGill-Queen's University Press 1976.

– "Publishing and Bookselling in Kingston, Ontario since 1810." *Historic Kingston*, no. 10 (1961): 23–36.

Hamil, F.C. "The Reform Movement in Upper Canada." In *Profiles of a Province*, edited by Edith Firth. Toronto: Ontario Historical Society 1967.

Hannay, James. *History of the War of 1812*. Toronto: Morang and Co. Ltd. 1905.

Hansen, Marcus, and Brebner, J.B. *The Mingling of the Canadian and American Peoples*. New York: Russell and Russell 1940.

Haworth, Eric. *Imprint of a Nation*. Toronto: Baxter Publishing 1969.

Henderson, J.L.H. *John Strachan, 1778–1867*. Toronto: University of Toronto Press 1969.

Herrington, Walter S. *History of the County of Lennox and Addington*. Toronto: Macmillan Co. of Canada 1913.

Hofstadter, Richard. *The Idea of a Party System*. Berkeley: University of California Press 1969.

Horsey, Edwin. "Cataraqui, Fort Frontenac, Kingston." Typescript, 1937. Special Collections, Douglas Library, Queen's University.

– *Kingston – A Century Ago*. Kingston: Kingston Historical Society 1938.

Houston, Susan. "The Impetus to Reform: Urban Crime, Poverty and Ignorance in Ontario, 1850–1875." PH D thesis, University of Toronto 1974.

Isaac, Rhys. *The Transformation of Virginia, 1740–1790*. Chapel Hill: University of North Carolina Press 1982.

Ivison, Stuart, and Rosser, F. *The Baptists in Upper and Lower Canada before 1820*. Toronto: University of Toronto Press 1956.

Jackson, Eric. "The Organization of Upper Canadian Reformers, 1818–1867." *Ontario History* 53 (1961): 95–115.

Johnson, J.K., ed. *Historical Essays on Upper Canada*. Toronto: McClelland and Stewart Ltd. 1975.

Johnson, Warren Bertram. *The Content of American Colonial Newspapers Relative to International Affairs, 1704–1763*. Washington: University of Washington, 1962.

Kass, A. *Politics in New York State, 1800–1830*. Syracuse: University of Syracuse Press 1965.

Kelley, Robert. *The Transatlantic Persuasion*. New York: Alfred A. Knopf 1969.

Keon, Daniel. "The New World Idea in British North America: An Analysis of Some British Promotional, Travel and Settler Writing, 1780–1860." PH D, thesis, Queen's University 1984.

Kerber, Linda. *The Federalists in Dissent, Imagery and Ideology in Revolutionary America*. Ithaca: Cornell University Press 1970.

Kerr, James, E. "Sketch of the Life of the Honourable William Dickson." *Waterloo Historical Society Papers* 4 (1916): 26–32.

Kesterton, W.H. *A History of Journalism in Canada*. Toronto: McClelland and Stewart 1967.

Korbe, Sydney. *The Development of the Colonial Newspaper*. Gloucester, Mass.: Peter Smith 1944.

Landon, Fred. *Western Ontario and the American Frontier.* 1941. Reprint. To-
ronto: McClelland and Stewart 1967.
Lee, James Melvin. *History of American Journalism.* Boston: Houghton Mifflin
Co. 1917.
Lewis, Benjamin M. *An Introduction to American Magazines 1800–1810.* Ann
Arbor: University of Michigan 1961.
Livermore, Shaw. *The Twilight of Federalism: The Disintegration of the Federalist
Party, 1815–1830.* Princeton: Princeton University Press 1962.
Lockridge, Kenneth A. *Literacy in Colonial New England.* New York: W.W.
Norton and Co. 1974.
Lower, A.R.M. *Canada – Nation and Neighbour.* Toronto: The Ryerson Press
1952.
– *Colony to Nation: A History of Canada.* 3rd ed. Toronto: Longmans, Green
and Co. 1959.
– "Immigration and Settlement in Canada, 1812–1820." *CHR* 3 (1922): 37–47.
Maccoby, S. *English Radicalism, 1786–1832.* London: George Allen and Unwin
1961.
Machar, A.M. *The Story of Old Kingston.* Toronto: Musson Book Co. 1908.
McLean, Mary. "Early Parliamentary Reporting in Upper Canada." *CHR* 20
(1939): 378–91.
McLean, M. "The Peopling of Glengarry County: The Scottish Origins of
a Canadian Community." CHA *Historical Papers* (1982): 156–71.
McMurrich, Ronald. "Joel Stone and the Founding of Gananoque." *Historic
Kingston,* no. 15 (1967): 30–6.
Maier, Pauline. *From Resistance to Revolution.* New York: Alfred A. Knopf
1972.
– *The Old Revolutionaries.* New York: Vintage Books 1980.
Martin, James K. *Men in Rebellion.* New York: New Brunswick 1973.
Matthews, Donald. *Religion in the Old South.* Chicago: University of Chicago
Press 1977.
Mecredy, Stephen. "Some Military Aspects of Kingston Development during
the War of 1812." MA thesis, Queen's University 1982.
Merritt, Richard L. *Symbols of American Community, 1735–1775.* New Haven:
Yale University Press 1966.
– "Public Opinion in Colonial America: Content Analysing the Colonial
Press." *The Public Opinion Quarterly* 27 (1963): 356–71.
Milani, Lois Darrock. *Robert Gourlay, Gadfly.* Thornhill: Ampersand Press
1971.
Miller, Marilyn G. "The Political Ideas of the Honourable Richard Cart-
wright, 1759–1815." MA thesis, Queen's University 1975.
Mills, David. "The Concept of Loyalty in Upper Canada, 1815–1850."
PH D thesis, Carleton University 1981.

Mitchell, Austin. *The Whigs in Opposition, 1815–1830.* Oxford: Claredon Press 1967.

Moore, Christopher. *The Loyalists.* Toronto: Macmillan Company of Canada 1984.

Mott, Frank Luther. *A History of American Magazines, 1741–1815.* New York: D. Appleton and Co. 1930.

– *American Journalism: A History, 1690–1960.* 3rd ed. New York: Macmillan Co. 1962.

Murrin, John. "The Great Inversion of Court versus Country." In *Three British Revolutions*, edited by J. Popock. Princeton: Princeton University Press 1980.

Nelson, William. *The American Tory.* Boston: Oxford University Press 1961.

Nursey, Walter R. *The Story of Isaac Brock.* Toronto: William Briggs Co. 1908.

Osborne, Brian S. "Trading on the Frontier: The Function of Peddlers, Markets and Fairs in Nineteenth-Century Ontario." In *Canadian Papers in Rural History*, vol. 2, edited by D.H. Akenson. Gananoque: Langdale Press 1979.

– "The Settlement of Kingston's Hinterland." In *To Preserve and Defend: Essays on Kingston in the Nineteenth Century*, edited by Gerald Tulchinsky. Montreal: McGill-Queen's University Press 1976.

Palmer, R.R. *The Age of Democratic Revolution*, 2 vols. Princeton: Princeton University Press 1959.

– *The World of the French Revolution.* London: George Allen Unwin 1971.

Patterson, G.C. *Land Settlement in Upper Canada.* Toronto: King's Printer 1921.

Patterson, Graeme H. "Whiggery, Nationality and the Upper Canada Reform Tradition." *CHR* 56 (1975): 25–44.

– An Enduring Canadian Myth: Responsible Government and the Family Compact." *Journal of Canadian Studies* 12 (1977): 3–16.

– "Studies in Election and Public Opinion in Upper Canada." PH D thesis, University of Toronto 1969.

Payne, George Henry. *History of Journalism in the United States.* New York: D.D. Appleton-Century Co. 1940.

Pense, F.B. "Kingston Newspapers." Typescript, nd. Douglas Library, Queen's University.

Peterson, Carl Howard. *The Politics of Revival, 1783–1815.* Stanford: Stanford University Press 1974.

Phillips, C.E. *Development of Education in Canada.* Toronto: W.J. Gage 1957.

Plaunt, Dorothy R. "The Honourable Peter Russell." *CHR* 20 (1939): 258–74.

Playter, George F. *The History of Methodism in Canada.* Toronto: Anson Green 1862.

Popock, J.G.A. *The Machiavellian Moment.* Princeton: Princeton University Press 1975.

Potter, Janice. *The Liberty We Seek: Loyalist Ideology in Colonial New York and Massachusetts*. Cambridge, Mass.: Harvard University Press 1983.

Preston, R.A. "The History of the Port of Kingston." *Ontario History* 46 (1954): 291–11.

Pringle, J.F. *Lunenburgh or the Old Eastern District*. 1890. Reprint. Belleville: Mika Silk Screening 1977.

Quealey, F.M. "The Administration of Sir Peregrine Maitland, Lieutenant Governor of Upper Canada, 1818–1820." PH D thesis, University of Western Ontario 1968.

Rae, E. *Alexander MacDonnell and the Politics of Upper Canada*. Toronto: Ontario Historical Society 1972.

Rae, James E. "Barnabas Bidwell, A Note on the American Years." *Ontario History* 60 (1968): 31–7.

Rawlyk, George. *New Light Letters and Songs*. Hantsport: Baptist Heritage in Atlantic Canada 1983.

– "The Federalist-Loyalist Alliance in New Brunswick, 1784–1815." *The Humanities Association Review* 27 (1976): 142–60.

– "Loyalist Military Settlement in Upper Canada." In *The Loyal Americans*, edited by Robert S. Allen and Bernard Pothier. Ottawa: National Museum of Canada 1983.

– and Potter, Janice. "The Honourable Richard Cartwright." *DCB*. Vol. 4. Toronto: University of Toronto Press 1983.

Read, D.B. *The Canadian Rebellion of 1837*. Toronto: C. Blackett Robinson 1869.

Richard, Elva M. "The Jones of Brockville and the Family Compact." *Ontario History* 60 (1968): 169–84.

Roberts, Stephen George. "Imperial Policy, Provincial Administration as a Defence in Upper Canada, 1796–1812." D. Phil. thesis, Oxford 1975.

Robertson, J. Ross. *The History of Freemasonry in Canada*. Toronto: The Hunter, Rose Co. 1899.

Romney, Paul. "A Conservative Reformer in Upper Canada: Charles Fothergill, Responsible Government and the British Party." CHA *Historical Papers* (1985): 42–62.

Roy, James A. *Kingston, The King's Town*. Toronto: McClelland and Stewart 1952.

Ryerson, Egerton. *The Loyalists and Their Times*. Toronto: William Briggs 1880.

Sanderson, J.E. *The First Century of Methodism in Canada, 1775–1839*. Toronto: William Briggs Co. 1908.

Scadding, Henry. *Toronto of Old*. Toronto: Oxford University Press 1966.

Shepperson, N.S. *British Emigration to North America*. Oxford: Clarendon Press 1957.

Shortt, Adam. "The Economic Effects of the War of 1812." In *The Defended Border*, edited by Morris Zaslow. Toronto: Macmillan Co. of Canada 1964.

Shy, John. *A People Numerous and Armed*. New York: Oxford Press 1976.

Smith, Alison. "John Strachan and Early Upper Canada, 1799–1814." *Ontario History* 52 (1960): 159–73.

Smith, Allan Charles. "The Imported Image: American Publications and American Ideas in the Evolution of the English Canadian Mind, 1820–1900." PH D thesis, University of Toronto 1972.

Smith, W.L. *The Pioneers of Old Ontario*. Toronto: George N. Morang 1923.

– *Political Leaders of Upper Canada*. Freeport: Books for Library Press 1931.

Splane, Richard. *Social Welfare in Ontario*. Toronto: University of Toronto Press 1965.

Spragge, G.W. "Elementary Education in Upper Canada," *OH* 43 (1951): 107–22.

Spurr, John. "Garrison and Community, 1815–1870." In *To Preserve and Defend: Essays on Kingston in the Nineteenth Century*, edited by Gerald Tulchinsky. Montreal: McGill-Queen's University Press 1976.

– "The Kingston Gazette, the War of 1812 and Fortress Kingston." *Historic Kingston* no. 17 (1969): 16–30.

Stacey, C.P. "The Defence of Upper Canada in 1812." In *The Defended Border*, edited by Morris Zaslow. Toronto: The Macmillan Co. of Canada 1964.

Stagg, J.C.A. *Mr Madison's War: Politics, Diplomacy and Warfare in the Early American Republic*. Princeton: Princeton University Press 1984.

Stanley, George F.G. *The War of 1812*. Ottawa: Carleton University Press 1983.

Stevens, Abel. *Life and Times of Nathan Bangs, D.D.*. New York: Carlton and Pater 1863.

Strum, Harvey Joel. "New York and the War of 1812." PH D thesis, University of Syracuse 1978.

Talman, J.J. "The United Empire Loyalists." In *Profiles of a Province*, edited by Edith Firth. Toronto: Ontario Historical Society 1967.

Temperley, Howard. "Frontierism, Capital and the American Loyalists in Canada." *Journal of American Studies* 13 (1977): 5–27. Reprint. Cambridge University Press 1979.

Thistlethwaite, Frank. *The Anglo-American Connection in the Early Nineteenth Century*. Philadelphia: University of Pennsylvania Press 1959.

Thomas, Isaiah. *The History of Printing in the United States*. 2 vols. Albany: Joel Munsell 1874.

Thompson, E.P. *The Making of the English Working People*. Middlesex: Penguin Books 1963.

Thompson, F.F. "Reflections upon Education in the Midland District, 1810–1816." *Historic Kingston*, no. 11 (1963): 8–20.

- "A Chapter of Early Methodism in the Kingston Area." *Historic Kingston*, no. 6 (1957): 32–45.
Tulchinsky, Gerald, ed. *To Preserve and Defend: Essays on Kingston in the Nineteenth Century*. Montreal: McGill-Queen's University Press 1976.
Tupper, Ferdinand, ed. *The Life and Correspondence of Major General Sir Isaac Brock*. London: Simpkin, Marshall and Co. 1845.
Walden, Keith. "Isaac Brock, Man and Myth." MA thesis, Queen's University 1972.
Wallace, W.S. *The United Empire Loyalists*. Toronto: Glasgow Brook and Co. 1938.
- "The Periodic Literature of Upper Canada." *CHR* 12 (1931): 4–22.
Waltman, Marla Susan. "From Soldier to Settler: Patterns of Loyalist Settlement in Upper Canada, 1783–1785." MA thesis, Queen's University 1981.
Walton, John Bruce. "An End to All Order: A Study of Upper Canadian Conservative Response to Opposition 1805–1810." MA thesis, Queen's University 1977.
Weir, Robert. "The Role of the Newspaper Press in the Southern Colonies on the Eve of the Revolution: An Interpretation." In *The Press and the American Revolution*, edited by Bernard Bailyn and J.B. Hence. Worcester, Mass.: American Antiquarian Society 1980.
Weitenmann, Herman. "The Interlocking of Nation and Personality Structure." In *Nation Building*, edited by Karl Deutsch et al. New York: Atherton Press 1963.
White, R.J. *Waterloo to Peterloo*. London: Mercury Books 1963.
Wilson, Bruce. *The Enterprises of Robert Hamilton*. Ottawa: Carleton University Press 1984.
Wise, S.F. "The Origins of Anti-Americanism in Canada." In *Fourth Seminar on Canadian-American Relations*. Windsor 1962. Pp. 297–306.
- "God's Peculiar People." In *The Shield of Achilles*, edited by W.L. Morton. Toronto: McClelland and Stewart 1968.
- "Upper Canada and the Conservative Tradition." In *Profiles of a Province*, edited by Edith Firth. Toronto: Ontario Historical Society 1967.
- "Sermon Literature and Canadian Intellectual History." In *Canadian History before Confederation: Essays and Interpretations*, edited by J.M. Bumsted. Georgetown: Irwin-Dorsey 1972.
- "John Macaulay, A Tory for all Seasons." In *To Preserve and Defend: Essays on Kingston in the Nineteenth Century*, edited by Gerald Tulchinsky. Montreal: McGill-Queen's University Press 1976.
Wise, S.F., and Brown, Robert. *Canada Views the United States*. Toronto: Macmillan Co. of Canada 1967.
Wise, S.F.; Carter-Edwards, D.; and Witham, J. *None Was Ever Better: Loyalist Settlement in Ontario*. Cornwall: Ontario Historical Society 1984.

Wood, Gordon S. *The Creation of the American Republic 1776–1784*. New York: W. W. Norton Co. 1979.

Wright, Richardson. *Hawkers and Walkers in Early America*. Philadelphia: J.B. Lippincott Co. 1927.

Wroth, Lawrence C. *The Colonial Printer*. 2nd ed. Charlottesville: University Press of Virginia 1938.

Young, Alfred F. *The Democratic Republicans of New York*. Chapel Hill: The University of North Carolina Press 1967.

Index